DECONSTRUCTING SPECIAL EDUCATION AND CONSTRUCTING INCLUSION

2nd edition

INCLUSIVE EDUCATION

Series Editors:

Gary Thomas, Chair in Inclusion and Diversity, University of Birmingham, and Christine O'Hanlon, School of Education, University of East Anglia

The movement towards inclusive education is gathering momentum throughout the world. But how is it realized in practice? The volumes in this series examine the arguments for inclusive schools and the evidence for the success of inclusion. The series fuses a discussion about the ideals behind inclusion with pictures of inclusion in practice. The aim is to straddle the theory/practice divide, keeping in mind the strong social and political principles behind the move to inclusion while observing and noting the practical challenges to be met.

DECONSTRUCTING SPECIAL EDUCATION AND CONSTRUCTING INCLUSION

2nd edition

**Gary Thomas and
Andrew Loxley**

 Open University Press

Open University Press
McGraw-Hill Education
McGraw-Hill House
Shoppenhangers Road
Maidenhead
Berkshire
England
SL6 2QL

email: enquiries@openup.co.uk
world wide web: www.openup.co.uk

and Two Penn Plaza, New York, NY 10121-2289, USA

First published 2001
Second edition published 2007

A catalogue record of this book is available from the British Library

ISBN13: 978 0 335 22371 8 (pb)   978 0 335 22370 1 (hb)
ISBN10: 0 335 22371 0 (pb)   0 335 22370 2 (hb)

Library of Congress Cataloging-in-Publication Data
CIP data applied for

Typeset by RefineCatch Limited, Bungay, Suffolk
Printed and bound by CPI Group (UK) Ltd, Croydon, CR0 4YY

The **McGraw·Hill** Companies

Contents

Series editors' preface

'Inclusion' has become something of an international buzzword. It's difficult to trace its provenance or the growth in its use over the last two or three decades, but what is certain is that it is now *de rigeur* for mission statements, political speeches and policy documents of all kinds.

But although it is used so often now, people barely seem to think about its meaning any more. The word 'inclusion' is often merely a filler in the conversation. Politicians sometimes seem to use the words 'inclusion' and 'inclusive' merely to add a progressive gloss to what they are saying. When they talk about the need for a more inclusive society they know that they will be seen as open minded, enlightened and right thinking. And they will be confident that such is the power of the halo effect that accompanies mention of 'inclusivity' that it will be possible to circumvent all sorts of difficult practical questions. If this happens, and if there is insufficient thought about the nitty gritty mechanics, those who do work hard for inclusion can easily be dismissed as peddling empty promises.

This series is dedicated to examining in detail some of the ideas that lie behind inclusive education. Inclusion, much more than 'integration' or 'mainstreaming', is embedded in a range of contexts – political and social as well as psychological and educational – and our aim in this series is to make some examination of these contexts. In providing a forum for discussion and critique we hope to provide the basis for a wider intellectual and practical foundation for more inclusive practice in schools and elsewhere.

In noting that inclusive education is indeed about more than simply 'integration', it is important to stress that inclusive education is really about extending the comprehensive ideal in education. Those who talk about it are therefore less concerned with children's supposed 'special educational needs' (and it is becoming increasingly difficult meaningfully to define what such needs are) and more concerned with developing an education system in which tolerance, diversity and equity are striven for. To aim for such developments is surely uncontentious; what is perhaps more controversial is the means by which this is done. There are many and varied ways of helping to develop more inclusive schools and the authors of this series look at some of these. While one focus in this has to be on the place and role of the special school, it is by no means the only focus: the thinking and practice that go on inside and outside schools may do much to exclude or marginalize children and the authors of this series try to give serious attention to such thinking and practice.

The books in this series therefore examine a range of matters: the knowledge of special education; the frames of analysis that have given legitimacy to such knowledge; the changing political mood that inspires a move to inclusion. In the context of all this, they also examine some new developments in inclusive thinking and practice inside and outside schools. *Deconstructing Special Education and Constructing Inclusion*, one of the first books in this series and the first to be published in a second edition, looks both backwards and forwards. Back to the intellectual schemas within which special education was built and forwards to the kind of education appropriate for the inclusive society for which many people are striving. It is critical of the thinking of the past, while taking seriously the challenges presented by inclusive ideals.

Gary Thomas
Christine O'Hanlon

Preface

The need for a second edition of *Deconstructing Special Education* surprised and delighted us. When we came up with the idea for the original volume back in the 1990s we assumed that a book that had nothing to do with 'how to' and gave little in the way of advice about 'what works' would have limited appeal. We feared that lack of popular appeal would mean that we would have to make do with quoting extremely selectively from reviews, rather in the style of the reviews parodied in *1066 and All That*: 'this slim volume'; 'extraordinary'. Happily, when the reviews came they didn't need such radical excision (some of the best bits are quoted on the back cover) and we've been pleased with the consistently strong sales of the book over five years. Pleased, not only because one's ego benefits if it seems that people want to hear what one has to say, but, more importantly, because we think that these consistently good sales have proved the appetite among educators – teachers, students and academics alike – for something other than 'how to' and 'what works'. For the assumption that that kind of recipe book is what teachers want seems to us to devalue teachers as thinking, independently reasoning professionals. We hope that the sales of the book demonstrate the appetite among professionals in education for ideas, argument and scholarship. Professional development surely depends far more on engagement in a community that shares and argues about ideas than it does on being spoon fed tips, bullet points and too easy answers.

More specifically, we hope that the sales of the first edition of the book reveal the demand for vigorous challenge to the shibboleths of special education and for some assertive discussion and argument about inclusion. Preparing for this second edition, we went back to our notes for the first edition. In reopening the original files, we saw that one of the titles that we had mooted for the book was *Mad, Bad or Stupid: the Thinking Behind Special Education*. Remembering our discussion from the time, we liked the title, but we weren't quite brave enough to push forward with it. Like all UK academics, we twitch at the sound of the letters 'RAE' and timidly imagined that a book that began with two simple monosyllabic words might do us less good in the dreaded research assessment exercise than one that began with a good four-syllable word: *deconstructing* – a four-syllable word that conjured up, to boot, images of clever late twentieth-century French philosophers. 'Deconstructing' was a word to impress with.

Pretentiousness apart, however, 'deconstructing' did seem to do the business. We did, after all, want to 'take apart' – to deconstruct – the thinking behind special education. If the book were to be called *Deconstructing Special Education*, it would do what it said on the tin. And we do, in passing, mention a few late twentieth-century French philosophers (whose musings have more relevance for an analysis of special education than one might at first think).

The second part of the original, sadly dropped title, *the Thinking Behind Special Education*, would have been apt, for the book is indeed about the thought underpinning both special education and inclusion. It grew out of a feeling that the frames of analysis, usually psychological or sociological, often used to organize thought about special education, on their own restrict an understanding of the whole picture – a bit like watching a film without the sound. In writing the book, we have therefore tried to avoid writing just about, for example, the place of psychology in special education – or even a sociology of special education's development. A panoply of factors have to be considered in understanding the growth of special education and the recent desire of people to move to inclusion. All of them interconnect and it serves little purpose, we repeatedly argued then, and continue to argue in the second edition, carefully to dissect out a particular disciplinary understanding. Each of these disciplinary understandings, with its own methodological instruments, its own preference for focus, and its own insights, loses something of the whole picture.

In what follows, then, we avoid simply juxtaposing different disciplinary evidence and analysis. Instead, we have discussed the validity or otherwise of that evidence and those arguments in the context of a wider picture. We argue that much of the theoretical understanding behind special education can lead its followers on wild goose chases. We argue for a loosening of hold on the erstwhile theoretical knowledge behind special education and for more reliance on our own knowledge, as people, of what we know about learning and what we want from schools. We argue that schooling should be guided by principles and that those principles are more or less the same whoever the participants in the schooling are taken to be. And our starting point is that education should be guided more by the understandings laid down by the great educators of yesteryear – Rousseau, Pestalozzi, Froebel, Montessori – and continued in the twentieth century by the likes of John Dewey, Lev Vygotsky, John Holt, Lawrence Cremin, Paulo Freire and Frank Smith. It is to their simple truths about teaching, learning and thinking (rather than to the theories and methods of psychologists or grand theoreticians) that we should look in constructing inclusion.

We begin the book with a discussion of some issues concerning the knowledge of special education and in the middle of the book take two case studies – the first of the way special education has considered behaviour difficulty and the second of reading difficulty – to illustrate the ways in which these considerations exemplify that knowledge. Lessons, we think, emerge for special education and inclusion. In the last part of the book, we discuss notions of difference and how politics and policy have their influence on these notions. This discussion leads into two final chapters that make an argument for inclusion on the basis of the foregoing critique and discussion. In the very last chapter, new to this second edition, we examine some of the ways in which we feel that inclusive thinking now has to move forward, building on the developments that occurred in the 1990s.

When writing it is helpful to imagine who one's reader is likely to be and in writing this book we have had in mind a reader who is undertaking some kind of advanced study in education, perhaps a master's degree or a doctorate. For we have, in being critical of established positions and knowledge, assumed a little familiarity with those positions and that knowledge. But we hope that the book will be of interest also to a wider readership – professionals, advisers, psychologists, administrators, parents and carers – who wish to engage with a critical perspective on special education and inclusion. With all these inevitably busy readers in mind we have provided short summaries of each chapter to help define the shape and direction of the book. We hope, however, that the summaries will provide tasters and not substitutes for the full chapters, for there is a limit to the extent to which complex arguments can be condensed.

Chapter 2 is an amended version of a paper by one of the authors published in *Discourse* 21 (3), and we are indebted to the editor of *Discourse* and its publishers, Carfax Publishing, members of the publishing group Taylor & Francis, London, for permission to use it. We are most grateful also to Kath Sayer, whose work we draw on in that chapter, for permission to reproduce the barchart in Figure 3.1.

We would like to thank Shona Mullen from Open University Press, whose inspiration led to the project not just of this book, but of the series in which it is embedded, and to John Skelton and Anita West for their help and forbearance in seeing the project through during Shona's maternity leave. Thanks go also to Fiona Richman and Catriona Watson from OU Press and McGraw-Hill for their encouragement and help with the second edition. Thanks go to the many colleagues and students at Oxford Brookes University, the University of the West of England, the University of Leeds, Trinity College Dublin and the University of Birmingham with whom we have discussed special education and inclusion and whose ideas have contributed incalculably to this book. Especial thanks go to Hilary Cremin, Georgina Glenny, Ian Grosvenor, Peter Hick, Ann Lewis, Caroline Roaf and Jane Tarr, and to Mark Vaughan of the Centre for Studies on Inclusive Education, for their inspiration, friendship and help. Thanks to Christie and Fionn Cremin and to Kate and Emily Thomas for their inside intelligence on the workings of schools and in particular their contributions to Table 3.2.

Gary Thomas
Andrew Loxley

Special education – theory and theory talk

Brainstorming around a table at Frontier College, Toronto, in July 1988 sat a group of educators, writers and parents, together with adults who had in their youth been taught in special schools. Concerned about the deficiencies of mainstreaming as it was then happening, they came up with a new idea: *inclusive education*. Their ideas about rejecting exclusion and encouraging participation for all spread rapidly to inspire a global educational community about the benefits of inclusion.

In developing notions of inclusion, the focus of the Frontier pioneers was disability and desegregation (see O'Brien and Forest 1989). But there has been a progressively broadening compass to that original idea of inclusive education and 20 years hence the focus of inclusive thinking is diversity and social justice just as much as it is mainstreaming and disability. The 1990s saw thinking about inclusion billow out from a one-dimensional plane, along which one viewed the integration and the valuing of children with disabilities and difficulties, to a three-dimensional terrain that now incorporates a more extensive spectrum of concerns and discourses – about the benefits that come from valuing diversity.

A major part of this book is about these changes in thinking about inclusion: an examination of the growth of inclusion and a rationale for this growth lies at the core of the second half of the book. But it is important to remember here, right at the beginning of the book, that the revolution that has occurred in thinking and practice has taken, relatively speaking, only a short while in the history of education. It appears ephemeral and frail when contrasted with nexus of thinking and practice that represented the century-long tradition of special education. It thus sometimes seems at something of a disadvantage when looked at alongside the seemingly solid epistemological and empirical foundations of special education – a new kid on the block, still to prove it has any substance beyond 'ideology' and competing poorly with the knowledge claims of its predecessor.

So our aim in this book is to give some attention to the reasons both for the new and the traditional thinking. Our purpose is to examine the rapidly evolving changes that are occurring in the movement to inclusive education and also to look with a critical eye at the provenance and structure of the thinking that has led to special education. It is the latter with which we start.

Deconstructing special education

We start our examination by looking behind special education[1] to its intellectual foundations and to its construction. We look in this chapter at the growth of special education, at its many faces, at its reconstruction of itself in different forms and at its response to a changing political mood. Most importantly, however, and running through each part of this enquiry, is an examination of the *knowledge* of special education. Faith in certain kinds of knowledge provides the credence, the believability behind special education's status. Trust in this knowledge secures special education's reputation as a rational, sensible way of educating a portion of the population. But if one takes a questioning disposition to this knowledge, serious challenges to the legitimacy of special education begin to emerge.

Many excellent critiques have located the existence, growth and status of special education not so much in these knowledge-related matters, but in professional, structural and institutional interests at play in society. We do not deny the significance of these analyses; indeed we draw on them extensively in this book. We believe, however, that to assume that they can proffer anything like a full analysis of the growth of special education is to ignore, or at least to downplay, the impact of ways in which knowledge is arrived at, disseminated and used. At the risk of sounding pompous, it is these *epistemic* features in the growth of special education to which we give special attention in this book. There often existed over twentieth-century discourse about special education a presupposition almost of rock-solid knowledge. On this solid knowledge the edifices of special education could be confidently built. The very words which have been used to discuss not just special education but, more importantly, its key concepts – words like 'intelligence' – have been taken to have reasonably straightforward meanings, the *logoi* of Derrida (1978). But, as Derrida points out, there is no ordinary, uncontaminated language. If this is so – and there is a clear case for it to be especially so in the words surrounding the tenuous human 'sciences' from which educators have borrowed liberally – the argument must be strong for a close scrutiny of the underlying (usually unspoken and taken-for-granted) assumptions and frameworks that form the basis for thought and belief.

Our focus, then, is the knowledge held and promulgated by special educators, and the means by which this knowledge is secured. There have been assumptions in the empirical and rational arguments behind special education almost of a kind of special, privileged knowledge. In this book, this kind of knowledge – or at least assumptions that it can exist – will be critically examined.

Critiques

Before examining these epistemic features, it is important first to set such attention within the context of other critical examinations of special education, for
there have been many of these. We need to outline these in order to make clear
our points of agreement and, more importantly, disagreement, with them. For
much critique that gives rise to an inclusionary mindset emerges from committed theoretical positions which, it seems to us, share a need for scrutiny:
the topic of inclusion is hardly uncontroversial (see, for example, Croll and
Moses 1998; Dorn *et al.* 1996; Hornby 1999; Kauffman and Hallahan 2005)
and if fairness is being aimed for, the epistemological premises underpinning
these committed inclusionary positions need as much deconstructing as those
which preceded them.

What, then, are these viewpoints and critiques? Slee (1998) provides an excellent summary of the different perspectives from which disability and special
education have been viewed and, in certain cases, critiqued. Turning his analysis around notions of disability and basing it on earlier work by Fulcher (1989)
and Riddell (1996), he suggests that these perspectives comprise the following:

1 Essentialist perspectives – which locate children's differences and disabilities
   unproblematically in their individual pathology. This has sometimes been
   called a *deficit* or *medical* approach.
2 Social constructionist perspectives – which interpret and present disability
   as a socially contrived construct 'deployed against minorities enforcing
   social marginalisation' (Slee 1998: 128).
3 Materialist perspectives – which see disability as a form of exclusion created
   and maintained by the economic system. It is worth noting here that
   Abberley (1987), an exponent of this view, has said that 'the main and consistent beneficiary [of exclusion] must be identified as the present social
   order, or more accurately, capitalism'. These are, then, Marxist analyses
   (although are not offered explicitly by Slee as such).
4 Postmodern perspectives – which reject the theoretical explanations offered
   by materialist accounts, seeing the experiences of excluded children and
   adults as discontinuous and ungroupable. Although Slee does not give
   examples, it is worth noting that Young (1990) suggests that the mere
   existence of excluded groups forces us to categorize – and the categories
   encourage a particular mindset about a group, while in reality the 'groups'
   in question are 'cross-cutting, fluid and shifting' (Young 1990: 45). Meekosha
   and Jacubowicz (1996) make a similar point: there is no discrete class of
   people who are disabled.
5 Disability movement perspectives – which, Slee says, 'devote-less attention
   to the production of a coherent theoretical explication of disability in their
   eclectic quest for social change' (Slee 1998: 129).

Others have taken different angles on the conceptualization surrounding
disability and special education. Söder's (1989) stance is interesting since it is
critical of some of the received wisdom of critics themselves. He outlines four
distinct approaches:

1 The medical/clinical perspective (similar to Slee's first perspective).
2 The epidemiological approach – which sees disability as an abnormality but seeks to account for this abnormality with a range of social and other explanations.
3 The adaptability approach – wherein disability arises out of some maladaptation of the individual to the environment, due perhaps to the expectations imposed by people in that environment.
4 The social constructionist approach – in which disabilities are constructed on the basis of interpretations made because of social values and beliefs.

Söder sees much of the critical analysis surrounding this field as being off the mark. He suggests that there is an 'epistemological error' in the assumptions behind the fourth of the categories of analysis he identifies, namely the social constructionist approach, which has been at the root of much of the progressive thinking behind moves to inclusion. He suggests that this analysis rests in a hope that 'structure' can be changed – that the meanings ascribed to structures can be altered by goodwill. He calls this kind of thinking 'voluntarism' and puts it down to researchers trying to be reformers, change agents and politicians.

Many disagree with Söder's position. They would challenge his view that there is an epistemological error at the base of this and – in direct contradiction to his point that researchers are trying to be politicians – take the position that researchers' engagement with the political and social in this area is an imperative. Their view is, in other words, that critique and analysis cannot disengage itself from social and political issues (see, for example, Armstrong *et al.* 1998; Gitlin *et al.* 1989). It is from this perspective that analysis has taken into account what Tomlinson (1987) has called the 'social, economic and political structures of a society'. She locates her own critique of special education specifically in *critical theory*, which she finds useful 'in interpreting events and explanations in the expanding area of special educational needs' (Tomlinson 1987: 33). It is worth quoting her at some length since she summarizes her position and the position of many critics of special education with great clarity:

> Critical theorists have suggested that the answers to questions about 'why children fail' might lie as much in the social, economic and political structures of a society as in anything intrinsic to children or 'lacking' in a child. From a critical theorist's viewpoint, it becomes easier to question the deficit model of children, which assumes that negative properties intrinsic to children – low IQ, disability, inability – are wholly responsible for his or her educational failure. It becomes easier to examine the social processes by which 'achievement' is defined. Who, for example, decides what achievement is in a society where the highest achievers are almost always white, upper- or middle-class males? Why does being a poor reader *and* working class seem to have much more serious and long-term social consequences than being a poor reader and upper or middle class?
>
> (Tomlinson 1987: 34)

Not the first, Tomlinson is one of the most articulate advocates of this theoretical position and she has done as much as anyone to drive debate and analysis about special education forward. As she notes, her work has paid particular
attention to the institutional and professional[2] interests at play in the growth
of special education: 'I have been concerned in my work in special education
to use critical theories to question the part professionals and practitioners play
in the social and cultural reproduction of a particular class in our society'
(Tomlinson 1987: 39).

The resilience of special education

Such critical commentary is well developed and has since the mid-1970s helped
to lay the platform for many notionally progressive changes in legislation
across the world. The USA was among the pioneers in this legislative sea change
with its Public Law 94-142, which mandated public education for students
with disabilities in 'the least restrictive environment' – or, in other words, the
most natural, mainstream or integrated environment.

Despite the legislation, however, and despite the critical commentaries,
there has, as the analysis of Skrtic (1991) has pointed out, continued to be a
re-emergence of the kind of thinking which leads to ever newer forms of
segregative and exclusionary practice. As Skrtic (1991: 150) puts it, 'the new
practices associated with . . . mainstreaming simply reproduced the special
education problems of the 1960s in the 1980s'. The exclusionary practices
are still there: there is still labelling; exclusion shows no sign of declining
(see Parsons 1999).

The critical theorists might see the resilience of special education as a clear
demonstration of education's inevitable *reproduction* of the existing social system. As Tomlinson (1987: 34) puts it: 'Critical theorists have noted the way
that education often helps to *reproduce* the children of blacks, minorities,
working-class – and the handicapped – into inferior, powerless, social positions.' The process being referred to by Tomlinson is exactly the same as that
referred to (only half-flippantly) by the French social philosopher Simone Weil
in *The Need for Roots* ([1949] 2002): 'Culture is an instrument wielded by professors to manufacture professors, who when their turn comes will manufacture professors.' Educational culture, at whatever level, is predisposed to
remake itself and the society from which it draws. Pierre Bourdieu, the French
sociologist, has done most to explicate this process of reproduction (see, for
example, Bourdieu 1984; Bourdieu and Passeron 1977), pointing to the role of
'cultural capital' in this.[3]

Some observers of the social and political scene subscribe to a distinction in
the management of human affairs between what is popularly known as 'conspiracy theory' versus 'cock-up' (McLynn 1999). Those who do subscribe to
such distinctions will notice something of the conspiracy theory in analysis of
special education that rests in critical theory. For the existence of special education is seen through this particular theoretical template in terms of maintenance and reproduction of the existing social order for the benefit of those

who already possess power and 'cultural capital'. There is an assumption of intentionality in the system.[4] The system is assumed to be *about* the reproduction of the social order. There could be said to be strong and weak versions of intentionality here and one doesn't have to subscribe to a strong version of intentionality in order to assent to Archer's (1979) analysis of the development of educational systems as related to the interests of those who manage the system.

Clearly, the interests at play in the education system have contributed to the manufacture and maintenance of segregation. But there are other more prosaic ways of interpreting the perpetually re-emerging exclusionary practices of education – ways that avoid any kind of intentionality. A good example of an approach which might be considered less conspiracy oriented is the analysis of Skrtic (1991), which locates the phenomenon more in *functionalism*. If functionalism, which 'presupposes that social reality is objective, inherently orderly, and rational and thus that social problems are pathological' (Skrtic 1991: 152), is consciously or unconsciously adhered to by planners and practitioners, it will lead to a particular mindset about the way to deal with education's problems, namely the children who don't fit or won't learn. He continues:

> [W]hen industrialization and compulsory school attendance converged to produce large numbers of students who were difficult to teach in traditional classrooms, the problem of school failure was reframed as two interrelated problems – inefficient organizations and defective students.
>
> (Skrtic 1991: 152)

He is surely right about the framing of school failure in notions of bad schools or bad children and his analysis is borne out by the contemporary discourse of education and special education, with its discussion of effective (and, by implication, ineffective) schools. He goes further to suggest that it is what he calls the 'machine bureaucracy' of schools, itself a product of functionalism, which is responsible for the re-emergence of old thinking and old practice in new clothes – even when schools are notionally moving to inclusion. Instead of achieving the 'adhocracy' which he looks forward to, schools retain (presumably because they are tacitly cleaving to the tenets of functionalism) the organizational structure that perpetuates exclusionary responses to children who are difficult to teach. We do not demur from this analysis in any way; indeed, we find it helpful and draw on it, especially in Chapter 2 of this book (see also Thomas and Glenny 2002).

Theories of special education and theoretical critique: reasons to be different

However, we try to cast the net even wider and to avoid theoretical analysis.[5] If 'atheoretical analysis' in education is a contradiction in terms to some, it is anathema to others, who see any such analysis typifying a philistine and anti-intellectual stance. Some commentators – such as Garrison (1988) and Suppes

(1974) – have even claimed that atheoretical research in education is impossible. Non-theoretical research seems taboo for a large part of the research community in education.

But one of the problems, as we see it, of analysis in education is that it is discipline oriented: it tends to follow the theoretical and methodological furrows of disciplinary preference – of sociology, psychology, history or whatever. The trouble is that in education, and in special education in particular, foci for analysis do not usually lend themselves to the analytical instruments borrowed from the major disciplines. We take up this theme in the next chapter, borrowing from the neurologist-turned-anthropologist Oliver Sacks who argues that research and diagnostic instruments fashioned for one set of questions are inappropriate for another set. Back in the 1960s Barker (1968), in arguing for a more 'ecological psychology', made the same point. He highlighted the need for recognition of different forms of enquiry and analysis by giving an example of alternative, but equally valid, explanations for the same event. He asks us to imagine the movement of a train of wheat across the Kansas plains. How is this movement to be explained? An economist will explain it in one way, while an engineer will explain it in another. 'Both the laws of economics and the laws of engineering are true; both operate in predictable ways on the train' (Barker 1968: 12).

The train analogy is a nice one, for it points to the diverse number of analytical frames that can be lain over any phenomenon. The crude questions asked about an event (such as 'how is the train's movement to be explained?') disguise the multiplicity of levels at which analytical purchase can be made. It may be easy to ask certain questions, yet those questions may be wholly inappropriate for the task in hand.

Theory-shaped critique

Life is monstrous, infinite, illogical, abrupt and poignant; a work of art, in comparison, is neat, finite, self-contained, rational, flowing and emasculate.

Robert Louis Stevenson (Stevenson 1999: 85)

For the words 'a work of art' in Stevenson's presciently postmodern statement, one could easily substitute the words 'theory' or 'research'. Art, theory and research are all examples of artifice: the attempt to draw a narrative, a theme out of the 'monstrousness' and 'abruptness' of life. The theory of our educational scholarship and this applies especially to special education, seeks order. It is measured for its effectiveness by the extent to which it is logical, clear, tidy, parsimonious, rational, consistent. The disciplines in which theory is framed encourage attempts at explanation in a social world which is singularly lacking in order or intentionality. As Oakeshott (1967) puts it, the rational mind behind the attempt to forge theory has

none of that *negative capability* . . . the power of accepting the mysteries and uncertainties of experience without any irritable search for order and distinctness, only the capability of subjugating experience . . . [The rationalist has] no aptitude for that close and detailed appreciation of what actually presents itself.

(Oakeshott 1967: 2, emphasis in original)

It is a freedom to make a 'close and detailed appreciation of what actually presents itself' which a loosening of grasp on theory offers. If we are seeking to understand why one child isn't reading, or why another refuses to go to school, we should perhaps trust in our own knowledge as people – trust in our experience and understanding of fear, interest, friendship, worry, loneliness, boredom. We know what it is to be confident, over-confident or to feel self-doubt. We understand lying, openness, hypocrisy. We understand guile and the possibility of being deceived. We have self-knowledge, and this is our principal tool in helping us to understand others. As Joynson (1974: 2) puts it, 'Human nature is not an unknown country, a *terra incognita* on the map of knowledge. It is our home ground. Human beings are not, like the objects of natural science, things which do not understand themselves.'

We can use our understanding of these facets of being human, however, only if we feel confident in the knowledge that using them does not restrict our understanding – only if we feel that we are not missing out on some important empirical knowledge or missing some key theoretical insight. One of the points that we wish to make in this book is that the models, theories and intellectual castles created in the field of special pedagogy have helped little in improving learning – helped little in understanding why children fail at school[6] (and this is discussed further in the next chapter). This is unfortunate enough in itself, but the even more unfortunate corollary is that the existence of this kind of supposedly privileged knowledge has persuaded teachers in ordinary schools across the globe that they may not be sufficiently knowledgeable or sufficiently expert to help children who are experiencing difficulty: that they do not have sufficient technical expertise or theoretical knowledge to teach all children.

To say merely this, however, is to make the case too weakly: this privileged knowledge, these theories and models have, by satisfying Oakeshott's 'irritable search for order and distinctness' distracted attention from the ways in which we may use our common humanity to understand others and use our common sense to make schools more humane, inclusive places. For the knowledge is compartmentalized and disbursed according to the frames provided by academic disciplines most obviously adjacent to special education.

Free thinking is difficult in such an intellectual atmosphere. When Foucault (1970: 49) said that 'knowledge [has] closed in on itself' he was referring to the codification of knowledge into disciplinary compartments. It would be a brave set of practitioners who would dare to move outside the professional edifices and procedural imperatives generated by those codifications. Procedural arid professional responses and reflexes thus emerge from schools when problems with pupils arise, but these are often no more than what Skrtic (1991) calls 'symbols and ceremonies', distracting attention from more obvious and straightforward (but probably less prestigious, and certainly less immediately credible) action based on humanity and common sense. As Kohler (1947) put it in his masterpiece *Gestalt Psychology* (in the gendered language of the time – for which, apologies):

> I feel that I must take sides with the layman; that, for once, he rather than our science is aware of a fundamental truth. For the layman's conviction is likely to become a major issue in the psychology, neurology and philosophy of the future.
>
> (Kohler 1947: 323)

Kohler's prediction, made halfway through the twentieth century, looks to have been a little too optimistic at the beginning of the twenty-first. Even though there has been a turn away from the mechanistic behaviourism of his time, there is still strongly detectable a sense that those who urge the need for a more humanistic turn are slightly soft in the head. And this applies particularly at the 'applied' level of implementation: even in the 1970s and 1980s there was a feeling among applied psychologists that behavioural psychology had been drawn from the white heat of contemporary psychological discourse. This was despite the warnings of those like psychology's elder statesman Sigmund Koch (1964), who warned of the necessity to remember that:

> In every period of our history we psychologists have looked to external sources in the scholarly culture – especially natural science and the philosophy of science – for our sense of direction. And typically we have embraced policies long out of date in those very sources . . . Psychology is thus in the unenviable position of standing on philosophical foundations which began to be vacated by philosophy almost as soon as the former had borrowed them.
>
> (Koch 1964: 4–5)

The warning is about the transposition of one kind of thinking to a different arena and it applies today as much as when Koch wrote. Theoretical, model-making, grand explanatory effort is in a human field bound to be not only short of the mark, but possibly misleading. It is especially so if it leads to the belief that practice – practice in schools and with children – involving know-how knowledge (Ryle 1990) can be extracted from such endeavour.

The tack taken in this book is that the theories and models of special education are no exception in this respect. Indeed, they provide an exemplary case of how grand explanatory frameworks can be misleading and we give examples of this in Chapters 3 and 4 where we look especially at children's behaviour at school and at their difficulty with reading. Especially worrying in this is how these frameworks can seem to make us lose confidence in ourselves as teachers and, indeed, as people.

The problem as we see it, however, lies not just in these theories and models of special education and special pedagogy, but also in the theories employed in its critique. One of the difficulties of taking an explicitly theoretical stance – like that of critical theory – in trying to understand a phenomenon like special education is that things become shaped according to the theoretical lens through which one is viewing them. Barrett (1978) poses the danger thus:

> The greater and more spectacular the theory, the more likely it is to foster our indolent disposition to oversimplify: to twist all the ordinary matters of experience to fit them into the new framework, and if they do not, to lop them off.
>
> (Barrett 1978: 149)

The warning here is about the simplifying tendency of theory in the social and symbolic sciences in general – the problems are not restricted by any means to special education or even education. Theoretical moulds, from wherever they derive, the argument goes, are the Procrustean bed of the educator; there is the danger that in compacting, trimming and generally forcing the worlds with which we work into these theoretical moulds we may distort and misperceive those worlds. And education is by no means peculiar in this respect: Wright Mills (1970) described and attacked this theoretical tendency in socio-historical analysis, where he suggested that theory (in particular in the philosophies of Comte, Marx, Spencer and Weber) creates a 'transhistorical strait-jacket' into which the evidence of history is coerced.

Thus, while many have seen theory as the *sine qua non* of educational analysis, we view it here with profound scepticism. This is not to dismiss it: where it can provide what Bourdieu calls a 'thinking tool', it can be valuable, enabling the perception of something in a different light or from a different perspective. However, where it dominates thought, permanently dictating the direction of analysis, it can become hypnotic and even dangerous. This is how Bourdieu himself puts it:

> Let me say outright and very forcefully that I never 'theorise', if by that we mean engage in the kind of conceptual gobbledygook . . . that is good for textbooks and which, through an extraordinary misconstrual of the logic of science, passes for Theory in much of Anglo-American social science . . . There is no doubt a theory in my work, or, better, a set of thinking tools visible through the results they yield, but it is not built as such . . . It is a temporary construct which takes shape for and by empirical work.
>
> (Bourdieu in Wacquant 1989, cited in Jenkins 1992: 67)

Theory is, then, for Bourdieu, a thinking tool – a *temporary construct*. It is something that comes and goes: a brief model, a metaphor, an idea or set of ideas which come out of one's thinking, one's reading and one's experience of the world. It is evanescent and fragile, to be captured and cradled when useful but discarded when it begins to dominate and steer the analysis.[7] Foucault says something similar. For Foucault, while Piagetian or psychoanalytic theory may form useful stepping-off points, they are useful only in the sense that they are caricatured or theatricalized. The conclusions one draws thus emerge from a disrespectful tossing around of the notions of the grand theory builders. They cannot emerge, according to Foucault, from the very architecture of the theorists' palaces. To use theorists' ideas in this way, as totalities that provide a useful explanatory framework, can lead us on interminable wild goose chases and down infinitely long culs-de-sac. Foucault suggests that when social theories have been used as explanatory frameworks they have proved a 'hindrance to research' (Foucault 1980a: 81). Likewise with Bourdieu: theory should never be a dogma – an unvarying liturgy of principles for the operation of some analytical process.

This is important for three distinct reasons. First, it is important because of the direct effects which the grand theory of the Great Thinkers has had in special education. In Chapter 3, we examine how special education has suffered from the influence of psychoanalytic theory on the understanding of behaviour difficulty at school. That which is, notionally at least, 'theory' has a particularly powerful influence since it confers academic legitimacy on the subject of the supposedly 'theoretical' analysis.

So, in a field like special education, which has always suffered something of an inferiority complex about its academic status, there is the danger that 'theory' may be used to add cachet to simple ideas or propositions – and to claim some epistemological legitimacy and explanatory currency for these ideas and propositions. But those ideas and propositions lent credibility by theory are as likely to be incorrect as correct. Indeed, the imprimatur of correctness, while proffered by supposedly theoretical analysis, is probably entirely inappropriate for a field like education, given the plasticity of the stuff with which we work and which we study. There is no means in educational research of enabling what the philosopher of science Canguilhem (1994: 41) calls the 'elimination of the false by the true'. Educational theory is (and we are thinking here of its 'grand theory' which has been particularly influential in special education: Freudian, Piagetian, behavioural), unlike science's theory, non-progressive – in science there *is* an eventual elimination of false by true or at least (for those who balk at the starkness of false versus true) an elimination of less reliable knowledge by more reliable knowledge (Ziman 1991).

But in education that process of elimination of less reliable by more reliable is far more problematic – because of the kind of *knowledge* we trade in, as educators. The knowledge that we have and which we seek as educators of whatever kind – teachers, planners, researchers – is not progressive knowledge. Today's school student *knows* more about electricity than Faraday, *knows* more about chemistry than Mendeleyev and more about genetics than Mendel, because of the cumulative, transferable nature of the knowledge involved. It is unlikely, however, that today's student of education knows more about education than great educators such as Froebel, Pestalozzi or Rousseau – although today's experienced teacher in any and every school in the land may well 'know' more than these luminaries. The reasons for the contrast between the education student and the practising teacher lie in the difference between what the philosopher Gilbert Ryle (1990) called *know-how* knowledge and *know-that* knowledge. The know-how knowledge is practical knowledge – and the practising teacher's know-how knowledge may (or may not) be more sophisticated than that of Froebel. The 'know-that' knowledge is the accreted knowledge of facts, collectable and progressive and clearly demonstrable in the sciences; but this latter has offered little progress that one can discern in education: there has been little conspicuous elimination of the false by the true – and neither should we expect there to be. The problem with the cachet imputed by theory, however, is that it suggests that the truth, the right path *has* been found or at least is in some way *findable*.

All those who work in education, and particularly special education, should be concerned about this: concerned about the consequences of theory, since those consequences are in the real world of classrooms and the real lives of teachers and children. Theories are not simply the playthings of bored academics: they have often been used to 'explain' how children learn, and why they fail. Piaget's thinking, for example, has been responsible for many ideas and initiatives in education. Reliance on Piagetian theory and what Bruner (1966: 214) calls 'the cloying concept of "readiness" ' led to wholly mistaken notions about readiness for reading. Bryant (1984: 257), indeed, contends that 'there can be no question that the implications of Piaget's theories about children's logical skills are, as far as teachers are concerned, restrictive and negative'. It is surely not too early to say that certain elements of that theory proffer a serious misrepresentation of the way children think. This has happened for two main reasons: from unrealistic expectations about the place and limits of theory in education and from the understandable fascination of professional and academic communities by a particularly powerful nexus of theoretical knowledge.

It is worth saying a word or two about Vygotsky here, since his genius in thinking about learning has often been presented as the anti-venom to Piaget's genetic determinacy. One wonders whether his reputation is entirely justified or whether the fascination with him is due to his romantically short life, his clever flirting with the apparatchiks of the USSR (in contrast to the leaden political correctness of Lysenko)[8] and his bright acceptance of the importance of the social element in learning. His, after all, was an optimistic way of seeing learning – and the message with which Vygotsky leaves the teacher contrasts with that left by Piaget, which Bryant (1984: 257) says is 'a pretty bleak one'. But while Vygotsky's ideas are refreshing, most educators (outside the scholarly world of Vygotsky interpreters) would probably flounder if asked to expound, without waffling, in more than three or four sentences exactly what Vygotsky said. Their answers would probably be of the variety: (i) 'Learning is social: children learn from those – usually adults – who know more than they do about something' and (ii) 'Learning happens best when children are being stretched a little bit – but not too much; what they are learning shouldn't be too easy and it shouldn't be too hard.'

The extraordinary fact is that neither of the latter ideas is particularly startling and neither is particularly new. Their consistency rings through the work of all the great educators: Pestalozzi, Froebel, Montessori, Rousseau. The reason that they have been so interesting recently is that they have presented an alternative to the crystal-hard theorizations with which they were contemporary. Theorists like Freud and Piaget seemed to be constructing channels within which our ideas about children's thinking were to be constrained. Vygotsky, along with these other educators, returns to unadorned knowledge of learning which comes from our knowledge, as people, of what it is to learn. That knowledge is, then, by no means new to us: it has not been revealed by some remarkable theoretical disclosure. It comes from Ryle's 'know-how' that

we gain of others (as learners, friends, deceivers, trusted colleagues, or whatever) and that knowledge arrives from our experience as teachers and as
people. While Rousseau shocked the world with *Émile* ([1762] 1993), he said
only what *good* teachers know (and probably have always known) about
learning:

> Instead of keeping [Émile] mewed up in a stuffy room, take him out into a
> meadow every day; let him run about, let him struggle and fall again and
> again, the oftener the better; he will learn all the sooner to pick himself
> up. The delights of liberty will make up for many bruises. My pupil will
> hurt himself oftener than yours, but he will always be merry; your pupils
> may receive fewer injuries, but they are always thwarted, constrained, and
> sad. I doubt whether they are any better off.
>
> (Rousseau [1762] 1993: 49)

The contrast drawn by Rousseau seems remarkably prescient, and rather like
a contrast between good nursery education and that which might be offered
by Direct Instruction, Doman Delacato or one of the other miracle methods
of special pedagogy. No miracle pedagogy has been discovered since his day
or is ever likely to be revealed by the theoretical endeavours of educators or
psychologists.

We reject the view, then, that special educators (or, indeed, any educators)
have to adopt some formulaic schema for collecting data, some analytical sieve
for sifting them or some theoretical frame for synthesis. As the historian of
ideas Isaiah Berlin (1979: 86) says: 'What do the greatest classical scholars of
our time know about ancient Rome that was not known to Cicero's servant
girl? What have they added to her store?' If, in other words, practitioners are
immersed in the practice and observation of education, its traditions, literatures and the literatures of cognate areas, there is no need for some external
validation of their action.

The second reason for mistrusting theory, as we have indicated already, is
that theory may dominate analysis when one is seeking to understand a phenomenon like special education. This is so even with a theoretical system as
open ended, personal and 'emancipatory' as critical theory.[9] The argument of
critical and emancipatory theorists is that theorizing that excludes or ignores
meaning, significance and social and historical contexts denies the possibility
of social critique. Theory, these advocates would say, has to emerge out of
political stance. In addressing the critique of Clark *et al.* (1998) of certain
kinds of sociological theory applied to special education, Slee (1998) says the
following:

> There is a failure to recognise that imported sociological theorising of
> disability and education is not a quest to force theoretical closure to elimi-
> nate doubt. It is essentially a political project demanding ever-clearer
> explanations of complex realities in order that we know 'what's going on,
> why and how we change it' (Troyna 1994). In this respect it is what Troyna
> (1995) referred to as partisan research.
>
> (Slee 1998: 129)

Stanley Fish (1989) is one of the most forthright critics of the kind of theoretical enterprise of which Slee speaks here. The disavowal of forced 'theoretical closure' is not enough, Fish would argue, not only because it is contradicted by the subsequent commitment to 'partisan research' (which surely loads one's reasoning toward some expected endpoint), but because the analysis that is sought and proffered with the honorary title 'theoretical' assumes some kind of privileged status. But in reality this discourse, this 'theory talk', possesses no epistemological advantage over any other. There is no way of showing that it is right or wrong. Neither is there any way of showing that the undoubted commitment to social and personal improvement – the partisan-ness of which Troyna writes, and which lies behind it – can in any way be validated. Many sincere people at the turn of the century, for example, believed – no doubt after due dialectic and reflection – that it was right and proper to ship children from England to Australia for a 'new life' (Newman and Roberts 1996). It is now recognized, of course, from the personal accounts that have come from the recipients of such well-meaning policy, that it often caused unquantifiable misery. The problem is that critique and theory which comes out of one political stance is as likely to be right or wrong as another. That which determines to provide critique is liable to be undermined by it. Fish (1989) notes that the critical theorist:

is unable to show that critical self-reflection is something it is possible to do . . . [this] means that critical theory is faced with two unsatisfactory alternatives: either it admits an inability to distinguish between its own agenda and the agenda it repeatedly exposes, admits, in short, that it is, like everything else, merely 'interested' and not possessed of a special interest called the emancipatory or it preserves its specialness by leaving its agenda without content, operating forever at the level of millenarian prophecy, issuing appeals in the name of a generalised human potential, calling for actions that have no particular content, celebrating goals that remain unachievable because they remain unthinkable.

(Fish 1989: 455–6)

The problem stems not from taking a political stance, for part of our argument is that to pursue a value-oriented education system is just as valid a project as the seeking of an evidence-led one (and this is explored in Chapter 7). Rather, the problem stems from the assumption that a particular stance is validated and given credibility by its association with a certain theory. Again, the problems emerge from the privileges that theory confers.

The third reason for mistrusting theory, aside from its Procrustean and legitimizing tendencies, is that it may distract us from action and from concern with the kind of social justice that is necessary for a movement to inclusion. This may seem a strange proposition and is certainly one which would be disputed by those who promote their theoretical analysis as 'emancipatory'. The argument for the proposition is articulated powerfully by Richard Rorty (1998). Academics since the mid-1960s, he says, have become so preoccupied with the weighty matters of theory and theorizing that they no longer bother to concern themselves with the mundanity of reform – of the kind of efforts at social justice that are behind inclusion. It is the 'mundanity' that is important:

effecting social justice is, for Rorty, about a difficult, dirty agenda of change in statute, regulation and ways of operating public organizations like schools. Recently, however, concern with this kind of agenda has become submerged under a welter of theorizing. Academics nowadays, he asserts, in their fascination with theory, have turned away from secularism and pragmatism. Academics seem to want always to see things 'within a fixed frame of reference, a frame supplied by theory' (Rorty 1998: 36).

The 'fixed frame of reference' argument is the one articulated by Barrett and others and which was addressed earlier. But Rorty is going further: he contrasts the contemporary academy with pre-1960s' reformers whose uncomplicated agenda was to protect the weak from the strong. Rorty's message, if it is right, surely has particular resonance for special educators. The message is that for those in fields like education, the priority should be change. Change is effected only through an unremitting focus on the particular – by concentrating energy on a detailed, unglamorous agenda of administrative, legal and financial matters. But a focus on these mundane but necessary matters is subverted by the contemporary intellectual's obsession with theory. The product of the theorizing academy has been 'many thousands of books which represent scholastic philosophizing at its worst' (1998: 93). Rorty asserts that this kind of academic theorizing 'produces dreams not of political reforms but of inexplicable, magical transformations' (1998: 102).

This theorizing (and these dreams) of academic special educators would be harmless enough if they didn't have consequences. But the trouble is that our theories in special education do have consequences – consequences of both omission and commission. On the omission side, if we are too busy theorizing, we may neglect to act, as Rorty asserts; we become too obsessed with our own theory projects. On the commission side, theory – of whatever kind – legitimizes some potty ideas and practices. 'Theory' carries with it such academic cachet that it is taken to be a sound basis from which to proceed. That which is 'theoretically grounded' is taken to be more worthy of respect and support than that which, more simply and prosaically, seems right and sensible.

Rorty says that this theorizing often offers 'the most abstract and barren explanations imaginable' (1998: 93) and that it distracts from the proper job of the academic in the social sciences, which is to reform. Special education is surely one of the clearest cases in point, where reform should supersede theorization. This is one of the clearest messages from this book: that the kind of theory employed by all branches of social scientific endeavour over the twentieth century often channelled thinking about special education inappropriately. Further, it provided misleading metaphors for understanding some of the social and psychological processes in which we are most interested.

Think small: the need for local enquiry

Because of this, we would want to reassert, theory should be seen better as the 'temporary construct' of Bourdieu: the thinking tool. Dewey said much the same: take Meiklejohn's (1966) summary of Dewey's position:

It is unwise, Dewey tells us, to philosophize, to have and to use 'general theories' ... 'What is needed,' Dewey says, 'is specific inquiries into a multitude of specific structures and interactions. Not only does the solemn reiteration of categories of individual and organic or social whole not further these definite and detailed inquiries but it checks them.'

(Meiklejohn 1966: 83)

Dewey's emphasis on 'specific enquiries' is very similar to Rorty's emphasis on a particular, detailed agenda and Skrtic's *adhocery*. The corollary of such a way of thinking is that we should invest less dependence in the grand theoretical edifices and rigid castles of metaphor constructed by education's intellectual heroes. And we should place less faith in theory's methodological handmaidens. As the iconoclastic critic of social science, Stanislav Andreski (1972: 108–9) puts it: 'The overemphasis on methodology and techniques [in social science], as well as adulation of formulae and scientific-sounding terms, exemplify the common tendency ... to displace value from the end to the means.' In education in general, and special education in particular, there has been this tendency to displace value from the end to the means as the legitimacy and value of research is determined less by common-sense evaluations of its status and likely impact, and more by notions such as 'reliability', imported from the natural sciences.

Not only does a focus on means rather than ends deliver a particular kind of knowledge, one that may well distort the sort of practice we feel that it is right to implement, it also may, again in Andreski's (1972: 116) words, provide 'an alibi for timorous quietism'. It may, that is to say, distract attention from important yet challenging matters for the educator – away, in other words, from critical thought, inquiry and innovation about the curriculum; away from children as people.[10] It may lead the gaze instead towards the less challenging paraphernalia of measurement and research procedure. Postman (1995) puts it well. He notes that Confucius:

insisted on students studying what we would call 'good manners'. Can you imagine a school today requiring as a major subject the study and practice of good manners? Surely, no one can say it is not an important subject. Perhaps it is not in the curriculum because the Educational Testing Service would be hard-pressed to figure out how to assess it.

(Postman 1995: 104)

Thus, for example, with the kudos which learning theory invested in behavioural methods, more attention was devoted to the proper application of task analysis procedures or the correctness of behavioural objective specification[11] than was given to the question of what was actually wanted from an education of children for whom the procedures were devised. It was only when critical voices reached sufficient volume – from a number of directions (see for example, Stenhouse 1975; Wood and Shears 1986) and from the protestations of teachers – that serious questions began to be asked about what was going on.

If one doesn't think small, one is in danger of being guided by the safety of prestigious theory, by the putatively secure knowledge emerging from the findings of supposedly empirical enquiry. The problem with a theory, as distinct from Bourdieu's 'thinking tool', is that it always returns to a guiding path. The underlying assumption is that there is a proper way of examining things. As Foucault put it (in discussion with Gerard Raulet) in interpreting the behaviour of revolutionary Marxists in the 1960s, there came to be an 'antidogmatic violence':

> *Gérard Raulet:* An antidogmatic violence in search of references [. . .]
> *Foucault:* And looking for them, on occasion, in an exasperated dogmatism.
> *Gérard Raulet:* Via Freud or via structuralism.
> *Foucault:* Correct. So, once again, I would like to reassess the history of formalism [. . .] within the larger phenomenon of formalism in the twentieth century, as important in its way as Romanticism or even positivism during the nineteenth century.
>
> (Foucault 1994: 111)

None of this is to deny the particular and specific insights that may come from particular kinds of theory and which may be used as thinking tools in considering particular problems that arise out of children's reluctance to learn. It is the seeking of form, in Marx, Freud, the Frankfurt School or wherever, that is of concern – and this is important when we are looking to explain the history of special education, since the grand theory postulated by the Grand Theorists has been highly influential. Even to the present day, as we discuss in Chapter 3, notions of emotional disturbance dominate explanations of behaviour difficulty and these rely for their legitimacy on a Freudian ontology, even if that ontology is, as Crews (1997: 298) has put it, an 'ontological maze peopled by absurd homunculi'.

Even with, as Rorty (1998: 76) puts it, a 'partial substitution of Freud for Marx as a source of social theory', there remains the seemingly willing dependence on the structure of a theory or what Dewey (1982: 187) called the 'logic of general notions under which specific situations are to be brought'. Dewey asserted that instead of these general notions, 'What we want is light upon this or that group of individuals, this or that concrete human being, this or that special institution or social arrangement' (1982: 187).

When Foucault says that his 'genealogy' entertains 'the claims to attention of local, discontinuous, disqualified, illegitimate knowledges against the claims of a unitary body of theory which would filter, hierarchise and order them in the name of some true knowledge', he sounds distinctly like the Dewey of nearly a century ago who warned of theory – of 'true knowledge'. Indeed, Rorty (1991: 193) suggests that 'Foucault can be read . . . as an up-to-date version of John Dewey.'

Concluding comment

The picture drawn in this chapter is of special education as something of an epistemic jumble. Its 'jumbleness' has not evidently been a source of concern to many, or even a source of note. Indeed, the very legitimacy of special education is proudly constructed out of its 'theory', even though the theory is an agglomeration of bits and pieces from Piagetian, psychoanalytic, psychometric and behavioural theoretical models.

We make an argument here for a loosening of hold on the erstwhile theoretical knowledge behind special education, contending that less of our inquiry into children's difficulties at school – and, more importantly, less of our response to those difficulties – should be defined and tackled in the way that it has hitherto. An argument is made, if we are looking to the shape of an education system for the future, for more reliance by all in education – practitioners, planners, academics, researchers – on ideals about equity, social justice and opportunity for all. In pursuing these ideals, in improving the education system, we should accept rather than deny the insights that emerge by virtue of being human – insights that emerge from our own knowledge of learning; our own knowledge of failure, success, acceptance or rejection. There is nothing to be lost in so doing, for the evidence is that there are no magic fixes or startling insights to emerge from the traditional knowledge base of special education. Indeed, there is a great deal to be regained through a recourse to our common humanity. Joynson (1974) begins his book *Psychology and Common Sense* by précising a G.K. Chesterton story that makes the point well:

> [A] man dreams of emulating the great explorers. One day he sets sail from the West Country and heads out into the Atlantic, confident that he is destined to discover an unknown land. For many weeks he wanders across the ocean, buffeted by storms and uncertain of his position. At last, a coastline comes in view and, as he approaches, he sees the towers and domes and minarets of a strange civilisation. Greatly excited, he makes his way ashore. To his astonishment, the natives speak English. He has landed at Brighton.
>
> (Joynson 1974: 1)

Maybe the research indicating the ineffectiveness of special education (reviewed briefly in Chapter 2) has landed us at Brighton. Maybe the realization that we haven't found a new civilization and neither are ever likely to leads us to a separate set of questions about failure at school. Maybe it leads us to re-evaluate our research and its methods and to place more value in what we – as people – already know and want.

Analysis framed by the research methodology of special education and the discourse that surrounds it tends always to push discussion about alternatives to special education into boxes. Discussion tends to lead to this method versus that method, or segregation versus integration, or exclusion versus inclusion. In Vygotsky's metaphor, words are the tools we use for thinking and the words we use in our discourse here tend always to channel discussion along predictable furrows. The tools for thinking – the vocabulary, the theory, the research methodology – encourage particular ways of thinking. Worked with these tools, failure – whether it is perceived to be failure of children at school, or failure of schools to educate children – becomes yet another special education discourse.

In the next few chapters we proceed to examine the consequences of this discourse, such as the influence it has had on professional and popular thinking about learning difficulty. Suggesting that much of the 'knowledge' of special education is misconceived, we proceed to make the case that arguments for inclusion have to emerge out of ideas about social justice and human rights.

Summary

Much critique has focused on the place of special education in the wider social system. Special education has been taken by critics to act as a kind of service industry to the mainstream; acting in that role, the argument goes, it is discriminatory and oppressive. While such critiques are not invalid, they leave much unsaid. The point made in this chapter is that notions of learning difficulty that underpin special education and special pedagogy rely for their status on some questionable kinds of knowledge and reasoning. They rely on notions that have been elevated by 'scientific' methodology and theory to something more than they really are. The Great Thinkers of the 'ologies' (usually psychology) have built impressive theory, which gives credibility and kudos to particular (and often mistaken) ways of viewing learning, viewing children and viewing the difficulties that they experience at school. Often, these theories distract attention from simpler explanations for children's failure to thrive. An argument is made for a renewal of confidence in practitioners' knowledge as teachers in understanding the failure of children at school. Only outside the confines of the disciplinary and professional knowledge that enjoys such status in special education will there be a restoration of faith in the kind of principles which must guide inclusive practice.

Notes

1 Special education is taken throughout to mean not just segregation in special schools, but also the special procedures and systems – sometimes in the mainstream – that exclude certain children.

2 It is worth noting that Fish (1989) makes a critique of 'anti-professionalism', which highlights what he takes to be an epistemological arrogance among anti-professionals. He notes that the anti-professional position assumes: 'let us free ourselves from the confining perspective of particular beliefs (even when they are our own) and with the help of *acontextual* and transcultural algorithm . . . come to see things as they really are' (Fish 1989: 277). He argues that what anti-professionals 'seem never to realise . . . is that power not only constrains and excludes, but also enables, and that without some institutionally articulated spaces in which actions become possible and judgments become inevitable (because they are obligatory), there would be nothing to do and no values to support' (Fish 1989: 239).

3 By cultural capital, Bourdieu means the accumulated resources and insignia which can be 'cashed in' for society's goods and services.

4 Intentionality in the philosophical sense is different from intention in the familiar sense. Deliberate intention to oppress others may or may not be assumed (in the people who populate a society) by theorists to exist. The existence of *intentionality*,

however, on the part of the model maker or theory constructor is different. It is described by Dennett (1996: 46–8) as 'aboutness': 'Something exhibits intentionality if its competence is in some way *about* something else . . . Intentional phenomena are equipped with metaphorical arrows, you might say, aimed at something or other . . . But of course many phenomena that exhibit this minimal sort of intentionality do not do anything *intentionally*, in the everyday sense of the term.'

5 Many would seek to disabuse us of the notion that we are not theorizing (see Rajagopalan 1998). However, one needs to draw in for support again Stanley Fish, who has had a lot to say about the overuse of the notion of 'theory'. He (1994: 378) highlights the highly varied activities shoved under the billowing cloak of 'theory', concluding that 'to include such activities under the rubric of theory is finally to make everything theory, and if one does that there is nothing of a *general* kind to be said about theory.' He distinguishes between theory and what he calls *theory talk*; the latter being 'any form of talk that has acquired cachet and prestige' (Fish 1989: 14–15). When informed analysis occurs, we are in Fish's terms 'not following a theory, but extending a practice, employing a set of heuristic questions' or, as E.D. Hirsch (1976) puts it, 'making calculations of probability based on an insider's knowledge'. This is *not* using theory. We can, says Fish, always call such kinds of thinking 'theory' but nothing whatsoever will have been gained and we will have lost any sense that theory is special. We discuss this further elsewhere (Thomas 1997b; 1999a; 2007).

6 As Baker *et al.* (1995: 14) put it: 'There is no separate knowledge base for teaching children classified as mildly retarded or learning disabled.'

7 Bourdieu's drawing of this distinction is not unique. Mouzelis (1995) makes the point that there is a classic distinction (drawn by S.K. Nadel) between (i) theory as a set of substantive statements, provable by empirical investigation, which try to tell us something new about the world, and (ii) theory as a set of tools. Mouzelis further points out that Althusser makes a similar distinction between theory as tool/means (which he calls Gen. II) and theory as provisional end product (which he calls Gen. III). In education (as distinct from sociology) Chambers (1992) identifies no fewer than nine meanings for 'theory' as it is used in this field. Only one of those meanings concerns theory as 'thinking tool'.

8 Trofim Denisovich Lysenko was the Soviet agronomist and geneticist who progressed in the Soviet scientific establishment by developing a genetic theory that was consistent with Marxist–Leninist thought. Darwinian evolution and Mendelian genetics, he asserted, could not be correct because it conflicted with Marxist–Leninist ideology. His ideas received official support, being taught in biology courses in the USSR and they were incorporated, with disastrous consequences, into agricultural programmes.

9 Commentators such as Armstrong *et al.* (1998) make a persuasive case for the social value of theory, arguing for a Habermasian extension of personal theory to critical and emancipatory theory.

10 James and Prout (1990) make the case persuasively with respect to the damage that has been done to our view of children as people. In particular they point to ways in which models such as those of Piaget have inappropriately 'constructed' notions of childhood. Readers of Piaget will have noticed that he calls himself not an educator or even a psychologist or a biologist but rather a 'genetic epistemologist'. The phrase gives some clues about Piaget's mission and his core beliefs. As Toulmin (1972: 424) points out, there are two ways in which this *epistemology genetique* can be understood: as 'intellectual phylogeny' of human cultures, on a collective level, or to 'intellectual ontogeny' of individual human beings. The former, he says, is the correct interpretation of Piaget's meaning. The rational adult is, in other words, seen as the butterfly at

the end of some ugly but necessary pre-rational stages. Seen through such a theoretical lens, all kinds of implications follow for teaching and for an understanding of failure to learn in the child.

11 It is worth noting that those who promulgated behavioural objectives insisted on the observability of the behaviour that was being promoted and that this insistence owes a lineage directly to logical positivism via Skinner's behaviourism. The insistence that a child be seen to *do* something, rather than merely be noted vaguely to *enjoy* it is traceable with no difficulty at all to the logical positivists' insistence on the verification of meaningfulness through observation. Carnap (leader of the logical positivists' Vienna Circle) would no doubt have turned in his grave at the knowledge that the philosophical school that he helped to form had, 50 years later, provided the intellectual lead for a system of teaching that involved breaking down learning into dozens of 'behavioural objectives'.

The knowledge-roots of special education

The twentieth century was a good one for special schools. They grew in number until they catered for around two per cent of the school population, a figure that was maintained until near the end of the century. The growth was not by chance: it happened because people felt special education was a Good Thing – there was a rationale for it. That rationale was built on arguments about the best interests of the separated children and it was buttressed by all kinds of theoretical and empirical ballast. Our argument in this chapter, however, is that this theory was usually empty and the empirical evidence often illusory.

As we noted in Chapter 1, special education has not been alone in the process of developing hollow theory and constructing evidence that is next to meaningless. It has been a process general to education and the social sciences throughout the twentieth century – a process about which many have commented (see, for example, Andreski 1972; Dewey 1920; MacIntyre 1985; Popper 1989; Rorty 1998; Wright Mills 1970). Dewey suggested that theorizing – that is, the process of trying to develop theories – in fields like education does little good. Indeed, it 'detains thought within pompous and sonorous generalities' (Dewey 1920: 189–99).

If the pomposity and sonorous generality spoken about by Dewey have been features of the theorizing of education, they have been an especially prominent feature of the thinking and research behind special education. Prominent, for the children for whom psychologists and educators have so diligently toiled have experienced such conspicuous difficulties at school that the work done on their behalf has seemed automatically praiseworthy. This is not to claim that the theorizing and empirical work of those who have worked in these fields has been motivated by anything other than the highest motives or ideals. But these individuals may nevertheless be open to the charge that they have been too often indiscriminate in pursuit of immediate goals and ambitions and in so doing may have overlooked the wider effects of their intellectual and professional empires. The problem is that the structures – intellectual, academic, commercial and professional – that have surrounded the expansion of special education have been responsible for producing sterile arenas of study and practice. In such infertile land for enquiry important questions about the meaning and nature of education have often been glossed over.

Special education has grown for many reasons. Prime among these has been the setting on a pedestal of certain kinds of 'knowledge': theoretical, empirical, and above all, scientific. It is our contention that the putative character of this knowledge – it has been projected as stable, objective, reliable – has created a false legitimacy for the growth of special education and the activities of special educators; indeed, the reification of scientific knowledge in a field in which it is inappropriate amounts, we shall argue, to a kind of scientism.

Growth of special education – a new epistemology

The twentieth century saw a great expansion in special education. It was only in the century's last two decades that the expansion halted. If a graph were to be drawn showing the proportion of children educated in special schools, the line would show a very gradual increase during the nineteenth century, with an acceleration in the early years of the twentieth century and a significant rise again after the Second World War. The gradient would only have levelled off in the 1980s and 1990s.

If the first special school in the UK was the School of Instruction for the Indigent Blind, established in Liverpool in 1791 (see Hurt 1988 for a detailed history), the next decades saw many schools following suit. During the nineteenth century special schools began to emerge for blind, deaf and 'dumb' children; philanthropists began to offer support for these deserving unfortunates and government even provided special relief for children with such disabilities under the Poor Law Amendment Act 1834.

The increase in the proportion of children being educated at special schools was by no means a smooth one and at the beginning of the twentieth century there was a jump in the special school population. This was not due to some sudden boost of humanitarian impulse on the part of benefactors, government and the public at large. Rather, the changes occurred out of a changing mindset about education and about children who were different. Around the end of the nineteenth century, assumptions about that which made a child worthy of special education shifted. Around this time, a cluster of ideas was emerging that gave strength to the notion that not simply those with conspicuous disabilities – the blind and the deaf – should be educated separately, but that those who were, more prosaically, just *different* could and should be educated separately, for their own benefit and for the benefit of the majority.

The new ideas emerged out of a new worldview which had arisen at that time. Popularly held views about children who were different, deviant or disabled were transformed from mere common sense by a new way of investigating and understanding. New ways of finding out about the world and new theories and models for looking at the world gave educated laypeople entirely fresh perspectives on the natural world.

It is important to remember how powerful this new epistemology was and to reflect – before taking a brief case history on an element of it – what some of its consequences were before the last quarter of the twentieth century. Age-old notions about affliction, about stupidity, about what it is to be mad or bad are at the root of ideas about specialness and what to do with people who are special. Although these notions have recently been challenged, it is only in the last 20 years or so that challenge and critique have taken the place of a less questioning disposition among the intellectual establishment. Ideas that are generations old – ideas, for example, about cleverness and stupidity – have rarely been unravelled by this intellectual establishment. Rather, words like 'intelligence' have been taken as without-problems descriptors of God-given phenomena that were taken manifestly to exist. Psychologists and educators have seen it as their duty merely to seek out, reveal and measure such phenomena rather than explicate them or problematize them. Although there are some notable exceptions, academics in the fields most closely associated with education have seldom proffered incisive insights into the ideas that have shaped the ways in which we think about the schools children inhabit.

It has been left to others – artists, novelists, philosophers, historians – to provide the most interesting commentary and to pose the most critical questions about the operation of institutions that care for and educate 'different' people. Ken Kesey's *One Flew over the Cuckoo's Nest*, Christy Nolan's *Under the Eye of the Clock* and, more recently, Ruben Gallego's *White on Black*, for example, have arguably done as much to shape contemporary thinking and policy about people with differences than all the academic research and writing of the last half-century.

Special education research – the magic of the method

The last sentence in the previous section makes a large assertion, but we believe it to be correct. It would be a brave special educator who would venture to proffer for critical scrutiny a putative advance in practice-from-research that has occurred over the last one hundred years. Certainly there have been advances in thinking about the proper form education should take – advances in thinking about care and humane treatment. But these are advances that have come more from changes in the political and social climate than from research in special education.

The challenge is to identify what beneficial effects have emerged in special education practice from a particular piece of research – about assessment, or pedagogy, or whatever – which have not, on evaluation, proved to be as good as the effects emerging from the next non-research-based (and probably cheaper and simpler) method. The research that has happened in special education and educational psychology has tended to follow the find-what's-wrong-and-cure-it paradigm. Thinking within this paradigm starts with enthusiasm but is usually followed by what Hargreaves (1978: 5) calls a certain 'cycle of events':

> After the initial phase in which the original ideas and instruments are developed by psychologists there follows a phase in which over-zealous educational psychologists make somewhat premature applications of, and exaggerated claims for, these ideas and instruments and use them in ways which are not strictly warranted. Then follows a third phase in which teachers receive these ideas in a severely attenuated form, and as the ideas become diffused they also become distorted and abused. This stimulates a fourth phase in which the abuses are subjected to critical scrutiny and this in turn generates a final phase in which the original enterprise is denigrated and held to be wrong in principle.

But it is not just that the methods are attenuated and abused in practice. There also seems to be something about the practice emerging from the dominant model of research that makes it overconcerned with 'fix-it' matters. The problem is that often these fix-it cures are shown empirically to have effects, sometimes dramatic, and these are then drawn into Hargreaves's cycle. However, in the messy field of research about people and their social environments, where it is difficult if not impossible to delineate variables for inspection of their effects, new techniques can acquire potency for any number of reasons: the charisma of a pioneer; the energy of dedicated a research group; the support of a government or the publicity machine of a publishing house. Thus, special education has come up with a panoply methods and techniques over the years, all of them claiming some empirical justification: instrumental enrichment, Doman Delacato, conductive education, Direct Instruction, diagnostic-prescriptive teaching (see Johnson and Pearson 1975 for the 'denigration'; and see Pawson 2006 for a discussion of how early evaluations of success are never somehow matched by later ones).

Examples are almost too easy to find – and a study of the history of each discloses a pattern strikingly concordant with the 'cycle of events' which Hargreaves describes. Of late, the overuse of the technology of behavioural psychology with children with severe learning difficulties provides an excellent case study of Hargreaves's process. Great hopes were placed in the potential of behavioural techniques both to help children learn and to help them behave appropriately. While there is no doubt that they provided some assistance in thinking about pedagogy for some children, there can be equal certainty that they oversimplified the nature of learning and led, in widespread practice, to a kind of curricular desertification – as sensible, cautious thinking about educational aims was replaced with the certainties of behavioural analysis.

Direct Instruction, another technique in which great hopes were invested, rested in a hyper-rational set of ideas about teaching and learning formal skills. Specifying exactly what should be taught, how it should be taught and how learning should be evaluated, early forays into its use showed great promise. Longer-term evaluation, however, in the large American Follow-Through project (DeVault et al. 1977) indicated that the great benefits attributed to it may have been due as much to the generous resourcing allocated to it as to the specific pedagogic elements. More worryingly, recent analysis has indicated that on leaving school those children who were part of a Direct Instruction curriculum were significantly more likely to have been involved in crime, were less well adjusted and engaged in fewer community activities than those who partook at an earlier age in traditional nursery activities (Schweinhart and Weikart 1997).

Likewise, in diagnostic-prescriptive teaching – another wonder cure – the appealing notion that one could assess where a child's difficulties lay and then prescribe a programme of help spawned a rash of specialized assessments – such as the Illinois Test of Psycholinguistic Abilities (ITPA) – and associated remedial programme writing. Unfortunately, the evidence (which has still evidently to hit many people) is that all of this assessment and programme writing is an elaborate waste of time. A brood of evaluations undertaken in the mid-1970s and since show that help based on this kind of approach is no more effective than help based on the teacher's own gut assessment of the difficulty and his or her own solution to it. The evidence to back up these assertions has been around since the mid-1970s, when an excellent analysis of diagnostic-prescriptive teaching was undertaken by Newcomer and Hammill (1975) and a scholarly appraisal of research findings and the tenets on which the diagnostic-prescriptive approach is based was undertaken by Arter and Jenkins (1979). Brown and Campione (1986) are also worth reading for a review of special assessment procedures over the past century. They interestingly relate the nineteenth-century psychologist William James's failure to boost his 'memory muscle' by doing memory exercises to the current failure to find evidence for the idea that children can have academic skills boosted through training in putative sub-skills. In the same context, Rueda and Mehan (1986) provide evidence for the possibility that it is social interchanges which get in the way of learning when children do badly at school. Far from lacking 'meta-cognitive skills', children who were labelled 'learning disabled' managed to do all the things they weren't supposed to be able to do: checking, monitoring, evaluating and so on. And they also used sophisticated planning in avoiding tasks expected of them. Rueda and Mehan conclude that supposedly context-free metacognitive activities are in fact context bound: it is almost as though the ability to use them is switched on or switched off by the surrounding social circumstances. In boredom and/or fear, other systems will kick in.

Frank Smith, the Canadian educator, gives a vignette that provides a glimpse into the sort of thinking underpinning the sterile diagnose-and-prescribe approach behind so much special pedagogy:

> The author of a highly successful commercial instructional program that employed all of these fragmented techniques told me why they had to be so detailed and specific – 'You can't trust teachers to teach.' His program was so detailed it even told teachers when to smile, and to ignore student questions if the program hadn't provided answers.
>
> (Smith 1998: 72)

It is the sort of approach that assumes that when a child's time at school appears to be going wrong, special measures are needed: special assessment, special pedagogy – in short, special education. Strangely, when such a mindset kicks in, common-sense knowledge about learning and teaching is doubly mistrusted.

Unfortunately, special education has been so successful at continually devising more glossy and more elaborate forms of assessment and pedagogy that teachers have begun to lose confidence in their own ability to assess and teach all the children in their charge. Children who are difficult to teach have become by default 'special' children. Teachers have really begun to believe that they are not skilled enough to deal with 'special' children – children who are finding their work at school difficult. If, after all, someone has gone to the obvious trouble and expense of producing a test such as the ITPA, then it stands to reason that the test does *something*. The natural assumption will be that such a test crystallizes and holds a great deal of knowledge about the ways that children learn and think.

The truth is that such tests – and more importantly the logic behind them – mask what is really going on when a child is learning, or not learning, at school. Worse, they give the impression that for some children a separate set of procedures is needed to assess and help them. The truth that seems to have emerged is that for all children the best way to assess them is, quite simply, to look at what they are doing and to talk to them about it (see Lunt 1993 for an elegant discussion of this in relation to Vygotskian thinking). Certainly, some children will learn more slowly than others. Some people pass their driving test on the first try, while others don't make it until the sixth or seventh attempt. This doesn't mean that the latter have learning difficulties or special driving needs. It may mean that they have lost confidence or they are anxious – but their learning needs are still exactly the same as anyone else's. Children are no different from adults in this respect. Children who are slower to learn – for whatever reason – need the same in order to learn as any other child. They need the kind of things which, as discussed in Chapter 1, our humanity tells us they need: interest, confidence, freedom from worry, a warm and patient teacher. The legacy that 100 years of special education has given to teachers is the idea that this isn't enough; that you need all sorts of special procedures and qualifications to help you understand them and all sorts of special techniques before you can make any sort of a job of helping them.

If one reviews the history of some of the methods and instruments of special education, one cannot fail to be impressed by the fact that children learned anything at all when they were used. The remarkable resilience and plasticity of children's learning processes never ceases to be both surprising and impressive. There is little enough ground for believing that effort spent in developing ever newer and ever better methods of teaching will do any good – especially when compared with ways of helping children which are simpler. Indeed, it sometimes even appears that it doesn't matter what teachers do as long as they do it with commitment and enthusiasm and as long as they do it frequently enough. The person helping the child doesn't even need to be a teacher, let alone need sophisticated instructional systems. There were plenty of studies in the early 1980s (e.g. Jackson and Hannon 1981; Tizard *et al.* 1982) showing that children can make extraordinary progress when having help from their parents and carers, whatever techniques were being used to help them:

> Of much greater practical significance is the fact that teachers and parents working in collaboration did improve the academic performance of the children *without the parents being given any special training in the techniques of tutoring.*
>
> (Tizard *et al.* 1982: 13, our emphasis)

One doesn't have to be a rocket scientist to realize that what is common to the success of this and a whole range of other methods spawned by special educators is not the special techniques being used – not, in other words, the magic of the method. Instead, it is, more mundanely and prosaically, the amount of help being given and the sensitivity with which it is given. It seems that given a few fairly broadly defined parameters within which any reasonably sensitive adult works with a child (e.g. enthusiasm, patience, starting at a level which is not too difficult, the ability and willingness to give encouragement) such help can hardly fail to be successful. If this is the case, why are we wedded to the idea that further study in the old tradition will do any good?

Faith in defunct methods

The answer to all this lies partly in faith in the methods behind special education research. Admittedly, methodology is not an obvious place to look for an explanation for our predilection for 'fix-its' in special education and, as noted in the previous chapter, many have looked instead to vested professional and commercial interests to explain the continual re-emergence of the same kinds of solution by educators to learning or behaviour difficulty (see, for example, Abberley 1987).

These interests have certainly played their part, but too little has been attributed to the effects of methodology. Perhaps 'methodology' locates the problem too precisely, for methods represent merely the manifestation of a mindset, a paradigm, a way of viewing the world. The mindset in question emerged at the end of the nineteenth century and grew during the twentieth century. For the best part of the twentieth century, there had been the optimistic assumption that the path of progress in knowledge would be a smooth one – that progress would follow naturally out of scientific advance. It was assumed that the highly successful methods of scientific investigation were appropriate not just for physics and chemistry but also for social enquiry. For many years, therefore, 'social scientists' emulated their peers in the natural sciences – in assumptions about the nature of knowledge, theoretical advance, research design and the use of inference. It is only of late that there has been a recognition of the limits of supposedly scientific enquiry in determining the ways in which we should examine schools.

While neurologist Oliver Sacks would no doubt eschew the role of scientific myth slayer, in *An Anthropologist on Mars* (1995) he provides an excellent example of the change in research style to which we are alluding. In this book, he sets aside the methods of the scientific discipline, neurology, in which he was trained in favour of the tradition of the storyteller and the anthropologist. In so doing he offers a set of sparkling insights and understandings into the worlds of a number of people who behave differently. Such insights have been largely curtained off from us by the understanding offered by traditional analyses. As part of Sacks's discourse on our understanding of difference – of the 'borders of human experience', as he puts it – he quotes G.K. Chesterton:

> I don't deny the dry [scientific] light may sometimes do good, though in one sense it's the very reverse of science. So far from being knowledge, it's actually suppression of what we know. It's treating a friend as a stranger, and pretending that something familiar is really remote and mysterious.
>
> (Sacks 1995: xvii)

Things have moved on since the rationalist assumption that any subject could be reduced to what Thayer (1995: 530) calls 'an ontology of individual particles'. A theme of contemporary epistemology is that there are no certainties – and, more important, that there are no special means of getting to knowledge about the human world. 'Life,' as Samuel Butler put it in his *Notebooks*, 'is the art of drawing sufficient conclusions from insufficient premises' and it is a recognition of the truth of this in our dealings with others that has led to a search for and a recognition of other forms of understanding than those that are offered by the tight, delimiting methods of science.

When trying to understand people – *people*, as distinct from gases in a test tube – we each have to use our own humanity, recognizing our 'failings', our frailties, misunderstandings and prejudices. These 'failings', it increasingly seems to have been realized in the last 20 years or so, have to be used in our understandings of the predicament of others and not 'controlled out' in our investigative procedures. There is not likely to be discovered some special method for unearthing data about people or some rational calculus for interpreting their trials and tribulations. The methods of a 'scientific' psychology or sociology have encouraged not only an illusory vision of a set of certain answers regarding human existence. They have led also to a garbled, two-dimensional discourse, which has stripped from our study of people any of the recognition that we, as people, have ourselves of the plight of others. In this desiccated study there is no use of what Oakeshott (1989: 65) called 'historic languages of feelings, sentiments, imaginings, fancies, desires, recognitions, moral and religious beliefs, intellectual and practical enterprises, customs, conventions, procedures and practices, canons, maxims and principles of conduct'.

It is perhaps too kind a judgement on twentieth-century psychology and sociology to say merely that these disciplines have failed to take stock of and use the 'historic languages' of which Oakeshott speaks. For it is not as though psychologists and sociologists have merely mislaid this kind of understanding, have merely put it down somewhere and forgotten where they put it. The process has been far more conscious and deliberate than that. It has involved an intentional casting off of certain kinds of knowledge – the knowledge we have of other human beings that comes by virtue of our own membership of the human species – in the assumption that these kinds of knowledge would contaminate a dispassionate, disinterested understanding of others. And in doing this, a strange kind of professional and academic language has been encouraged. Straightforward understandings have often been puffed up into something to look impressive and 'scientific'. As the iconoclastic American sociologist Wright Mills (1970: 40) put it of Talcot Parsons's classic sociological treatise, *The Social System*: 'One could translate the 555 pages of *The Social System* into about 150 pages of straightforward English. The result would not be very impressive.' The point here, however, is not just that the understanding wouldn't be impressive; it is that it would – even if stripped of pomposity and verbosity – be irrelevant, dry and empty.

All of this is relevant for the study of special education, for it is this branch of education that has suffered most from assumptions that have been made in the twentieth century about the proper way to study the individual and social behaviour of human beings. If education as a field of study has always suffered from something of an inferiority complex about its academic status – borrowing its epistemological tenets and research methods only too readily from its clever cousins psychology and sociology – special education has suffered the inferiority complex even more profoundly. Not only have those tenets and methods of psychologists and sociologists been eagerly snapped up, but special education has always seemingly been only too easily influenced by the prevailing cultural orthodoxy – the spirit of the times, the things that are taken for granted without having to think, or what Bourdieu (in Bourdieu and Eagleton 1994) calls *doxa*.

It has been vulnerable to such swaying in the wind since it has never had an intellectual homeland of its own – no core of beliefs or understandings. It has thus been prey to passing intellectual fashion and transient cultural whim. It has occupied a place on the periphery of education where its *raison d'être* has been as a kind of service industry to mainstream education. There has been little in the way of intellectual lead. Where movement has happened it has taken place as a result of broader social movements, supported by what Foucault (1991: 23) calls the ' "epistemological-juridical" formation'. The knowledge produced by the scientific study of psychology and psychiatry have merely buttressed our everyday constructions about disability, difference or disorder.

To the practically minded, Foucault's ideas may seem to be superfluous to a discussion of special education. In fact, however, his analyses are strikingly relevant to the world of education and special education. Foucault's analyses help one to understand that social structures – in our case special schools, special assessments and special teaching – far from being God given, are made by people acting intentionally. The interesting insight which Foucault provides is that the intellectual apparatus that has emerged ostensibly to add objectivity, humanity and disinterested 'science' to an analysis of social structures, in fact, does nothing of the kind. In the messy world of human beings and human relations, this intellectual apparatus does little other than provide in new words and garb what we already recognize and know.

But the trouble is that this apparatus does not merely rename and smarten up old ideas. The real trouble is that the shining instruments of the social sciences add legitimacy to common-or-garden ideas and prejudices. The notion of a gradient of cleverness, for example, was given a shot of adrenaline by the scientific paraphernalia of assessment testing. Mental infrastructures have emerged to support these social structures – paradigms, theories, research methods, research findings – but it is increasingly recognized that these are less disinterested and less informative than was once assumed. Philp (1990) sums up Foucault's contribution to this change of assumption excellently:

> The normal child, the healthy body, the stable mind . . . such concepts haunt our ideas about ourselves, and are reproduced and legitimated through the practices of teachers, social workers, doctors, judges, policemen and administrators. The human sciences attempt to define normality; and by establishing this normality as a rule of life for us all, they simultaneously manufacture – for investigation, surveillance and treatment – the vast area of our deviation from this standard.
>
> (Philp 1990: 67)

Let us give an example.

Intelligence and special education: a case study in the construction (and deconstruction) of ideas

At the turn of the twentieth century, there was a strong feeling in Great Britain that in the newly structured council schools, set up in 1904, there should be no difficulties imposed on the majority of children by those who were 'imbeciles' or 'unworthy' (an idea that is by no means uncommon even now). Where did such an idea come from? Is it enough merely to blame 'Victorian values'? Certainly, such Victorian values existed and were exemplified in the writings of 'eminent Victorians' such as Thomas Arnold, whose notions of 'good poor' and 'undeserving poor' (see Strachey 1971) were rooted in an unquestioning devotion to biblical teaching. But if one is interested to see how such ideas may have become cemented together more firmly and acquired a momentum of their own, it is necessary to look further to the events of the time.

Then, at the turn of the twentieth century, the successes of science meant that the methods of the natural sciences were looked on increasingly favourably. The influential philosopher-sociologist Herbert Spencer was able to promote the notion, in a reification of science's methods that has come to be known as 'scientism', that the only reliable knowledge of the universe was that found in the sciences. Darwinism was beginning to slough off its lunatic ecclesiastical critics and was quickly acquiring respectability and status. The new status, however – in line with the general direction provided by scientism – gave credence also to some biological fictions, most notably the idea that for society it was important that the 'weakest' should not be allowed to infiltrate the genetic stock. If degenerates and ne'er-do-wells were to mix and interbreed unhindered with others, the argument went, the inevitable result would be the decay of the stock of the race. Social Darwinism, as this school of thought came to be called, was promulgated enthusiastically in Britain by the prominent scientific polymath Sir Francis Galton, who in *Hereditary Genius, its Laws and Consequences* (1869), proclaimed that it would be perfectly possible to 'produce a highly gifted race of men by judicious marriages during several consecutive generations'. The uselessness ascribed to education in counteracting the effects of heredity in accounts such as this amounts almost to contempt. If education was not entirely futile, it was certainly of no benefit for the purpose of raising the achievement of the least able. The feeling of the intellectual establishment of the time is summed up by one of Galton's protégés, Karl Pearson, who at the beginning of the twentieth century was able to claim that 'No training or education can create [intelligence] . . . You must breed it' (in Kevles 1985).

It was not only in Britain that such ideas were being touted. The same enthusiasm for engineered genetic change was felt also in continental Europe, where the German embryologist Haeckel, with his Monist League, concocted a history of nations which explained their rise, decline and fall on the basis of natural selection.

It is worth noting that simultaneously in continental Europe, cognate ideas, but of a different provenance, were being promoted by Elisabeth Nietzsche, sister of Friedrich, who twisted her brother's increasingly influential philosophy into an aberration of its original form (see Macintyre 1992). Notions of the 'Superman' and Nietzsche's somewhat anarchic iconoclasm were cleverly bent by Elisabeth into a justification for anti-Semitism and eugenics. As Macintyre says: 'A measure of her success is the fact that Nietzsche's name has still not fully shaken off the taint of fascism.' For the record (since some accounts of the history of special education still link Nietzsche himself with the eugenic *Zeitgeist*), Macintyre (1992: xiii) concludes that 'Nietzsche would have been appalled at the use which the fascists (ably abetted by his own sister) made of his philosophy [and] . . . he would have damned Nazism comprehensively.' He quotes Nietzsche in *The Gay Science*: 'To enthusiasm for the "German national character" I have indeed attained very little . . . but even less to the wish to keep this "glorious" race *pure*. On the contrary, on the contrary' (ibid.: 115).

While eugenic views are wholly unacceptable now, it is important to realize how prevalent such views were at the turn of the twentieth century. It wasn't the prerogative of a right-wing zealot fringe to hold them. They held great popular currency. Indeed, even prominent intellectuals such as Sidney and Beatrice Webb in the emergent socialist movement were persuaded by eugenic arguments. The successes of the natural sciences at the time meant that the methods of science were held in high esteem. Philosophies such as Haeckel's Monism lent the cachet of science to a ferment of prejudices and half-truths incorporating racism, nationalism and eugenics.

It needed only a minor extension of the eugenic logic to lead to the proposition that defectives and degenerates should be removed from society's mainstream institutions, notably schools. When Cyril Burt was appointed as the first psychologist for London in 1913 further momentum was added to this logic. Burt was fond of the young technology of psychometrics (that is, mental measurement, including intelligence testing) being developed principally by Alfred Binet in Paris. Although Binet himself was cautious about the benefits of a mental quotient, Burt and others, notably the German psychologist William Stern, were less circumspect, as was the American psychologist Lewis M. Terman, who in 1916 coined the term 'intelligence quotient' or IQ. Psychometrics gave the promise of effectively calibrating levels of ability and sorting the population for the most and least intelligent. If this was possible, of course, it was possible also to separate out and educate differently children of differing levels of ability. Burt's growing reputation – built on a phenomenal energy and a prolific and well-written set of publications – his fondness for psychometrics and his commitment to the idea that intelligence was inherited and more-or-less immutable all combined to give great stimulus to a segregative education system based on the categorization of the child.

An argument can be made for the case that it was an enthusiastic embracing of Social Darwinist thinking that led to Burt's notorious fraud in the construction of his evidence about the heritability of intelligence. Although the now received interpretation of the facts is contested by some, there is very strong support (see Hearnshaw 1979; Kamin 1977) for the thesis that Burt constructed data about the heritability of intelligence from non-existent identical twin studies. The interesting phenomenon in this is not that Burt was willing to do this out of personal ambition, professional rivalry, or whatever, but rather that the self-evident truth – the doxa – was, for Burt, so plainly *there* to be supported by any means. The folklore, in other words, took precedence in the epistemology: empirical support for the folklore assumption was almost an afterthought in the process.

The focus in public analysis of Burt's fraud has been on the man and his ego. As Hearnshaw (1979) puts it of Burt's invented castlist of researchers and reviewers:

> Of the more than forty 'persons' who contributed reviews, notes and letters to the journal during the period of Burt's editorship, well over half are unidentifiable, and judging from the style and content of their contributions were pseudonyms for Burt. Howard and Conway [Burt's putative assistants] were members of a large family of characters invented to save his face and boost his ego.
>
> (Hearnshaw 1979: 245)

While Burt's ego clearly played a part in all of this, the invention of material, data and people cannot be attributed solely to the man's psychology. More interesting than personal psychology in this chapter of deceit is Burt's conviction in the legitimacy and correctness of the cause for which he was contriving evidence. Here was a man who had the highest respect for science, yet was prepared, it seems, to put conviction in a deeper truth – that of the genetic basis for intelligence – above its systems and procedures.

The problem is not simply fraud – to assert this would be to reduce what happened to human frailty. The problem is one almost of epistemology – of ways of knowing. Burt knew, viscerally rather than rationally, that he was right. Neither can it be simply dismissed as Burt being some kind of 'bad apple' – the sort of person that the scientific community vigorously discourages, but who sadly emerges very occasionally. The problem, in a social scientific community hypnotized by the methods of the natural sciences, is of a kind of trance induced by those methods' success. The fact that the conspicuously messy world of people's behaviour, where variables cannot be held constant and experiments cannot be conducted with anything approaching the rigour of the laboratory – the fact that this world is in no way congruent with the world of chemistry or physics was not allowed to disturb the hallucination that the natural sciences' methods must be appropriate. The worldview, a hangover from the scientism of Herbert Spencer, generated a very particular way of thinking about people and thinking about the way in which people could be understood.

There was a faith in science's methods. But the problem with faith, as distinct from doubt, is that constitutes the very antithesis of the scientific method it seeks to emulate. With faith there is none of what Haldane (1965) called 'the duty of doubt'. Since the method is elevated and is assumed to comprise some canonical and almost magical set of procedures, there is little or no scrutiny of ways of knowing, of the protocols and procedures which a scientific culture has of checking its facts or assuring their reliability. And these methods of the scientific culture are as important – as Feyerabend (1993), Kuhn (1970), Popper (1977) and others have shown – as the assumed-to-be-important methods in science's success. Burt's hoodwinking of his own scholarly community was allowed to happen because no one checked the facts. And this pertains to this day. There is all the impedimenta of scientific scholarly culture surrounding much of the knowledge of educational and psychological science, yet little in the way of self-scrutiny of those procedures.[1]

Neither is this some shabby but forgettable episode. The data that Burt constructed were used by Jensen (1969) in his influential *Harvard Educational Review* paper about the heritability of intelligence. Hearnshaw describes (in a generally sympathetic biography of Burt) Burt's process of deception in constructing this very material: Burt had started his letter in reply to American psychologist Jencks, who had asked for details of twin pairs used by Burt:

> 'I apologise for not replying more promptly; but I was away for the Christmas vacation, and college (where the data are stored) was closed until the opening of term.' As a matter of fact Burt had not been away for Christmas; his data were not stored at college; and the college had only been closed for a week. So every single particular in his apology was untrue.
>
> (Hearnshaw 1979: 247)

One is forced to the conclusion, Hearnshaw asserts, that Burt had taken so long to reply only in order to have time to fabricate a suitably convincing set of scores and statistics. The details of the fraud are fascinating, for this was no slip of the pen: no oversight, as some have asserted that they must be, given Burt's reputation as a first-rate psychologist, statistician and scientist. This was a calculated deception in the name of an intuitively held truth.

Burt was influential in the way that thought developed about children who had difficulties at school and his influence persisted until the disclosures of the 1970s. Remember that the fourth edition of *Mental and Scholastic Tests* was published as recently as 1962 and this was a volume that could unashamedly give as one of its index entries: 'Special school children, *see* Mental defectives' (Burt 1962: 548). His aim, as he expressed it, was 'the diagnosis of mental deficiency' (ibid: xxix) and it was clear that he saw mental deficiency as some kind of affliction: 'when speed is demanded, their incapacity becomes as sadly apparent as that of a wooden-legged cripple when his companions break into a run' (ibid: 440). Talking of the learning of arithmetic and English, Burt says 'the young normal child is just learning the rudiments of these subjects; but he is learning them with great rapidity. The defective, on the contrary, learns them with laborious slowness – in truth, by comparison, with a diminishing speed' (ibid: 440).

Burt was one of the most influential voices in the climate that gave rise to the 1944 Education Act, insofar as it related to the differentiation of children according to their ability. The 1944 Act constructed a highly segregative post-war education system with its 10 categories of handicap for which special schools would cater. Although Hearnshaw insists that Burt should not be seen as the architect of the selective system, he himself sees Burt's role as highly significant in it:

> By the time the Hadow committee had produced its report on *The Primary School* in 1931 its members had been persuaded that before the age of twelve 'children need to be grouped according to their capacity, not merely in separate classes or standards, but in separate types of schools'. The process which culminated in the Education Act of 1944 had its beginnings in the early experiments of Burt a quarter of a century previously.
>
> (Hearnshaw 1979: 96)

Burt had advised the consultative committee that had given rise to selection thus: 'It is possible at a very early age to predict with some accuracy the ultimate level of a child's individual power' (cited in Hearnshaw 1979: 115). This confidence in psychometrics and in the fixity of intellectual functioning had been expressed a lot earlier in the USA, where Terman (1924: 336) had asserted that: 'The first task of the school would be to establish the native quality of every pupil; second, to supply the kind of instruction suited to each grade of ability.' The consensus about the good sense embodied in eugenics in this climate of opinion is evidenced by the fact that at the end of the 1920s 24 American states had passed laws enabling sterilization.

The feeling was not all one way, however. The political scientist Walter Lippmann (1922) had published a series of articles in the USA in which he argued that intelligence testers cleaved to a dogma about the heritability of intelligence and that: 'Intelligence testing in the hands of men who hold this dogma could not but lead to an intellectual caste system.' The perspicacity and prescience of Lippmann were borne out by later events. In the selective and segregative systems enabled by psychometrics were to be found precisely the caste system predicted and feared by Lippmann.

Other shifts of thinking have occurred. The Second World War put paid to discussion of eugenics. It should be noted also that the crude Social Darwinism of the early part of the twentieth century was displaced at the end of the twentieth century (in a renewed social interest in Darwinism prompted by greater understanding of genetics) by a far more sophisticated discourse about potentially evolved characteristics. With books such as Robert Axelrod's *The Evolution of Cooperation* (1984) came the realization that evolution concerns not merely the survival of the 'fittest' but also the development of cooperation and altruism. This recent understanding of the complexities of evolution leads the Darwinist Peter Singer (1999) to advocate social thinking which would have been unthinkable for Herbert Spencer and his contemporaries. In *A Darwinian Left: Politics, Evolution and Cooperation*, Singer concludes with the comment that 'A Darwinian left would . . . [r]eject any inference from what is "natural" to what is "right" . . . [p]romote structures that foster cooperation rather than competition' (Singer 1999: 61).

It is interesting to note the demise of the eugenics/psychometrics viewpoint, since there are parallels in the way in which, later on in the twentieth century, arguments for special education have lost ground. Before the result of the Second World War killed off any respectability that an overtly eugenic position might hold, the findings of more sophisticated research were beginning to eat into the confidence of the eugenicists. As Fienberg and Resnick (1997: 11) put it: 'In the course of the 1920s, true believers became skeptics, and it appeared that the mainstream of American psychology had made a major paradigm shift, from race to culture, and from nature to nurture.' This change, they note, was due to the accumulating weight of evidence available in the psychological literature. Evidence came from many and varied sources: from exposure of the inappropriate statistical treatment of environmental influences in studies on racial difference; from studies showing that blacks raised in the north had higher scores than whites from the south; from studies of southern-born black children raised in New York showing that the longer they had lived in New York, the higher their scores.

Despite all this, and Burt's alleged fraud and powerful arguments against the case for eugenics notwithstanding, the momentum gathered by the eugenic cause has enabled the arguments to be put again and again through this century. In the 1960s Jensen (1969) was able to ask, in an influential paper in the *Harvard Educational Review*: 'Is there a danger that current welfare policies, unaided by eugenic foresight, could lead to the genetic enslavement of a substantial segment of our population?' The arguments continue to be made, as they have been recently in *The Bell Curve* (Herrnstein and Murray 1994).

Although there is a regular bubbling up of hereditarian views such as these, no one now, at the beginning of the twenty-first century, could claim that hereditarian views are in the ascendant. Argument about the provenance of human ability now recognizes the complexity at play and this recognition had its origins in the paradigm shift of the 1920s to which Fienberg and Resnick refer. But parallel evidence to that concerning racial differences did not emerge about special schools for several decades. Assumptions about the effectiveness of the special school system were largely built on notions of the importance of nature over nurture. It was received opinion that special schools provided a sensible way of meeting the needs of a minority of children, at the same time as safeguarding the efficient education of the majority in the mainstream. The common-sense view stood on the well-established platform of inherited and immutable intelligence. Since the facts as to its utility were plain, evidence to support it seemed unnecessary. This orthodoxy became so firmly embedded in the individual and institutional consciousness that no serious challenges were made to the idea until the mid-1960s. It was only after the successes of the civil rights movement in the USA that a changing social conscience gave rise to open questioning of what seemed to be another kind of segregation – segregation by ability and disability rather than race.

As these doubts emerged, research evidence was less equivocal than anyone would have expected. Evidence emerged about the surprising lack of success of the segregated system. Never mind about the rights and wrongs of segregating, these schools did not appear to work – even with the very generous resources allocated to them. Generosity has been the hallmark of special education funding: indeed, in some US school districts a quarter of the budget is spent on special education (see Wang *et al.* 1995) and internationally, around eight times as much money is spent on a special school pupil as on a mainstream pupil (OECD 1994). In the UK, 4.5 times as much is spent on each special school pupil as on each mainstream pupil, and the multiplier is rising consistently and significantly (Audit Commission/HMI 1992).

But despite the abundant resources flowing into special education, it did not appear to make much difference: children with similar difficulties educated in mainstream or special schools left school with similar results. This knowledge has been available since the early 1960s. As Johnson (1962) put it then:

> It is indeed paradoxical that mentally handicapped children having teachers especially trained, having more money (per capita) spent on their education, and being enrolled in classes with fewer children and a program designed to provide for their unique needs, should be accomplishing the objectives of their education at the same or lower level than similar mentally handicapped children who have not had these advantages and have been forced to remain in the regular grades.
>
> (Johnson 1962: 66)

The kind of evidence that gave rise to Johnson's statement began to accumulate with such consistency that it could not be ignored (e.g. Anderson and Pellicer 1990; Birch *et al.* 1970; Christoplos and Renz 1969; Dunn 1968; Galloway and Goodwin 1979; Lipsky and Gartner 1987; Mercer 1970; Reynolds 1988; Wang *et al.* 1987).

As the nineteenth century turned to the twentieth, then, there had been a collection of ideas that had little natural cohesion and which, in fact, had their roots in simpler notions – those notions springing from little more than cultural myth, folklore and prejudice. What gave great impetus to these ideas, and in particular the idea that certain children should be separated off from others and educated on their own, was the legitimation of these simple notions by their association with philosophy and science. The philosophy of

Nietzsche, the science of Darwin, were bent and misused. The new technolo-
gies of psychology, and in particular psychometrics, came to bolster the
developing epistemology. No one set out intentionally, of course, to set up a
new epistemology. What was happening was that a new way of knowing and
understanding was being inappropriately being created out of the 'thinking
instruments' of the time.

New ways of knowing and understanding difference: new kinds of evidence

In the previous section, a parallel was drawn between the loss of confidence in
knowledge about inherited ability and a loss of confidence in the benefits of
special schools. Our own drawing of this parallel, valid as we the authors feel it
to be, perhaps acts as a tiny case study of the potential dangers in making
connections – of imputing cause from association. Too much, it could be
argued, is being made here of the sequential nature of these realizations about
inherited ability and the benefits of special schools; too much of their temporal
juxtaposition. Likewise, it could be argued that it is easy to fall prey to the
temptation to denounce a certain model of research as inappropriate in conception and sterile in product, as we have done with research on special pedagogy, but to be happy to use that same model of research (as in the case of
special school outcome research) when its findings support one's own position.

The possibilities of making unjustified connections or of imputing causation
on too little evidence always exist. Such possible errors underline not only the
need continually to doubt the techniques and processes by which we come to
knowledge but perhaps, more importantly, the need to look carefully at the
questions we pose about special education. Too often in the past these have
been questions that relate to grand themes – about, for instance, why children
fail or why they behave inappropriately – and they provoke grand answers: an
explanatory model or, as Wright Mills (1970) put it of much of the social
scientific enterprise, 'Grand Theory'.[2] The emphasis has been on finding solutions: a special way of teaching or a new method of behaviour management.
That the solutions often appear so transitory or illusory, as we noted earlier in
this chapter, is as much down to the kinds of questions we ask about 'failure' as
the methods we use to answer those questions. As clinical psychologist David
Smail (1993: 8) puts it in the context of what he calls 'unhappiness': 'To proffer
solutions for problems we are barely beginning to understand does nobody
any service.' The problem, as Clark *et al.* (1998) indicate, is about naive
assumptions of linearity – from this cause to that outcome. In the world of
education things are rarely that simple.

In short, caution is needed when considering many of the issues which may
be of interest in special education. This isn't to say that questions shouldn't be
asked. But wherever simple relationships are sought – of the variety, 'What's
wrong with this child?' – many obstacles bar the way to an answer. Where
questions of this kind are posed, the focus is being directed to the child and his
or her mind and several problems emerge from this kind of focus.

First, there are problems that emerge from what has variously been called a medical, within-child, or deficit model – a model of putative diagnosis and treatment. Medical models of disorder are fine in their place, when thinking about measles or chickenpox. But they are less helpful in the consideration of people and their relationship to the organizations in which they live and work. Here, where the interplay between individual and organization is more subtle and multifaceted the medical model breaks down (Thomas 1992). Other, related, problems emerge from the supposed location of the problem in the person, as Laing (1965) and Szasz (1972) have pointed out. This is pursued further in Chapter 3.

But second, there are questions that special educators and educational psychologists have been less ready to ask. Perhaps 'questions' is too strong a word: doubts about the status of knowledge is perhaps nearer the mark. As the philosopher of mind Gilbert Ryle (1990) has pointed out, much of our thinking about mind is based on metaphor and that metaphor can be profoundly misleading. As he notes, what the metaphorical consideration of mental processes involves is the presentation of facts belonging to one category in the idioms appropriate to another. In our case in special education, failures in learning are often presented in the language and idioms of capacity. Children's lack of ability to do certain things at school is discussed in the language of buckets and other instruments of capacity measurement. Children are said, for example, to lack intelligence, to have weak sequential memory or (more commonly nowadays) poor phonological awareness. A child may lack a 'proper moral sense' (a real example given to one of the authors when working as an educational psychologist). As we point out in Chapter 4, the results derived from such metaphorical assays achieve narrative plausibility, but little else. The problem is that once such metaphor exists it is difficult to displace it, especially when all the paraphernalia of experimental endeavour comes to surround and bolster it. The impressive vocabulary and statistical impedimenta of psychometrics cements in place edifices of explanation that rest in little more than analogy. This kind of analogy, far from being helpful as some analogy unequivocally is, leads to what Ryle calls 'myth' and this myth leads researchers and practitioners down many a cul-de-sac.

Caution, then, is needed in our investigations. However, being circumspect and always questioning about the status of knowledge does not mean that the baby has to be thrown out with the bathwater. Smail (1993: 8) puts it well: 'There may be a lot to be said for trying to refract some of the inspired ideas of European (in particular French and German) thinkers through the kind of commonsensical prism one tends to acquire from British empiricism.' The aim should surely be to arrive at what Ziman (1991) called *reliable knowledge*. If there are better ways of coming to an understanding about the matters in which we are interested, this does not mean that existing methods are always entirely inappropriate for simple questions. Sometimes traditional techniques and processes will be appropriate for helping to answer the questions we pose and for producing knowledge on which we can rely. At other times, however, particularly where someone appears to be suggesting that they have discovered a better method of teaching, or of 'understanding' a child's misbehaviour, all our critical scrutiny should be employed to the full. The larger the claim, the more acutely one should be aware of the need to approach it with caution. In circumstances like this, the frailty and tenuousness of knowledge about human behaviour – about why and how people do things – should be pushed to the fore.

It is that tenuousness of knowledge about human behaviour and learning to which we now turn. An understanding of human behaviour, ever changing and fickle, appears usually to elude our understanding when the investigative methods of psychology have been adopted. As the highly respected American experimental psychologist J.J. Gibson (1967: 142) concluded, after a lifetime's work in the field, about the gains made by psychologists: 'These gains seem to me puny, and scientific psychology seems to me ill-founded.' Harré (1985: 14) goes even further in saying that it is a 'tragedy' that so many able people waste their time on the methods and products of a field that is 'disappointing in content and quality'. After a highly intelligent review of recently used psychological knowledge in special education, Swann (1985: 35) concludes that: 'Much knowledge derived from scientific psychology is not applicable in any straightforward sense. Psychology and education are enterprises guided by radically different ground rules. Much confusion has been wrought, much of it unrecognised, by the failure to understand this.'

Nevertheless, special education has over the twentieth century doggedly put faith in the methods and findings of psychology – faith in what we earlier called a defunct methodology. This reliance is picked up by Claxton (1985), who compares the different reaction of academic educational psychologists to the work of John Holt, a writer who with an informal perspicacity narrates the learning experiences of children at school, and Cyril Burt, some of whose failings have been chronicled earlier. Claxton notes the contempt academics have had for Holt, who prefers to eschew the flimsy insights available from scientific educational psychology, and the continuing respect for Burt, who 'may have been a Bad Boy, but he was One Of Us, and his crimes seem to provoke, within our community, much less vehement and self-righteous indignation than the acute and informal observations of John Holt' (Claxton 1985: 23).

Recently things have begun to change. What have become to be known as 'qualitative methods' have gained credibility as valid research tools in education and psychology and there are excellent examples already available of the use of such methods in critical analysis of the special education enterprise (see, for example, Benjamin 2003; Ferguson *et al.* 1992). While the genealogy of these methods is usually attributed in the methodological literature to the anthropologists and their emphasis on participant observation, it may be helpful to look more widely at their intellectual history – especially to the roots of the ideas in critical studies and linguistics, for it is here that one finds more of an extended and intelligent discussion of their provenance in a more general critical disposition about the character of knowledge. It is this character of knowledge that we have focused on in relation to some of the activities and findings of special education researchers and it is perhaps worth giving this some consideration, since it is significant not only for the way that investigation is approached but also, and perhaps more importantly, for the way in which people are treated during such investigation.

The legacy of positivistic science when transplanted to a focus on human beings was that one should deny what we know, as people, and put faith in a certain kind of disinterested knowledge. As Skinner (1972: 160) put it: 'What, after all, have we to show for nonscientific or prescientific good judgment, or common sense, or the insights gained through personal experience? It is science or nothing.' Unfortunately (for the key to analysis promised by Skinner was a potent one), 40 years of behavioural technology enable the question to be turned around: What has the putatively scientific (some would say 'scientistic') approach to human behaviour given us that we didn't already know? What has it caused us to disregard? To return to the quotation from G.K. Chesterton given earlier in this chapter, 'So far from being knowledge, it's actually suppression of what we know.'

Calls for a recognition of the validity of self-knowledge are not recent, however. It is Hans-Georg Gadamer who is credited with transforming the idea of 'hermeneutics' from one in which a person aimed to understand something in as disinterested and unprejudiced a way as possible to one where 'pre-conceptions or prejudices are what makes understanding possible' (Outhwaite 1990: 25). These preconceptions and prejudices, these 'sentiments, imaginings and fancies', as Oakeshott (1989: 65) put it, are what go to construct our understanding of others. To deny their significance in making sense of other people – their utterances, feelings, fears and failings – is to ignore the most important research tool at our disposal. Until recently the knowledge base of special education self-consciously disavowed the messy sentiments, imaginings and fancies, rejecting as valid data anything that could not be judged to be at least notionally objective.

Gadamer's ideas have been important in shifting the intellectual gaze in the human sciences from the supposedly objective to the personal – reinstating the validity of personal knowledge. He was not, however, unique in arguing for this process and nor has he been the major influence on changes in thought about how to approach the study of human beings. In the last two decades of the twentieth century the philosopher-historian Michel Foucault has induced among more reflective social scientists – educators included – a profound sense of unease about the disciplinary castles within which we have constructed knowledge about our social worlds. In special education this has forced a review of the utility of the professional knowledge within which we have come to understand the difficulties children experience at school. Many of those difficulties, when looked at through the set of lenses which Foucault provides, appear in an entirely different perspective.

Such changes are not attributable entirely to Foucault neither would we want to claim that the highly questioning disposition, which a reading of him inspires, leads to the most practical set of immediate consequences. However, if one follows Foucault and examines the disciplinary history of special educa-tion one is led to ask questions about why things are as they are – and why people have suggested that we should change. One is led to the position that over the last century certain influential schools of thought have dominated the ways in which we think about children and the form their education should take. The new disciplines of psychology, psychiatry, sociology and their outgrowths in other areas – psychoanalysis, psychiatric social work and educational psychology, for example – dominated the academic and professional scenes.

Special education grew in step with the development of the new disciplines and drew in large measure from the new forms of 'scientific' truth which they proffered. Our position is that far too much has been made of the contribution these schools of thought have had to make and that they have exercised a disproportionate influence on special education, on our understanding of why children fail at school and our prescriptions for action when they do. Too much has been invested in their significance. Their status as frameworks within which thinking can be usefully constructed has been overplayed and the extent to which practice can usefully follow from research generated within their parameters has been exaggerated. Barely a century old, these agglomerations of certain kinds of knowledge and technique have assumed an enormous importance in the growth of educational institutions and, in particular, in the growth of special education.

If these edifices of ideas, models, methods and techniques are construed merely as fallible cognitive frameworks it should be much easier than it has hitherto been to question their findings. For until recently those frameworks have presented a seemingly insurmountable challenge to the critic. Complete with what has come to be known as 'theory', they have enabled a crystallization of the received wisdoms and commonplace assumptions that have always existed. 'Intelligence' (the example of the case study above), measurable and researchable, came to replace cleverness and stupidity. The commonplace had become scientific. Maladjustment and emotional difficulties – the subject of our next chapter – came to replace naughtiness.

It would perhaps be an oversimplification to say that the mental frameworks of which we are thinking are solely the disciplines of psychology, sociology and psychiatry. Neither is it enough merely to blame 'science' or positivism. Perhaps the culprit is what some have called 'ideology', but even this is insufficient, for ideology, as Eagleton (1991) has pointed out, is an imprecise word, often used merely to denote that which we feel is in some sense structured on a body of knowledge with which we disagree.[3] The nearest idea to encapsulate what we are talking about is one to which we have referred a couple of times already, namely Bourdieu's notion of doxa – a kind of everyday knowledge that we take for granted. The benefit of hindsight shows that in special education, as in other areas of social policy, the tools of the intellectual establishment have done little to shift, disentangle or even examine that doxa. Almost always, scientific knowledge has weighed in behind received opinion, reinforcing it and strengthening it. The epistemology we have revered has reinforced that doxa.

How is all this relevant for special education and how we think about an inclusive future? We quoted earlier in this chapter from Oliver Sacks's *An Anthropologist on Mars* in which Sacks gave reasons for eschewing many of the procedural and methodological habits of his own discipline, neurology.

Neurologists are like special educators in many respects: they try to help people who are, for whatever reason, uncomfortable, unhappy, disaffected, unable or unwilling to 'fit in'. Sacks's insight is that the methods which have been used to examine this discomfort or disaffection, while they can be successful up to a point, fail to address the real issues at stake, which are human issues. It is worth quoting from him:

> The exploration of deeply altered selves and worlds is not one that can be fully made in a consulting room or office. The French neurologist François Lhemitte is especially sensitive to this, and instead of just observing his patients in the clinic, he makes a point of visiting them at home, taking them to restaurants or theatres, or for rides in his car, sharing their lives as much as possible. (It is similar, or was similar, with physicians in general practice. Thus when my father was reluctantly considering retirement at ninety, we said, 'At least drop the house calls.' But he answered, 'No, I'll keep the house calls – I'll drop everything else instead.')
>
> (Sacks 1995: xvii–xviii)

Maybe we need to keep the house calls. To study and to think about the shape education should take for those who can't or don't want to fit, maybe we should leave aside the investigative methods that have been developed by psychologists and educators during the twentieth century and look to new ways of understanding. As Clough (1995) puts it in the context of special education research:

> Method in social science subverts a profound human impulse to tell stories about the world as we see it. Method undoes the truth, for we put in method a trust it could not start to understand, being without feeling. We ask method to do something – to validate our work – which we cannot do ourselves.
>
> (Clough 1995: 126)

When children are excluded from the mainstream it is because someone feels that they will not fit. To examine why people don't fit, and to help organizations to enable them to fit, we have to understand them as people and to understand the people in the organizations that accept or reject them. The reductionist thrust of special education research has not in general led us to do this, and this has meant that special education has followed a particular route – one that has sought to analyse and fix instead of seeking to include. But as Rorty (1982: 201) puts it, drawing on Hilary Putnam's analogy: 'If you want to know why a square peg doesn't fit into a round hole you had better not describe the peg in terms of the positions of its constituent elementary particles.'

Concluding comment

The discussion of the previous chapter noted that critical analysis of the growth of special education has tended to focus on the professional, structural and institutional interests at play in its expansion. That analysis has said (to oversimplify the argument) that the emergence of a bipartite system, with mainstream and special growing hand in hand, has represented a kind of symbiosis: troublesome children were removed from the mainstream schools to benefit existing interests (e.g. Fulcher 1989; Tomlinson 1985) and simultaneously a burgeoning special education industry was being nourished. For some, the focus in all of this has been on what Abberley (1987) and others have called 'oppression'.

For other critical commentators, the growth of special education has been as much about expediency as oppression. Weatherley and Lipsky (1977) take this stance, focusing on the psychology of the politicians, planners and administrators who have to make decisions about the kind of developments that are worthwhile in special education. These individuals have a duty not only to do something about the problems they are paid to identify but, more importantly as far as their livelihoods, careers and salaries are concerned, to be seen to be doing something. Such a requirement means that the solutions they devise for the problems children experience in schools – solutions such as projects, services, policies – have to be visible. The more visible the better. For them to come up with the most inclusive solution – simply to devolve the substantial additional resources of special education directly to mainstream schools for those in the schools to devise their own solutions – would seem almost like an abdication of responsibility. The special system is thereby geared toward providing visible 'services' designed to help.

There are, then, different strands to critical commentary, each with its own emphasis. But whatever the intellectual provenance of this commentary, it is now well developed and has, indeed, since the mid-1970s formed the platform for notionally progressive changes in legislation across the world. But despite these critical commentaries, and despite the legislation, there has, as more recent analysis has pointed out, continued to be a re-emergence of the kind of thinking that leads to ever newer forms of segregative and exclusionary practice. Children are still labelled, albeit with 'gentler' labels (EBD instead of 'maladjusted' or 'disturbed', 'special needs' instead of 'educationally subnormal'), and exclusion from school is at a higher level than ever (DfES 2004; Parsons 1999); new forms of fix-it-and-get-better treatment are forever being devised.[4] Admittedly these newer kinds of practice are more subtle in their operation, but they are similar in their effects.

As we pointed out in the previous chapter, in his analysis Skrtic points to the 'machine bureaucracy' for the re-emergence of old thinking and old practice in new clothes. We do not demur from this analysis in any way; indeed, we find it enormously helpful. However, the point being made in the present chapter is that the structural features of society and schools and the educational machine cannot be the whole answer when the phenomenon of re-emergence is noted. Thus, we have not attempted in this chapter to add to it. Instead, we have tried to examine in more detail the intellectual roots out of which the credibility of special education has grown. We have looked at the doxa, the epistemology and the methodology of the thinking systems which have given credence to the special education enterprise. We have looked at the ways in which simple notions about difference are hardened with the catalyst of method into psychological constructs that are used to justify continuing separation and segregation. It is these that have created the crucible out of which the professional and institutional interests that have come to support special education have been created.

In the next two chapters, we take a closer look at the building blocks that go to construct two of the most important notions which continue to create a 'need' for special education. First, in Chapter 3, we look at the idea that children who behave unacceptably at school have emotional and behavioural difficulties. Then, in Chapter 4, we examine the idea that children who find difficulty with reading have an identifiable constitutional problem that needs to be remedied.

Summary

Most of the assessments and pedagogies developed by special education have failed on mature evaluation to live up to the hopes their early use excited. Experience does not dim faith, however, and faith certainly remains in the seductive 'fix-its' of special education. Partly, this is because the mindset and methodology underpinning this faith – of diagnosis and supposed cure – have an enduring allure. That allure is enhanced with the epistemological lustre of science, which gave credence in the middle of the twentieth century to assertions about the significance of intelligence in children's failure at school. Not only could natively endowed intelligence explain difference and failure, its method of assessment – IQ tests – could, it was asserted, accurately separate out those who would benefit from certain kinds of education. Belief in the importance of intelligence and in the tests that purportedly measured it gave rise to a selective and segregative education system, following the high-profile work of some influential educational psychologists. Intelligence, and the way it was studied and measured, provides a powerful case study for the dangers that inhere in a certain kind of thought – one which elevates certain kinds of supposedly empirical analysis and rational theorization – about teaching and learning. And this kind of thought is still revered, especially in considering children's failure at school. An argument is made for reinstating the worth of other kinds of thought and knowledge: personal knowledge that teachers hold about how and why their students are failing and how they might be helped. We argue for more reliance on our own knowledge as people of what we know about learning and what we want from schools.

Notes

1 Look, for example, at the stringent procedures of the medical profession in scrutinizing its peer review processes. It is significant that a recent edition of the prestigious *Journal of the American Medical Association* could devote its entire output to potential abuse of the peer review structure (see Rennie and Flanagin 1998). Following concern about whether similar processes were used in education (Thomas 1999b), an international literature search revealed no such equivalence in education: while 132 papers

were written over a 15-year period in medicine, only four existed in education (Speck 1993).

2 Wright Mills coined the term 'Grand Theory' to describe the expectation among social scientists that their disciplines should attempt to build systematic theory of 'the nature of man and society' (p. 23); he saw this effort as an obstacle to progress in the human sciences.

3 See the final chapter of this volume and Tarr and Thomas (1997) for a discussion of the use of the notion of 'ideology' to attack the concept of inclusion.

4 There are two interesting facts about recent exclusions and attendance. One is that the proportion of pupils excluded from special schools is far higher than from any group of mainstream schools. The other is that although the government in 2002/3 invested nearly £470 million in measures 'to improve behaviours and attendance' (DfES 2004), attendance has continued to deteriorate.

The great problem of 'need': a case study in children who don't behave

In the previous chapter we asserted that arguments for special education rest in particular ways of thinking and understanding. Those arguments have, we suggested, set on a pedestal certain kinds of theoretical and empirical 'knowledge' and favoured particular methodological avenues as routes to such knowledge. We contended that the putative character of this knowledge – stable, objective, reliable – has created a false legitimacy for the growth of special education and the activities of special educators. This chapter takes that theme forward, focusing on children who don't behave at school. It makes the point that the metaphors and constructs that are used to generate understanding about such difficult behaviour are often misleading, evoking as they do all kinds of quasi-scientific explanation – explanation that has popularly come to be known as 'psychobabble'. While 'psychobabble' is hardly a scholarly term to employ in a volume such as this, which purports to make a serious critique of special education, it is nevertheless an apt one. For the mélange of disparate metaphor and theory around which under-standing of people's behaviour is popularly constructed – in both lay and professional circles – rests in the reification of what is little more than tentative psychological conjecture. Perhaps more scholarly than 'psychobabble' would be Crews's (1997: 298) characterization of this knowledge, particularly that which rests in Freudian theory, as an 'ontological maze peopled by absurd homunculi'.

Whatever the register in which one chooses to discuss it, there have, we argue in this chapter, been some unfortunate consequences of this kind of discourse for schoolchildren. Further, in the more recent school-oriented approaches to helping avoid troublesome behaviour at school – approaches that put the emphasis on change *by the school* rather than the change *in the child* – are found merely a replication of the exclusionary phenomena of the past. Those phenomena are created by certain kinds of mindset and profes-sional system that accentuate rather than attenuate difference – and these mindsets and professional systems themselves rest in the thinking about difference, of both deficit and disadvantage, that we outlined in the previous chapter.

We contend that a relatively recent concept, that of 'need', has come to reinforce these concepts of deficit and disadvantage. Intended to be helpful, to place emphasis on a child's difficulties rather than simply naming a supposed category of problems, the notion of need has instead come to point as emphatically as before at the child. It has allowed to remain in place many of the exclusionary practices associated with special education.

The notion of emotional and behavioural difficulties: the root of the problem

A search through the last 10 years' issues of five leading national and international journals[1] finds not a single paper that discusses in any detail the provenance, status, robustness, legitimacy or meaning of the term 'emotional and behavioural difficulties' (EBD). This is surely a cause for concern. The term – often now relabelled ESBD, with the 'S' standing for 'social' – is widely and unquestioningly used in the UK (and other countries have their own equivalents) as an administrative and quasi-clinical category. Uniquely, it proffers a category that is specific to children, which combines legal, medical and educational connotations and meanings.

Although EBD/ESBD is not an official category in Britain, it exists as one in everything but name. Categories officially ceased to exist following the report of the Warnock Committee (DES 1978) and the 1981 Education Act. Yet it would be clear to a Martian after five minutes' study of the British education system that for all practical purposes EBD/ESBD is indeed a category and that it forms in the minds of practitioners, professionals and administrators one of the principal groups of special needs. It has been used as a category in the local statementing procedures which have followed from section 5 of the 1981 Education Act and the Education Acts which have succeeded it. It appears unquestioningly in papers in reputable academic journals (for example, Smith and Thomas 1992), and it appears as a descriptor in official documents and papers (for example, DES 1989a; 1989b; DfEE 1995; DfES 2003; Mortimore 1997).

The term 'EBD/ESBD', then, reveals no frailty; indeed, it displays a peculiar resilience and this makes it particularly interesting and useful as an example of a special education concept. The resilience it shows is demonstrated in its ability to survive and prosper over recent years, when attention has moved from the child to the institution, with for example, the Elton Committee's (DES 1989c) emphasis on whole-school approaches to discipline. Over the last decade or so academics and policymakers have proposed that in tackling the question of difficult behaviour at school, attention should be paid not only to analysis and treatment of the child's behaviour but also to the operations and systems in the school that may cause or aggravate such behaviour.

But behind this sensible development in thinking there resolutely continues a powerful subtext that the real causes of difficult behaviour lie in deficit and deviance in the child. Respected academics could, for example, as recently as 1994 frame their book (Chazan *et al.* 1994: 27) around section headings such as 'Identification of EBDs' and 'Factors associated with EBDs in middle childhood' (ibid: 36). Another could entitle his book *Treating Problem Children* (Hoghughi 1988). The agenda is of deficit, deviance and disadvantage in the child, and while school systems are usually mentioned in discourse such as this, they seem to appear almost as an afterthought. It is clear that the real problem is considered to be dispositional: that of the child – and the emphasis is thus on individual treatment. The term 'EBD' induces a clinical mindset from which it is difficult to escape. The clinical mindset is demonstrated even in recent interpretations of what ESBD means: one local authority in England (there are probably more) could, unabashed, in 2005, publish a review of provision about what it called 'Emotional, Social and Behavioural *Disorders'* [emphasis added] (Kramer 2005).

This mindset – of within-child difficulties or disorders – operates inside more all-encompassing ideas about need. The notion of need is seldom questioned. It is seemingly so benign, so beneficial to the child that it has become a shibboleth of special education thinking and policy. But we contend in this chapter that 'need' is less than helpful and that it is a chimera when difficult behaviour is being considered. The notion of need here is based on a belief that a *child's* problems are being identified and addressed. 'Need' in this context, however, is more usefully seen as the school's need – a need for calm and order. The language of the clinic, moreover, invariably steers the response of professionals toward a child-based action plan.

This focus on emotional need substitutes a set of supposedly therapeutic practices and procedures for more down-to-earth and simple-to-understand sanctions. It also diverts attention from the nature of the environment that we expect children to inhabit. The ambit of the 'helping', therapeutic response invoked by the idea of EBD is unjustifiably wide, being called on neither at the request of the young person involved (or at least very rarely so) nor because of some long-standing pattern of behaviour which has demonstrated that the young person has a clinically identifiable problem, but rather because the behaviour is unacceptable for a particular institution. But because these therapeutic practices and procedures notionally constitute 'help', they are peculiarly difficult to refuse.

Likewise, it is difficult to refute the kindly, child-centred, humanitarian tenets on which they supposedly rest. The tenets on which therapeutic practice rest may be all these good things (kind, humanitarian, child centred) but they have developed during an era when the intellectual climate eschewed – or, rather, failed even to consider as meaningful concepts – ideas about the rationality and rights of the child. In such a climate, it was considered appropriate and necessary for decisions to be made about and for children by concerned professionals. Whereas systems for rule-breaking adults have come to incorporate strict procedures to protect rights, systems could develop in schools to deal with rule infraction that would incorporate no such protections – since the protection was considered to be automatically inherent in the beneficial action of the professionals acting on the child's behalf.

But those actors and advocates would often be the very same people who were offended by the child's behaviour. In the adult world, political and legal systems are particularly sensitive to the boundary between wrongdoing and mental illness and it is a commonplace that in certain circumstances in certain political regimes it is only too convenient to brand wrongdoers and rebels 'mad'. In more favourable political circumstances, by contrast, fastidious care is taken to differentiate between law breaking, rebellion and mental illness. Alongside this fastidiousness, there is a range of protections for both the wrongdoer and for the person who is depressed or schizophrenic – sophisticated protections against unfair conviction or the too convenient attribution of mental illness to unwelcome behaviour.

But for children and young people at school, because of assumptions about their vulnerability and their irrationality, and presuppositions about the beneficial actions of professionals acting on their behalf, those protections do not exist. Their absence has enabled in education a label such as 'EBD/ESBD' to be compiled out of a range of disparate ideas about order and disturbance. Those ideas are elided yet their elision is rarely acknowledged or addressed.

The elision of ideas represented in the notion of EBD/ESBD has done little, we contend, for the individual child. Yet it also exercises an influence even on supposedly whole-school approaches to behaviour management at school. The notion of EBD/ESBD distorts the way that management or organizational issues at school are defined and handled. A whole-school approach to behaviour difficulties existing in the same universe as a thriving notion of EBD/ESBD means that behaviour difficulties are invariably seen through a child-centred, clinical lens. For this clinical lens is more convenient for everyone: it offers immediate response (often the removal of the child) rather than the promise of an improvement in a term or a year; it offers ready-made routes into existing professional systems that distract attention from possible shortcomings of the school and it avoids the large-scale upheaval and expense of whole-school reform. Following episodes of difficult behaviour, traditional child-focused professional responses therefore tend to follow.

The language of need out of which we build ideas about problem behaviour therefore induces procedural responses whose main function is the appearance of doing something constructive. The mantra of need mechanically induces a set of reflexes from the school, but these are often little more than rituals – bureaucratic shows of willing. They constitute what Skrtic (1991) calls 'symbols and ceremonies'.

A different view about how to respond to difficult behaviour at school can emerge out of current thinking on inclusion. The inclusive school should best be seen as a humane environment rather than a set of pre-existing structures and systems for dealing with misbehaviour. These traditional structures and systems inevitably invoke already existing professional responses. But our contention is that schools contain such an odd collection of rules and practices that unless these are themselves addressed and altered, misbehaviour from children is an almost inevitable consequence.

Whose needs?

The blanket ascription of 'need' when behaviour is found difficult at school needs some examining. Whose needs are being identified and unravelled here? The route taken is nearly always to assume that the child needs something and the assumptions about need proceed to imputations of intent, weakness and problem in the wrongdoer.

Foucault (1991) analysed this process as it has taken place in juridical practice over two centuries. According to his analysis, modern times have seen a transformation in society's response to wrongdoing. Because historically responses to wrongdoing were often so shockingly cruel, new 'kinder' techniques of control have supplanted them. Foucault's *Discipline and Punish* (1991) begins with an example: a picture of a savage punishment in pre-Revolution France, where a prisoner, Damiens, has his limbs carved from his body. But it is not principally condemnation of this cruelty that follows from Foucault. Rather, he has drawn the picture to contrast it with the kinds of punishment that have come to succeed it. Because of the conspicuous savagery of punishment regimes in Europe until the mid-nineteenth century, Foucault says, a backlash forced attempts to be more gentle, to have 'more respect, more "humanity" ' (ibid: 16). It is these successors to the punishment of Damiens for which Foucault reserves his sharpest critique. For these systems – this 'gentle way in punishment' (ibid: 104) – are quieter, more insidious. These new techniques, relying on the constructs and knowledge of the new social sciences, constructed various forms of understanding of the wrongdoer which made imputations of intent and assumptions about motive. This would not be so bad were it not for the fact that the understandings provided by the new sciences depended on tentative, fallible theories which were treated as though they were scientific fact.[2] In fact, they were merely making new kinds of judgement about misbehaviour, but judgements which were given added credence and respectability by their association with supposedly scientific thinking and understanding – understanding which had been so successful in the natural sciences. In short, what has occurred, the analysis of Foucault suggests, has been a movement from simple judgement and punishment of someone's disapproved-of act, to complex and unjustified judgements about his or her 'soul'.

EBD/ESBD provides an excellent case study of this elision from punishment to judgement. It provides a clear example of a category created from an intermingling, on one side, of certain systems of knowledge (like psychology and medicine) and, on the other, of a need for institutional order.

To make this proposition represents perhaps not too sparkling an insight, since a critical recognition of the place of the medical model in special education is hardly new and we noted in Chapter 1 its consequences for many of the procedures and practices of special education. Our specific focus here, though, is on the almost explicit conflation of administrative need with quasi-medical category; of the transition from naughty-therefore-impose-sanctions to disturbed-therefore-meet-needs. It is the nature of the transition that we wish especially to examine: the gradient from punishment to 'help' down which the child tends to descend once 'need' has been established.

There are taken-for-granted assumptions of 'help' in the 'meeting need' mantra of contemporary special education protocols and these 'needs' have been silently transmuted with the assistance of the constructs of academic and professional psychology from the *school's* needs for order calm, routine and predictability to the *child's* needs – supposedly for stability, nurture, security, one-to-one help or whatever.

In the unspoken assumptions behind special education procedures there is no acknowledgement of the manoeuvre that has occurred here – no recognition of the frailty of the idea of an 'emotional need' – and no willingness to entertain the possibility that emotional needs may be a fiction constructed to escape the school's insecurities about failing to keep order.

Table 3.1 distinguishes between two kinds of need: that of the school and that of the child. Our intention is to point to the conflation of ideas and knowledges used in the notion of need and to suggest that the umbrella use of the construct disguises different kinds of problem that school staff confront. But unacceptable behaviour is rarely a problem of the child. While this behaviour is a problem for the school, it rarely constitutes a clinical problem. Neither does it point to some abnormality or deficit.

An elevation in the status of psychological knowledge has meant that simple understandings about what is right or wrong have in themselves become insufficient to explain difficult behaviour. A new epistemology has emerged wherein a lexicon of dispositionally oriented words and phrases govern and mould the way unacceptable behaviour is considered. Thus, if children

Table 3.1   What is meant by 'need'?

Schools' needs	*Children's needs*	
'Juridical' needs (but expressed as children's psychological needs)	Educational needs (but 'identified' using psychological constructs and instruments)	Physical needs (which may sometimes result in educational needs)
Category EBD/ESBD	*Category* Moderate learning difficulty (MLD)	*Category* Physical disability Hearing impairment Visual impairment
Characterized by Questions of order for the school	*Characterized by* Questions of how best to help children who are having serious problems with their work at school	*Characterized by* Questions of how best to help children who have physical or sensory impairments

misbehave at school, education professionals are encouraged to examine the background, motivations and supposed traumas of the students rather than the simple humanity of the school's operation – its simple day-to-day processes and routines.

Foucault (1991) warns against the assumption that the knowledge of disciplines such as psychology and sociology can inform the working practices of staff in schools and hospitals. It is not disinterested knowledge; in the context of prisons he says that it has acquired the status of an ' "epistemological-juridical" formation' (ibid: 23). As we discussed in Chapter 2, it is the same perhaps as what Bourdieu calls 'doxa': a kind of taken-for-granted knowledge, naturalized knowledge, 'things people accept without knowing' (Bourdieu and Eagleton 1994). In other words, the knowledge of psychology and psychiatry have infiltrated our everyday understanding of disorder and deviance so that they are now almost as one: disorder has somehow become melded with disturbance in such a way that thought about behaviour that is out of order at school can hardly be entertained without the collateral assumption of emotional disturbance and special need. This symbiosis of order and understanding is nowhere clearer than in the contemporary term 'EBD/ESBD'.

Meeting need

In education, this last reconceptualization occurs under the cloak of *meeting individual need*. The 'meeting need' notion satisfies two conditions for the educationist. First, it enables the labelling of madness (a Bad Thing) to be transformed into the identification of a need in the child (a Good Thing). Thus, the educator, with a wave of a wand is changed from labeller (this child is maladjusted) to benefactor and helper (this child has special needs and I will meet them). Second, an institutional need for order is transformed to a child's emotional need. The child who misbehaves has special needs rooted in emotional disturbance, the vocabulary at once invoking psychological, psychoanalytic and psychiatric knowledge. Once need is established, the psychological genie has been released.[3]

It is strange that psychologists and educationists should have managed to pull off such a feat of alchemy, since a moment's thought discloses the fact that the things that children habitually do wrong at school rarely have any manifest (or indeed covert) association with their emotional makeup. They concern the school's need to regulate time (punishing tardiness and truancy), activity (punishing lack of effort or overactivity), speech (punishing chatter or insolence) and the body (punishing hairstyles, clothes, the use of makeup or the tidiness of the individual).[4] As Cicourel and Kitsuse (1968: 130) put it: 'The adolescent's posture, walk, cut of hair, clothes, use of slang, manner of speech . . . may be the basis for the typing of the student as a "conduct problem".' And the term 'conduct problem', or more likely 'conduct disorder', is still alive and well in special education.

But being unpunctual, lazy, rude or untidy were never, even by early twentieth-century standards, qualifications for madness or even emotional difficulty. They concern, as Hargreaves *et al.* (1975) point out, rule infractions. They have little or nothing to do with an individual's emotional need, but everything to do with the school's need to keep order. Maintaining order through the upholding of these codes is necessary, school managers would argue, for the efficient running and indeed for the survival of the school.

Few could disagree. Institutions which require the collecting together of groups of 20 or 30 in classes, and hundreds in assemblies, need ways of keeping order. The energy of young people must be kept in check if these assemblages are not to descend into scrums. To maintain order, there is a need for disciplinary methods through the regulation of the use of space and the control of activity. Mostly, these work.

It is when they don't work, when children fail to conform and fail to respond to the 'gentle punishments', that the manoeuvre occurs in which need is passed from school to child. Unable to understand the stubbornness of the individuals concerned and fearful of the consequences for order, those responsible for order in the school then, following the precepts learned in teacher education and reinforced by the service system provided by the local education authority, reconceptualize the students as having emotional and behavioural difficulties.

Although changes in discussion about policy (e.g. DfEE 1997) have stressed the importance of an inclusive ethos in schools (that is, one in which the comprehensive ethos of the school is clearly articulated and the systems of the school are established to ensure inclusion), there remains a firm resistance to such an ethos. Croll and Moses (2000: 61), for example, found that more than half of the 48 headteachers they interviewed felt that, 'More children should attend special schools' and, in the case of 'children with emotional and behavioural difficulties', this figure rose to two-thirds (see also Mousley *et al.* 1993). More serious, there is an unspoken acceptance of need as a means of securing the removal of the child – an unthinking collusion with the process of need attribution. It is the doxa (Bourdieu and Eagleton 1994) which is troublesome: the establishment almost without thinking of the child as having needs. In the language of attribution theorists, the problem is that of 'fundamental attribution error' (Ross *et al.* 1977) – the easy over-attribution of events to the disposition of individuals rather than to the failings of institutions. (It is worth noting that of Croll and Moses's sample under 1 per cent of headteachers and only 2 per cent of teachers attributed 'emotional and behavioural difficulties' to 'school and teachers'.)

Once established as having emotional difficulties, children are diverted along a new path, which separates them and which ends in their being 'helped'. It shunts them sideways from a comprehensible and predictable system of practices and procedures that result in rewards and punishments to an alternative set governed by alternative professional personnel – psychologists, counsellors, social workers, psychiatrists – who listen, analyse and understand.

The new world is stripped even of the procedural certainties of the mainstream school as groundrules change and parameters invisibly move. The arcane paraphernalia of assessment procedures confirm the diagnosis of emotional difficulties. Once so labelled, your every word becomes untrustworthy.

Your complaints can be ignored, as the response to increasing irrationality is to pile on more and more 'help'.[5]

The result is incarceration by smothering: the entrapment of the child in a cocoon of professional help. One is launched on what Goffman (1987: 79) calls a 'moral career' in which both the individual's image of self and his or her 'official position, jural relations, and style of life' change in sequence as the child graduates through his or her career as sufferer and victim. Escape comes only by 'acknowledgement' and 'acceptance' of one's problems.[6] It helps if one can learn the vocabulary and the semiology of the therapeutic system and parrot it back to the therapeutic agent.

From simple wrongdoing to disturbance and treatment

How does all this happen? By a process not of judging the act or the behaviour in simple terms but by the judgement of what Foucault (1991: 17) calls the 'passions, instincts, anomalies, infirmities, maladjustments, effects of environment'. The impedimenta, vocabulary and constructs of the new professionals have come to invade the simple systems of judgement that preceded them. The act itself ceases to be condemned in simple terms; instead, it is an estimation of the *student* that is made. As Foucault puts it: 'behind the pretext of explaining an action, are ways of defining an individual' (ibid: 18).

The delineation of emotional disturbance interrupts the procedure of simply judging whether an act is right or wrong, good or bad. Simple moral judgement is suspended. It is displaced by a morass of half-understood ideas about disturbance, a jumble of bits and pieces from psychoanalysis, psychology and psychiatry, a bricolage of penis envy and cognitive dissonance, of Freudian slip and standard deviation, of motivation and maternal deprivation, regression and repression, attention seeking and assimilation, reinforcement and self-esteem – ideas corrupted by textbook writers and mangled by journalists and the writers of popular culture. Ideas which, as Crews (1997: 298) puts it, make 'an ontological maze peopled by absurd homunculi'. But these ideas are not only half-understood. Even if those who use the ideas in defining 'need' understood them as well as it is possible to understand them, they would be on shaky ground epistemologically and empirically (Cioffi 1975; Macmillan 1997; Nagel 1959), for the models which stand behind notions of emotional disturbance are, as Crews (1997: 297) points out, characterized by faulty logic, the manufacturing of evidence and facile explanation; they construct 'a cacophony of incompatible explanations'.

Explanatory and therapeutic currency is widely lauded by the psychological community in a small rainforest of 'scientific' journals, yet there is little sign of a diminution in unhappiness resulting from these supposed advances in understanding. Indeed, Smail (1993: 13) asserts that: 'There is certainly no evidence that the wider availability of psychological theories and techniques is leading to a decrease in psychological distress.' He suggests that in the burgeoning of psychological techniques to alleviate distress, there is far less a breakthrough in enlightened understanding, and more 'the success of an enterprise' (ibid: 13). The mass of techniques make a bazaar in which plausible homily, mixed with large portions of psychoanalytic and psychological vocabulary, take the place of a rational consideration of children's behaviour at school. Neither is there much evidence in education of the successful impact of this burgeoning enterprise: numbers of children excluded from school continue to rise. Indeed, they continue to rise even in *special schools*, which have prided themselves on their supposedly therapeutic skills. There were over 600 permanent exclusions from special schools in 1996/97, an increase of 21 per cent in relation to the 500 permanent exclusions in the previous year (DfEE 1998a). Twenty-eight per cent of special schools reported at least one permanent exclusion in 1996/97. All this was in the context of other key indicators of deprivation and social exclusion – such as the proportion of children living in a workless household or the proportion of children living in families of below average income – which showed improving trends (Howarth *et al.* 1998). Although exclusion fell between 1997 and 2000, it has been rising fairly consistently ever since, with a small fall in 2004/05 (DfES 2006).

It is strange that the therapeutic mindset behind notions of maladjustment and EBD/ESBD should have been so resistant to suffocation in the absence of supporting evidence. Smail suggests that an ostensibly therapeutic approach survives, first, because people want it to and, second, because it is impossible to demonstrate that it *is not* effective. The result of this quasi-scientific approach to behaviour is the sanctification of the agent of therapy (and even the agent of assessment), so that the whole assessment–therapy process surrounds itself with what Smail calls 'an aura of almost moral piety' in which to question putative benefits 'comes close to committing a kind of solecism' (1993: 16).

It is not only 'abnormal' psychology (as a sub-area of psychology) which is playing a significant part in the 'clinicizing' of unacceptable behaviour. For educationists, the notion of need *in the child* is reinforced by key psychological theories such as those of Piaget. Important for reports such as that of the influential Plowden (DES 1967), these theories have stressed the genetic determinacy of development, leaving explanation for behaviour problems or learning difficulties to be made in terms of developmental defect or emotional deprivation, the vocabulary again invoking psychological or social explanation for behaviour at school.

Many have pointed to not only the tenuousness of the theories on which such educational and social policy is based (e.g. Bryant 1984; Elkind 1967; Gelman 1982; James and Prout 1990; Rutter 1995), but also to the way in which attention is distracted from the nature and significance of the school environment in itself constructing the difficulties (e.g. Alexander 1984; Walkerdine 1983). But frail as these theories are, they are perennially attractive (as the persistence of Piaget's theories in teacher education syllabuses demonstrates) and it is the ideas which stem from them that influence the professional as he or she works with the reconceptualized child: the child with needs.

An illustration of the clinicizing of unacceptable behaviour is given in Figure 3.1, which shows some of the vocabulary used to describe difficult children in one secondary school. Recorded by a teacher participant–observer (Sayer 1993) in private settings (in informal conversation) and public settings

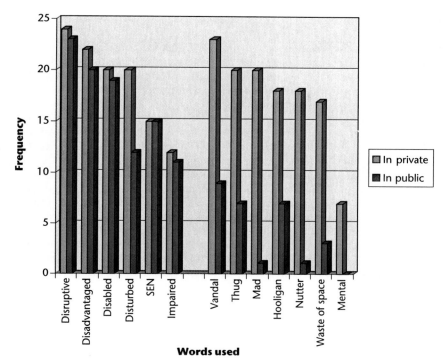

Figure 3.1 Vocabulary used to describe children

(at a staff meeting or with parents), the recordings reveal not only a set of highly 'psychologized' labels about pupils but also ones that are entirely focused on the disposition and character of the pupil.

Those labels used on the left of the figure (namely, 'disruptive' to 'impaired') are ones the user is comfortable about using in public and in private, while those on the right ('vandal' to 'mental') may have been used more frequently but are used more often in private than in public. The public acceptability of terms such as 'disruptive', 'disadvantaged' and 'disabled' in the discourse of school life shows the extent to which the psychiatric and the psychosocial have become fused and converted into acceptable psycho-educational labels. 'Disturbed' and 'disruptive' supplant 'nutter' and 'mad'. These labels merely make more palatable for public consumption the sentiments and beliefs revealed by the words used privately for the same pupils ('vandal', 'thug', 'mad', 'nutter', 'mental'). The substitution of the former set for the latter set does nothing, however, to displace an even more firmly ingrained set of beliefs about the origins of these young people's difficulties at school. For aberrant behaviour to occur, there has, in Foucault's (1980b: 44) words, 'to be something wrong with him, and this is his character, his psyche, his upbringing, his unconscious, his desires'.

Categories for children, not adults

Ideas about psyche, motivation and background form the substrate out of which these new descriptors emerge. They also contribute to and exaggerate the unequal power balance between adult and child, for in no *adult* system is the official process of packaging and labelling aberrant behaviour as well formed, sophisticated and widely accepted as it is in EBD/ESBD for these minors. Concomitantly, the rules, punishment regimes and labelling tolerated within schools would not be tolerated within any adult organization (other than the prison). It is perhaps significant that although 25 years ago a ferment of discussion under the leadership of Laing (1965) and Szasz (1972) surrounded the issue of whether difficult behaviour constituted mental illness, little of the significance of that discussion was assimilated into debate about what was then called 'maladjustment' – perhaps because a central pillar of the superstructure of children's services and special education has been the taken-for-granted assumption of doing good, of acting in *loco parentis*, of guardianship. These ideas have flourished partly because of a tradition of seeing the child as not only vulnerable and helpless but also as irrational.

The process of understanding children to be not only irrational but *also* emotionally disturbed effectively condemns them to voicelessness. Being seen as irrational (rather than simply stupid) is particularly damning, for it means that you are deemed unworthy even of consultation about what is in your best interests.

The system of soft categories (like EBD), spongy quasi-legal procedures – such as in the Codes of Practice (DfE 1994a; DfES 2000), quasi-medical diagnoses (like AD/HD) and quasi-scientific assessments, although it doesn't stand up to rigorous scrutiny, has its effects insidiously. Partly because children are taken to be not only irrational, but also in need of protection, it has been possible for a network of special procedures – supposedly protective and therapeutic – to grow around them, in a way that they have not grown around adults.

For adults, unacceptable behaviour is punished – but a comprehensible (if less than perfect) system of procedures and protocols protects them. Even if the protection is written in legal jargon, it is at least in the language of straightforward relations: you have done wrong, we will punish you with x, but you are entitled to y. For children, by contrast, repeatedly unacceptable behaviour leads them into a set of arcane official and semi-official procedures (detention, exclusion, referral to the psychologist, statementing, placement in special education) in which their rights are unclear not only to them and their parents but also to the administrators and professionals who work with them (and hence the need for the setting up of the Special Needs Tribunal). Ad hoc collections of people, such as governors in exclusions panels, decide about their rights to attend school and decisions (unrestricted by anything so mundane as a time limitation) are made by teachers, psychologists and administrators about their lives. For children, protection takes on a wholly different meaning from the protection the law gives to the adult suspected of law breaking. The protection given to the child is a paternalistic protection, for example in the 'protection' of a statement, where supposed 'needs' are constructed and then met. It is far harder to argue against someone who is meeting your needs than someone who is accusing you of breaking the rules.

Making schools more humane as environments: common talk in humane schools

Lest it appears that we are endorsing misbehaviour, violence or abuse, let us stress that we are not. We do not seek in any way to condone violence or to romanticize difficult behaviour. Neither do we seek to play down or underestimate the school staff's need for disciplinary techniques to keep order. Instead we are seeking to point out that misbehaviour seems to be an endemic part of institutions that organize themselves in particular ways and that if we seek to reduce such behaviour we have to recognize its provenance. We must recognize the possibility that the origins of misbehaviour lie less in children's emotions or even in their 'disadvantage' and lie more in the character of the organization we ask them to inhabit for a large part of their lives. It is an organization staffed by professionals whose response when faced with trouble is necessarily a professional one. Here, Skrtic (1991) suggests, is its main problem since it operates as a 'professional bureaucracy' (and Weatherley and Lipsky 1977, and Wolfensberger 1990 point to similar processes). Professional bureaucracies are organizations that, far from being designed to think creatively about how to change for the better, think rather about how to direct their 'clients' toward some existing professional specialism. Or they may consider how the problem can be absorbed in the professional procedures defined in a local policy document, as we discuss in Chapter 6. The mindset induced by the notion of disturbance fits happily into such a system, encouraging the view that specialized sets of professional knowledge exist to deal with misbehaviour.

It is odd that Skrtic's analysis occurs at a time when there has been optimism about the potential of school to influence 'outcomes' for children. For over the last decade or so, academics and policymakers have proposed that in tackling the question of difficult behaviour at school, attention should be paid not only to analysis and treatment of the child's behaviour but also to the operations and systems in the school which may cause or aggravate such behaviour. The positive arguments for such a shift in emphasis from child to institution rest in evidence and analysis from diverse sources. They rest in evidence about the significance of the school's role in influencing behaviour and achievement (e.g. Edmonds 1979; Hallinger and Murphy 1986; Jesson and Gray 1991; Levine and Lezotte 1995; Mortimore *et al.* 1988; Neisser 1986; Rutter *et al.* 1979; Sammons *et al.* 1993). They rest in recognition of the potentially damaging effects of labelling (in the work of theorists such as Cicourel and Kitsuse 1968). And they rest in arguments about the invalidity of interpreting aberrant behaviour as disturbed (in the ideas of Szasz, Laing and others). Resulting models for intervention and help which thus attach significance to the impact of the wider environment, and particularly that of the school, have been given added impetus by the development of thinking in areas such as ecological psychology (following pioneers such as Barker 1968; Bronfenbrenner 1979; Doyle 1977; Kounin 1967) and systems theory (Checkland 1981).

In fact, though, only a small amount of the school effectiveness research has related specifically to behaviour (e.g. Galloway 1983; Galloway *et al.* 1985; McManus 1987). The *Fifteen Thousand Hours* work (Rutter *et al.* 1979) looked at attendance and 'delinquency' but conceded that the process (independent) variables – that is, the school factors supposedly responsible for influencing outcomes – can contribute only in small measure to predictions concerning those outcomes. The authors say that other (unidentified) variables must be playing an important part in differences between schools on attendance and behaviour.

The tenuousness of the research evidence here has not prevented a widespread acceptance of the idea that schools make a difference when it comes to behaviour. Despite the clear caveat provided by Rutter and his colleagues about the generalizability of effectiveness findings when it comes to behaviour, there has been a near unanimous acceptance of the message which, it appears, policymakers want to hear.

Optimism in the face of lack of evidence is interesting and perhaps related to the laudable desire to do whatever can be done to make schools more congenial places for all who inhabit them. But the general body of school effectiveness literature and research has pushed whole-school responses in the wrong direction. Consistent with the conclusions which would follow from Skrtic's (1991: 165) analysis, the particular professional vocabularies – psychological and psychiatric – induced by the label EBD/ESBD discourage a move to the necessary creativity. They induce merely what Skrtic calls 'an assortment of symbols and ceremonies' that look and sound like sensible action – things of the sort that appear in the *Elton Report* (DES 1989c), such as writing a bullying policy or improving liaison procedures – but, in fact, shift attention from characteristics of the environment to what Skrtic calls aspects of the 'machine bureaucracy': things that have the appearance (but only the appearance) of rational reaction to a problem (see also Weatherley and Lipsky 1977 in this context).[7]

The system 'bureaucratises deviance' (Rubington and Weinberg 1968: 111), with a hierarchy of defining agents – and one may note how this hierarchy has been formalized over the years in the UK system, from Circular 2/75 to the 1981 Education Act to the Code of Practice (DfE 1994a).

The professional systems operating in schools to manage deviance in fact bureaucratize deviance as reliably today as they did when Rubington and Weinberg wrote about them 30 years ago. They now do so perhaps more sensitively and with more emphasis on the whole-school options suggested by Elton. However, the professional systems encourage and reinforce professional responses, thus diverting attention from ostensibly more mundane but potentially more significant aspects of the world that children have to inhabit. Thus, while a welcome move from the left-most column of Table 3.2 to the middle column has occurred in many circumstances, this move still represents attention to a narrow band of practices and activities that are professionally

Table 3.2   Approaches to misbehaviour

Therapeutic emphasis	Whole-school emphasis	Humane environment emphasis
• Counselling • Behaviour modification • Groupwork • Drugs (e.g. in AD/HD) • Family therapy	• Updating the bullying policy • Ensuring better liaison with school psychologist • Rationalizing report card systems • Establishing clearer and more explicit guidelines for transfer from Code of Practice stage 3 to stage 4 • Setting up a governor link with the learning support department	• Having more pay phones for students to use • Having more carpeted areas in the school • Ensuring that litter is regularly cleared • Ensuring that there is a plentiful supply of drinking fountains and that they are maintained regularly • Taking steps to discipline teachers who bully students • Staggering playtimes and school start and end times in large schools • Ensuring fair queuing systems at lunch in which staff don't automatically go to the front and older students can't routinely push in • Ensuring the minutes of the school council are routinely taken on the governing body agenda • Reducing the number of assemblies • Ensuring toilets are regularly cleaned and refurbished

interested. They ensure that the discourse is that of professionals, communicating in their habitual constructs. Discussion and debate about, for example, 'professional liaison' has more cachet than discussion about fair queuing systems at lunchtime, but the bullying policy thus engendered may be little more than an ineffectual sop, doing little to address the actual problems faced by pupils in the school. And liaison with the educational psychologist may do little to address the routine unfairnesses committed every day at school. As the great educator Rousseau ([1762] 1993) noted more than two centuries ago, some observations are considered too trivial to be true.[8] They have to have a theoretical or professional spin to make them seem significant.

A nice example of simple, non-theoretical, aprofessional thinking is given by Clarke (1997) as headteacher of a large urban comprehensive school. He notes:

> Some years ago, having taken issue with a teacher (male) for shouting at a student (female), I was invited at a staff meeting (under any other business!) to outline my 'policy on shouting'. Three points occurred to me:

i.   if mature adults disagree, they generally don't shout at each other;
ii.   it is hard to ask students to keep their voices down if the teachers shout;
iii.   it is impossible to say, hand on heart, that we do not have bullying if
     big, powerful men verbally assault small, powerless young women.

(Clarke 1997: 154)

This kind of intervention emerges from Clarke's values and beliefs as a teacher and as a person. It has nothing to do with any professional knowledge, theoretical archive or government code of practice. It is only this brave kind of thinking and action that emancipates one from the machine bureaucracy of which Skrtic writes.

An analogy can perhaps be drawn with successful action currently being taken on housing estates to manage the behaviour of unruly youngsters. This involves a deliberate move away from the pattern of response that would usually have taken place five or 10 years ago – a response involving 'understanding' the 'problems' of the young people involved, an understanding predicated on the theoretical assumptions of certain professional groups, which imputed 'need' to certain kinds of behaviour. The move is toward more community action, which involves – on one side – increasing the likelihood that the perpetrators of misdemeanours will be caught, disapproved of and, if necessary, punished, and – on the other – making systematic efforts to provide activity for the young people involved. It is through an engagement with the political (and a corresponding disengagement with the patronizing psycho-babble of 'understanding') that the patent truth of Postman's statement can shine out:

There is no question that listlessness, ennui, and even violence in school are related to the fact that students have no useful role to play in society. The strict application of nurturing and protective attitudes toward children has created a paradoxical situation in which protection has come to mean excluding the young from meaningful involvement in their own communities.

(Postman 1995: 103)

It is only by thinking in this way – outside the boundaries presented by the school walls – that genuinely inclusive solutions can emerge to the routine challenge presented by children's difficult behaviour. The champion of children's rights, Eric Midwinter, said something similar a quarter of a century ago:

I gaze half-benignly on cuts in public expenditure. If those cuts can mean (it is a large 'if') the properly directed deprofessionalisation and deinstitutionalisation of our public services and the controlled mobilisation of community resources, then I am convinced the overall quality of services would be improved.

(Midwinter 1977: 111)

The reflex response of education cannot in other words be a unilateral one using its familiar constructs and professional routes. Those constructs and routes inevitably involve separate action and sometimes segregated provision.

Concluding comment

In the use of the term 'EBD/ESBD', there is an indolent espousal of a term which too conveniently packages together difficult, troublesome children with emotional disturbance. In its use is an insidious blurring of motives and knowledges that imputes problems to children that, in reality, are rarely theirs. In the dispositional attributions which are therein made, unnecessarily complex judgements about putative need take the place of simple judgements about what is acceptable or unacceptable behaviour for a particular institution. Use of the term EBD/ESBD enables the substitution of the former for the latter – of the complex for the straightforward – and this, in turn, perpetuates a mindset about behaviour that distracts attention from what the school can do to make itself a more humane, inclusive place.

Recent understandings about the rights of the child have made little impact on the processes that formalize these attributions, fraught as those processes are with difficulties concerning the extra-judicial judgements being made on children's aberrant behaviour. Neither have questions posed about the effectiveness and appropriateness of 'helping' services in adult clinical psychology and psychiatry been addressed to anywhere near the same extent in children's services. In fact, the professional services that exist notionally to support children exist often in reality to support the institution (a distinction which is sometimes overtly and unselfconsciously made) and may set into train routines and rituals that have the appearance of effective response, but in practice do little other than distract attention from significant aspects of the environment that children are being asked to inhabit.

By retaining and using the label EBD/ESBD, sight is often lost of the fact that schools for many children present an environment with which it is difficult to come to terms. By packaging this difficulty as a problem of the children we divert our own attention from ways in which schools can become more congenial and inclusive places.

Summary

The legacy of the thinking behind special education is a set of ideas which perpetuate exclusion. In this chapter we focus on 'emotional and behavioural difficulties' (EBD) (or, commonly now, 'emotional, social and behavioural difficulties': ESBD), which we suggest represents a confused collation of notions. It rests on an unsteady foundation – a mélange of disparate ideas which, nevertheless, share one feature: the attribution of behaviour problems to the disposition of the child and his or her personal circumstances. Out of this mix of notions and attributions has emerged EBD/ESBD – a category that substitutes quasi-clinical assessments about putative need for more straightforward judgements about right and wrong. It enables and legitimizes clinically oriented judgements about the causes of misbehaviour – 'emotional difficulties' – which allow the school to evade serious scrutiny of its own routines and procedures. Moreover, the judgements made about children occur in the absence of the panoply of protections that exist for adults who behave oddly or unacceptably. This difference between the way adults and children are treated is an increasingly untenable anomaly at a time when policy debate correctly pays more attention to children's rights. The predominantly clinical and child-centred mix of notions and attributions behind EBD/ESBD influences also supposedly whole-school approaches to behaviour difficulties and distracts attention from ways in which schools can be made more humane, more inclusive places.

Notes

1 The *British Journal of Special Education*, the *Journal of Child Psychology and Psychiatry*, the *European Journal of Special Needs Education*, *Support for Learning* and the *British Educational Research Journal*.

2 Popper (1977: 264) makes a similar point about the nature of psychoanalytic theory, saying: 'Psychoanalysts of all schools were able to interpret any conceivable event as a verification of their theories.' The knowledge thus formed on such non-theory masquerading as theory is dangerous, disguising hunch and guesswork in the clothes of well-grounded science.

3 'Need' presents, in Corbett's (1996: 3) thinking, far from a helpful idea, but rather 'sugar-coated poison'. Carson (1992: 217) has also had something interesting to say about 'special needs', asserting that ordinary needs, concerned with children's humanity, are 'sacrificed on the altar of identifying and meeting their special needs'. Drawing from Murray, Fromm and Maslow, he points out that we all have needs to do with affection, security, belonging, fun, self-esteem and self-identity. These are ignored or downplayed in the obsession with special needs. The setting of the latter above the former can lead to the kind of 'solutions' to supposed learning difficulty which result in segregation.

4 Apologies to Miller (1993) for the paraphrase of his analysis of Foucault's position here.

5 It is worth noting the results of an increased willingness to listen to the child. The public enquiry into abuse at children's homes in Wales has disclosed 300 former residents who are now willing to testify in cases of abuse against 148 adults (Davies 1998; Waterhouse 2000). The abuse was physical and emotional, including sexual abuse, hitting and throttling children, bullying and belittling them. Punishments included being forced to scrub floors with toothbrushes or to perform garden tasks using cutlery. The fact that these young people did not consider it worth complaining at the time attests to the fact that they themselves perceived the extent to which they were disenfranchised, to which they were considered not to be rational, believable people – not people who would be taken seriously. The scandal was exposed only after Alison Taylor, a children's home head in Gwynedd, pressed her concerns at the highest levels. When the police first investigated Ms Taylor's concerns in 1986–87, the authorities constructed a 'wall of disbelief' at the outset. The subsequent decision not to bring prosecutions was greeted, the Waterhouse enquiry concludes, with 'inappropriate enthusiasm' by social services. The fear must be that this was not an isolated incident; that it was not a pocket of evil in an otherwise broadly satisfactory system. The fear must be that such is the invalidity accorded to the child's view that it represents the tip of an iceberg. According to the Association of Child Abuse Lawyers, there are 80 police investigations into institutional abuse. It says each one should prompt a public inquiry of its own. But the cost of the north Wales inquiry is put at £13.5m and it is therefore almost certain to be the last of its kind.

6 The idea in the popular mind that acknowledgement and acceptance help in the process of 'healing' is linked to many and varied contributory ideas stemming from psychoanalysis in particular. But, as Macmillan (1997) indicates, following a painstaking analysis of the original case notes of Breuer and Freud in the case of Anna O's talking cure, there was no empirical evidence for its success even in this bedrock case. One of the cornerstones of the almost universally held assumption that facing one's problems helps, is therefore on shaky ground.

7 Interestingly, Skrtic's analysis is similar to that of Toffler (1970: 364) who, before Skrtic, wrote of the need for a shift in schools from 'bureaucracy to Ad-hocracy', and likened the organizational system operating in schools to 'the factory model' (ibid: 368), rather like Skrtic's analysis of it as 'machine bureaucracy'. The diagnosis of the likely consequences is similar too. Nothing will change, asserts Toffler, if the basic machinery doesn't change – if the systems operating are not dismantled. As he puts it, 'much of this change [currently going on in schools] is no more than an attempt to refine the existent machinery, making it ever more efficient in pursuit of obsolete goals' (ibid: 366).

8 Rousseau's ([1762] 1993: 49) comment was: 'There is nothing so absurd and hesitating as the gait of those who have been kept too long in leading-strings when they were little. This is one of the observations which are considered trivial because they are true.'

Thinking about learning failure, especially in reading

The thrust of our argument so far has been that it is particular kinds of thinking which spark the segregative impulse that leads to special education. Much of the knowledge of special education, obtained via models derived from psychology, is far from being rock solid. While it looks, sounds and feels like empirical knowledge – and it undoubtedly displays these character-istics – its empirical face validity does not live up to its promise. The features of empirical enquiry that surround the knowledge of special education and educational psychology are merely surface features. There is, to borrow Chomsky's metaphor, no 'deep-structure' outside that provided by meta-phor. From the beginnings of scientific psychology to the present day, understanding of human thinking has rested in metaphor and analogy and it is notable how this analogy has always depended for its credibility on association with fashionable scientific and technological innovation. From the engineering analogies of the nineteenth century (railway network as nervous system) to the telephone exchange models of the early part of the twentieth century to recent computer and artificial intelligence analogies, the semiotics of mind have relied on these metaphors of movement, storage, input and output.

The surface-level metaphor being used in these models, however, disguises an even more profound, deeper-rooted and misleading metaphor: that of the homunculus. A *homunculus* (from the Latin meaning 'little man') is postulated to explain the complex – some would say ineffable – process of thinking by putting a little person in our heads who assimilates ('sees') inputs, and arranges for outputs (movements, speech or whatever) to happen. No one, of course, has ever actually believed that little people live in our heads: the hom-unculus is shorthand for any postulated *agent* that performs these functions.[1] It is an appealing and enduring notion and psychologists and educators have a predilection for inventing ever newer and ever better forms of homuncular metaphor. Dennett (1993: 262) notes that the ghostly notions of mind once held are updated in the micronemes, censor agents and suppressor agents of artificial intelligence. He notes that what has happened is merely a change in the 'grain size' of homunculi.

What is the relevance of this for special education? It is relevant since these are the very constructs and metaphors that are habitually employed to explain both learning and learning failure. It was such metaphor that led to notions of mind which gave such credence to psychometrics (and the compartmentalization of thinking) and thereby validated the use of tests to assess and categorize children. They operate even today. Take a look through any of the more 'scientific' literature of educational psychology and special education and you will find any number of models of mind that fall prey to the homuncular explanatory impulse. Indeed, diagrams of the brain are sometimes even summoned up in such literature (for example, Farnham-Diggory 1992) to add scientific gravitas and are adorned with arrows impressively going in and out – from this important area to that important area – to explain how and why people's behaviour is as it is.

The consequence in the practical and professional worlds of education is that children's difficulties are summarized through, and even explained via, these crude metaphors. As soon as it is possible, notionally at least, to crystallize this or that difficulty in poor 'sequential memory', weak 'phonological awareness', or whatever, it is possible to separate out and cater differently for such children. These then are a different set of discriminatory features from those examined in Chapter 3, those being associated with behaviour and these connected with learning.

As in Chapter 3, we focus in this chapter on one aspect of the special education enterprise, namely that associated with the analysis of reading. The purpose of this chapter is to examine some of the reasoning that may often lie behind the analysis of reading failure. Although reading has been chosen as an exemplar of this kind of reasoning, it is certainly not exclusive to reading and can occur to provide 'explanations' for almost any kind of learning difficulty.

There are many accounts seeking to examine the empirical evidence for or against this or that aspect of reading difficulty. But the findings of these are not our principal focus, save insofar as the implicit tenets or reasoning behind such studies demonstrates features of the kind in which we are interested here. Our purpose is critically to examine the notion that some facet of cognitive functioning can be used as the basis for accounting for reading difficulty. Our contention is that such explanations are merely *myth*.

Myths about mind

As Gilbert Ryle (1990) pointed out in *The Concept of Mind*, a myth is not the same as a fairytale. Rather, it is the presentation of facts belonging to one category in the idioms appropriate to another. Reading failure accounted for by a weakness or insufficiency with this or that kind of cognitive capacity is the presentation of the facts of reading acquisition in the language of cooking vessels, buckets, measuring jugs and other instruments of capacity measurement. It achieves narrative plausibility, but little else. In fact, while most myth, parable and analogy helps understanding, usually by simplifying a complex set of facts by association with a less complex set, the myth behind explanation of reading failure distracts and confuses rather than helps.

What then *is* this myth? The tendency of reading theoreticians over the second half of the last century has been to try to find specific bits of cognitive functioning that would account for a child's reading failure.[2] They have sought to understand what was going wrong in a child's head that caused his or her problems with reading.

In seeking these hypothetical phenomena, theorists began to separate out the reading itself from some shadowy interior processes that were assumed to lie behind the reading. With the invention of these interior processes, there ceased to be one practice – reading. Reading became merely the outward manifestation of the integration of several inner processes: visual memory, auditory discrimination, phonological awareness and so on.

This invoking of process x to account for process y has a long and not so illustrious intellectual history. It represents a kind of Cartesian dualism in which putative mental processes, such as phonological awareness, are made to account for actual behaviours, like reading. But what is found is illusory. As Harré (1998) points out, psychologists must be wary of creating nonsense phenomena, snarks and boojums, with nonsense properties.

The predilection of theorists to find mental constructions lying behind a phenomenon (such as reading failure) is by no means new. Nietzsche ([1886] 1990) even finds this tendency in Kant, whom he says resolved the problem of how synthetic judgements could be made *a priori* by the 'discovery' of a faculty:

> Kant asked himself: how are synthetic judgements *a priori* possible? and what really did he answer? *By means of a faculty*: but unfortunately not in a few words, but so circumspectly, venerably, and with such an expenditure of German profundity and flourishes that the comical *niaiserie allemande*[3] involved in such an answer was overlooked.
>
> (Nietzsche [1886] 1990: 41, original emphasis)

The 'twaddle' of which Nietzsche speaks here is an unfortunate characteristic of the tendency to find mental causes for behavioural phenomena. The defect in reasoning which leads people to say that faculty 'x' stands behind performance 'y' appears to need a good deal of camouflage and this is seen in much of the search for factors associated with reading failure today, for many of the papers which make the association between notional skill x and performance y are predicated with reference lists almost as long as the papers themselves.

Kinds of 'intelligence', 'skill' and 'awareness' are modern examples of Kant's *faculty thinking*. These modern *faculties* are used to explain some other performance, almost as though they comprised some box of tricks or (in more modern metaphor) neural circuits ready to be tapped. But although associations can, unsurprisingly, be found between people's performance at similar kinds of task (people who are fast at picking peas out of a bowl will also be fast at picking hazelnuts out of a bowl), extrapolations surrounding association of this kind to more complex assemblages of organizational ability (such as that purported to lie behind reading failure or success) are often found wanting. Take, for example, Klein's (1997) critique of 'multiple intelligence theory'.[4] Klein points out that:

> exceptional accomplishments may not be based on the domain-wide abilities Gardner proposes. For example, he claims that excellence in chess expresses spatial intelligence . . . But chess is one of the most-researched human cognitive activities, and general abilities, spatial or otherwise, seem to contribute little to its mastery . . . Highly ranked players are less likely to work in professions that involve solving spatial problems, such as engineering, than they are to work in professions in the humanities.
>
> (Klein 1997: 382)

Following the critique of Ericsson and Charness (1994) of the notion of multiple intelligence, Klein points out that expert performance is based on extended deliberate practice in the activity itself – not on broad underlying 'intelligences'. Such intelligence is merely another faculty, a shadow beyond the thing itself.

Nietzsche and others addressed the fallacy in this rush to identify explanatory faculties long ago and it is mildly surprising that psychologists continue to wish to find them. Nietzsche contends that the discovery of a faculty is not an explanation but merely the repetition of the question. He recalls Molière's doctor's answer to the question 'How does opium induce sleep?' with the notion that there is a faculty, namely the *virtus dormitiva*. Nietzsche suggests that answers such as this ought to belong in comedy only. It is perhaps significant that Quine uses exactly the same example of Molière's *virtus dormitiva* (and without any reference to Nietzsche) in similarly tackling contemporary manifestations of Cartesian dualism. Quine (1963: 48) says of the notion of 'idea': 'The evil of the idea idea is that its use, like the appeal in Molière to a *virtus dormitiva*, engenders an illusion of having explained something.'

Explanatory faculties?

The case is exactly the same with reading failure. There is an illusion of having explained something when a faculty such as 'phonological awareness' has purportedly been isolated. In reality, what has been discovered is an association of one kind of behaviour with another and many have pointed to the mistake of linking association with causation and of the problems of 'reciprocal causation' in the many associations found between supposed sub-skills and reading. Putting it baldly, does the lack, the deficit (of whatever kind) cause the difficulty with reading or does the difficulty in reading cause the lack?[5] Direction of causality is the issue and in real life not too many people have difficulty with this. Not many people on the Clapham omnibus believe that the wind is caused by trees shaking their leaves or assume that eggs are the right size for eggcups because of good planning by hens. Direction of causality does, however, seem to cause interminable problems for people who research into learning difficulty.

We will explore this issue of causality later under the heading ' "Inference tickets" in understanding failure at school' (p. 72). But before that it is necessary to look in more detail at the notion of association, for we take it to be an improper one to use for things that involve learning. The cognitive picture being drawn when these associations are postulated is a kind of modern-day phrenology – of this bit connecting to that bit and of this faculty being responsible for the development of that skill. It is thinking of learning as a kind of bricklaying operation in which tidy cognitive bundles are cemented together to produce sets of finished skills.

Tempting as such thinking is, it is misleading. It is built out of what Derrida (1978: 280) calls 'a desire for centre in the constitution of structure' – out of a feeling that a representation of the organization of our thinking should be of the same character as that for a flowchart for the distribution of urban water supplies. The fruitlessness of hankering after and perpetually making that kind of analogy – seeking that kind of order – is revealed by Wittgenstein in an oft quoted passage:

> [N]othing in the seed corresponds to the plant which comes from it; so that it is impossible to infer the properties or structure of the plant from those of the seed . . . So an organism might come into being even out of something quite amorphous, as it were causelessly; and there is no reason why this should not really hold for our thoughts.
>
> (in Kenny 1994: 218)

Our learning is our learning. There is no shadowy essence behind it, undergirding it or underpinning it. When we learn to drive, we do just that: learn to drive – and we do so in a car, on a road. There is no *virtus trafficiva* behind our learning that can be stimulated and developed to promote the ability to drive. We cannot sit in our sitting rooms, methodically raising and lowering our left feet to emulate clutch control skills, in order to kickstart the *virtus trafficiva* into action. There are no localized or specific skills that can be isolated, ordered and trained in order to promote the learning of another skill. Indeed, where simulation does appear to be useful – for example in flight simulation for pilots – it is worth noting that the skill being practised is precisely the skill ultimately to be performed. It is not some putative sub-skill that is mysteriously undergirding in some way the necessary performance. The notion that there ought to be such component skills is a product of our knowledge of models of machine organization in which components are essential – where the failure or insufficiency of a component necessarily entails its replacement or upgrading.

The idea that there ought to be such organization is understandably popular – for in its adoption is the possibility that remedy comes with simple training or upgrading strategies. But, unfortunately, its adoption is perennially barren as far as promoting learning is concerned. Its long history as an idea stretches back to William James who signally failed to boost his 'memory muscle' by doing memory exercises. As we noted in Chapter 2, Brown and Campione

(1986) relate James's failure in this respect to the current failure to find evidence for the idea that children can have academic skills boosted through training in putative sub-skills. These in turn, they say, can be related to the failure of currently fashionable metacognitive approaches to have any demonstrable long-term effect on functional ability. Each of these attempts represents a mistake in reasoning of essentially the same character: an attempt to explain a phenomenon with the fabrication of an organizing capacity, some 'faculty' lying beyond the behaviour itself.

These failures relate to the point made by Wittgenstein that there may simply be no structural organization of the kinds proposed. That there may be no faculties behind the performance is supported by neuropsychology stretching back 60 years to the physiological work of Lashley (see Orbach 1982). Even 60 years ago it was recognized that the association cortex showed great equipotentiality as far as complex learning was concerned. The logical corollary of Lashley's work – that impairment of learning ought to depend on the extent rather than the locus of a lesion – was also supported by empirical findings. Recent neuropsychology supports the idea that there are no simple relationships, no tidy bonding of cognitive bundles: Damasio (1994) argues that current knowledge of the brain provides a picture of indissoluble interconnection in which it is impossible to disaggregate, for example, the relationship of that which we call 'affect' from that which we call 'reason'. This knowledge, he argues, puts the final nail in the coffin of Cartesian thinking.

While none of this cannot conclusively prove that there is *not* some auditory memory faculty or some developed skill of phonological awareness lying behind the ability to read (for it is possible that the form of organization could simply be beyond the reach of our analytic tools), the empirical findings of neuropsychology are nevertheless in accord with the thrust of the argument of Ryle, Quine and Wittgenstein. They support the rejection of oversimple associative models that enable the explanation of failure in x with weakness in y. Instead, both the findings and the logic support the picture of holism and plasticity. They support a picture of learning for this or that purpose.

There should be mentioned here an unacknowledged difference in the kinds of skill or faculty that are assumed to lie behind, or at least form an integral part of, reading. On the one hand are the supposed memory and sequencing faculties, spatial awareness and left-right discrimination (for example), which, it seems, are all assumed to exist beyond the reader's consciousness in stronger or weaker forms. They exist for the psychometrician seemingly in the way that a car's power is represented in its engine's cubic capacity – and, indeed, in all the connective paraphernalia (from con rods to transmission to wheels) that enable the power to be converted to movement. On the other hand is the somewhat different 'phonological awareness', differing from these other faculties in the way that Ryle's 'knowing that' differs from his 'knowing how' (1990: 29). An *awareness* implies knowledge about something which is then used in the performance of some function.

But this, Ryle says, is part of the 'intellectualist legend' (ibid: 29) – the re-assimilation of knowing how to knowing that. It is a sleight of hand which provides a tantalizingly attractive solution to the child's failure in reading (or failure in whatever), but which, in fact, explains nothing. For in making the assumption that better phonological awareness confers some advantage on the naive reader, there is an assumption that some misty anterior process is preceding the performance of reading. But as Ryle indicates, 'When I am doing something intelligently . . . I am doing one thing and not two. My performance has a special procedure or manner, not special antecedents' (ibid: 32).

The problem comes partly, Ryle suggests, from a confusion between dispositions and occurrences. The confusion arises out of nothing more complex than grammar. Because 'know' and 'run' (for example) are both verbs, the assumption is that they behave as words in similar ways. But they do not. We do not say 'he knew so and so for two minutes'. We want to talk about what can be relied on to happen as well as what is happening. The verbs denoting those reliabilities are entirely different from those that describe episodes. Since episodic words, such as 'run' and 'read' offer no hope of explanation of failure (since they do not describe what normally or reliably happens) we turn to the dispositions – embodied in notions like memory and awareness – to explain this failure.

Reading, like running or sawing or driving, is concerned with episodes (as opposed to dispositions) and know-how (as opposed to know-that). Driving does not consist of all the learning I have done in order to move my arms and legs as though these movements constituted some antecedent necessaries. There is no 'ratiocination' (as Schön 1991 puts it) between thinking and doing. While my ability to drive depends almost too obviously on my ability to move my arms and legs, few would prescribe an arm movement development programme as part of a driving improvement course.

'Inference tickets' in understanding failure at school

None of this, of course, is to deny the existence of causal connections. As Ryle (1990: 117) notes: 'Bacteriologists do discover causal connexions between bacteria and diseases . . . and so provide themselves with inference tickets which enable them to infer from diseases to bacteria.' But, as he goes on to point out, these 'inference tickets' depend for their validity on the quality of the associated fact finding and reasoning. When, for example, the recent association was noted between *Helicobacter pylori* and the presence of ulcers in patients with abdominal complaints a wide range of additional work had to be undertaken to demonstrate that the *H. pylori* caused the ulcer (see Blaser 1996). (It was possible, for example, that the attenuation of the immune system produced by the presence of the ulcer enabled colonization by *H. pylori*, rather than the ulcer being caused by *H. pylori*.) Ryle's point is that the mere notion of association and the mere notion of inference, coupled with a metaphor such as 'the rails of inference' adds almost a third dimension to what is really only a narrative. The association in itself is insubstantial; the 'inference ticket' so painstakingly enabled by the additional work of the bacteriologist having found the association is not some third force. The problem, says Ryle, is that functional differences between arguments and narratives are obliterated.

Associations of the kind discovered in reading research offer, on their own, no inference tickets. They offer merely a narrative.

This is clearly evident to those who have been pioneers in the field of phonological awareness. Take, for example, what Goswami and Bryant (1990) have to say about their findings:

> We have had to come to two uncomfortable conclusions – uncomfortable, at any rate, for the authors of a book about phonological awareness and reading. The first is that there is very little direct evidence that children who are learning to read do rely on letter-sound relationships to help them read words. The second is that there is a great deal of evidence that these young children take easily and naturally to reading words in other ways.
>
> (Goswami and Bryant 1990: 46)

Such critical self-awareness is, however, evidently not present among many of those who use the construct of phonological awareness and who fashion for themselves inference tickets precisely of the kind discussed. Take, for example, what the respected reading researcher Farnham-Diggory has to say about phonological awareness in a book that is part of a series produced by Harvard University Press, edited by Jerome Bruner:

> Exactly what this ability [phonological awareness] involves physiologic-ally is not fully understood, but it is clear that some people are natively endowed with more of it than others are, and that low phonological awareness underlies reading problems.
>
> (Farnham-Diggory 1992: 119)

Here, then, is an extension of the simple proposition that training in skill x enables you to be better in skill y, behind which some proponents of the significance of phonological awareness might stand. This latter is in itself a tenuous proposition, of course, incorporating controversies about transfer of training which go back to James's memory muscle and introducing all kinds of confusion about reciprocal causation. But Farnham-Diggory is going further than that. Here in her comment is the explicit articulation by an academic of the assumption that is so commonly heard in professional life: poor readers are *natively endowed* with less ability in phonological awareness than others. Moreover, this *underlies* reading problems. According to her, it is 'clear' that this is the case. It is not evident (to the authors, at least) what kind of experimental design would enable one 'clearly' to disentangle heritable and environmental influences on any such language-linked ability (given that both influences are unequivocally operating from birth) and confer responsi-bility on the genotype. As Morgan (1996) makes clear the plasticity of the slowly developing human brain gives far greater likelihood to the possibility that use and utility are inextricably bound: *we become what we do.*

But let us allow this to pass for a moment and examine the seemingly more innocuous first part of the sentence. The sentence begins 'Exactly what this ability involves physiologically is not fully understood' and reveals an assumption that an ability *could* be understood physiologically, if only our instruments for finding out about this kind of thing were smart enough. The assumption is dualistic: that 'abilities' emerge out of 'physiological processes' in the brain. Whether or not the question could ever be this simple (and it couldn't), there is the question of whether it could ever be informative in the way that we go about teaching or designing an education system. It is rather like, in the example from Rorty and Putnam given in Chapter 1, wanting to explain why a square peg won't go into a round hole by reference to the interrelationships of the peg's constituent molecules. Harré (1985) suggests that Vygotsky's 'principle of unity' should always be used to forbid this kind of reasoning. The principle, says Harré:

> forbids the decomposition of a psychological phenomenon into elements which are below the level at which that phenomenon has meaning. To ignore Vygotsky's principle would be like trying to study syntax and semantics through attention only to the distribution of the letters of the alphabet.
>
> (Harré 1985: 14)

Stanovich (1994) is more circumspect in his use of language. Nevertheless, in a comprehensive research review which enables him to conclude that there is no support for the notion that a concept of dyslexia is needed that separates 'dyslexia' from more neutral terms such as 'poor reader', he feels able to conclude from his literature review that: 'Lack of phonological awareness inhibits the learning of the alphabetic coding patterns that underlie word recognition' (Stanovich 1994: 586). He feels able to suggest this because phonological awareness is the precursor to 'phonological coding ability' (15 separate references are given to support this single assertion) and problems with this 'phonological coding lead to the most diagnostic symptom of reading disability: difficulty in pronouncing pseudowords' (ibid: 586) (nine references are given here). Despite the evident stability of the associative link between phonological awareness, phonological coding ability and reading disability, there is nowhere in this an establishment of the 'inference ticket'. There is, for example, nowhere a recognition of the possibility that difficulty in pronouncing pseudo-words may be the most distinctive indicator simply because it is the task most similar to reading real words (and the word 'read' is carefully avoided in discussion of what youngsters do with these pseudo-words: they are said to be 'pronounced' and 'named'). In other words, it may simply be that a task which is the most effective predictor of a child's subsequent reading ability achieves this status merely by virtue of being most similar to the task in question: reading.

Findings consistent with the thesis being advanced here have come repeatedly from research over the last two or three decades and, as Norwich (1991) indicates in a comprehensive review, these findings have been broadly accepted by the research community. For example, the early hopes that the *Illinois Test of Psycholinguistic Abilities* would, following an in-depth breakdown of the child's specific abilities in memory, sequencing and so forth, furnish a key to how to help children read (by enabling a boosting of weak skills) were disappointed by the findings of, among others, Newcomer and Hammill

(1975) and Johnson and Pearson (1975). A scholarly appraisal of research findings by Arter and Jenkins (1979) confirmed these findings and sealed the conclusions which those researchers had drawn. Others such as Coles (1987) have elegantly and painstakingly shown the lack of relationship between putative specific neurological dysfunction and reading difficulty, at the same time as highlighting the not insignificant relationships between professional and academic knowledge bases.[6]

The genealogy of faculty-based explanations for human performance stretches back a long way, and sub-skill explanations for reading difficulty are only their most recent manifestation. Phonological awareness is another variant in this tradition and one of which researchers and practitioners should be wary.

Concluding comment

When children fail to learn in school, it is only too tempting to want to see something wrong with them. The perceived 'wrongness' may be affective, to do with their emotions, as we noted in Chapter 3, or it may concern their cognitive ability as we have noted in this chapter. Diagnoses of this kind lead to prescriptions about different kinds of treatment, either in a special school or with some kind of special teaching method. The point we have tried to make here is not simply that the empirical evidence for this kind of approach is, at best, equivocal (and Coles, following highly detailed and critical reviews – 1987; 2000; 2003 – claims baldly that the archive of research on reading failure represents 'bad science'), it is rather that the approach itself rests on notions of mind that are untenable.

Summary

Research effort in special education often seeks explanation for children's learning difficulties in hypothetical cognitive processes that are assumed to underpin competence. This is particularly the case with reading difficulty. Despite disappointing empirical evidence about the significance of such constructs, repeated efforts are made to discover them. An argument is made here for the case that the reasoning that lies behind these efforts relies on an artificial distinction between performances (such as reading) and faculties (such as memory or awareness). The construction of this distinction means that illegitimate cause–effect inferences are made about simple associations. The result of this sort of reasoning is a raft of assessments and special pedagogies whose benefits are, at best, dubious and whose ultimate effect is to exaggerate differences between children. The end product of the process is the logic of separating and segregating out those who supposedly need such supposedly different treatment.

Notes

1 Sometimes the term *homuncular functionalism* is used to describe this tendency.
2 There have been some notable exceptions, for example Gerald Coles (1987; 2000); Kenneth Goodman (1996); Frank Smith (1973; 1994; 1998).
3 This roughly translates as 'German twaddle'.
4 Gardner's (1983) widely read and quoted *Frames of Mind* proposes seven kinds of intelligence: linguistic, spatial, musical, interpersonal, etc. These purport to explain people's excellence or otherwise in various aspects of their everyday life.
5 Linguist and speech scientist Robert Scholes (1998: 182) makes the case that phonemic awareness 'is not an untutored component of the linguistic consciousness of speakers'. He concludes that 'any positive correlations between phonemic awareness and reading skill are based on a definition of reading that is misguided and potentially harmful' (p. 177).
6 As Smail suggested (discussed in Chapter 3) the commercial–professional enterprise encircling behaviour problems looks something like a bazaar. Coles suggests something similar for that, which surrounds reading failure. For Coles, however, this is not merely a benign growth that won't do too much harm; rather, it actively hurts children.

Modelling difference

One of the most enduring features of the world of special education is the construction and management of difference – the making of 'marginal identities' as sociologists would put it. The past 100 years have seen the development of mechanisms, procedures, measuring instruments and practices that have had the objective of identifying and moving pupils into segregated forms of schooling. The notion that special education operates as a filtering device to render more manageable the majority of the system has now become part of the received wisdom of critical thinking about special education, as we noted in Chapter 1. There are, however, several ways in which the process of constructing difference has been thought about and it is the purpose of this chapter to examine some of these, for they are relevant to the ways in which inclusion is conceived.

Difference or diversity? Celebrate or segregate?

To be called 'special' is to be given a new identity within the schooling system. How far this social identity becomes transferable to (or resisted by) other institutions or forms part of an individual's personal identity is highly debatable and it has been discussed through this book thus far. However, it is clear that this accreditation of difference represents in practice two phenomena: first, a transition from one state to another – that is from the 'non-special' to the 'special'; second, a set of interventions that reinforces this state of difference. There is at work a process of re-ordering that positions a pupil into different and possibly new sets of social relations – with teachers, peers and support staff.

This is what Munro (1997) calls a continual 'labour of division' and it is characteristic of much activity of institutions, not just schools. This notion of labour of division is, of course, an inversion of Marx's (1995) concept of the division of labour and it is used to signify the way institutions actively go about splintering and fragmenting previously given categories. It is about the drawing and continual redrawing of boundaries; of constructing points of demarcation, which, in turn, are used as indices to 'map' individuals or groups into appropriate classifications. This making of difference seems almost to be an endemic part of the process of being an institution. If this is the case, it presents problems for those who wish to see more inclusion in social and institutional life. What can be discovered about the process?

It is clear, first of all, that the recognition of difference is not necessarily anti-inclusional. Williams (1992), draws useful distinctions between diversity, difference and division:

> By *diversity* I mean difference claimed upon a shared collective experience which is specific and not necessarily associated with a subordinated or unequal subject position . . . *difference* denotes a situation where a shared collective experience/identity . . . forms the basis of resistance against the positioning of that identity as subordinate. By *division* I mean the translation of the expression of a shared experience into a form of domination.
>
> (Williams 1992: 70)

Williams is arguing that we cannot assume that difference will automatically be translated into some anti-inclusive domination. Not all forms of difference automatically imply marginalization and exclusion. Likewise, Munro (1997) points out that:

> considered as a feature of society, difference might be said to enjoy mixed fortunes. Sometimes difference is in vogue; it is a thing to be welcomed and may be referred to wholesomely in such terms as 'diversity'. On other occasions . . . it is viewed as something more shadowy, even malevolent, with any difference being treated as deviant.
>
> (Munro 1997: 14)

This then is the key issue: is difference something to be welcomed or is it, in Munro's terms, to be made into something 'shadowy', 'malevolent', 'deviant'? There are clearly variations in the way that educators handle kinds of difference. In the case of certain systems of symbols – sexuality, clothing, patterns of speech and behaviour – there is strong evidence that exclusionary pressure associates itself with this kind of difference.

But it is not just with difficult behaviour at school that the process of making difference works. While it is not as conspicuous in other areas it nevertheless occurs, despite the outward impression that inclusion is happening. As Barnes *et al.* (1999) and Geertz (1975) remark, different cultural groups mark out and categorize social difference by reference to localized criteria. And this has been especially the case as far as education is concerned and the concept of 'need' has played its part in this. The mark of difference has been used as a rationale for segregation rather than celebration, even though the markers of that difference are subtle and elude definition. For instance, notions of 'need' in physical impairment or, even more relevantly, 'learning difficulties' may have referents that are difficult to be specific about outside a local context. There is certainly evidence of this as far as reading difficulty is concerned: Thomas and Davis (1997) showed that 'reading difficulty' is not a clear-cut, unambiguous label; teachers in different schools will have different ideas about what constitutes 'a child with reading difficulty', depending on their local experience. As Lee (1996: 34) puts it of the near-certainty with which Warnock (DES 1978) and special educators talk of the existence of one in five children with 'special educational needs', 'given the inevitably contingent nature of special educational needs . . . the 20 per cent and 2 per cent estimates should be taken with a pinch of salt'.

The Audit Commission/HMI (1992) and Goacher *et al.* (1988) have said something similar, pointing to the difficulties in operationalizing the idea of one in five children with 'special needs' when its definition depends on relating the learning of one child to that of another. Intended to be positive – highlighting children with difficulties and directing resources to them – the idea of one in five ended up being 'reified' (Lunt and Evans 1994) and Fulcher (1989) has suggested that the effect of talking about a notion of one in five was to increase to 20 per cent the number of children who were deemed to be disabled. She points out that notions of SEN and disability are not so very far apart and that given that this is the case the inevitable consequence of the escalation (to 20 per cent) of numbers of children with 'special needs' was to marginalize more of the school population.

With Warnock (DES 1978), the number of children 'with special needs' rose from around 2 per cent of the school population – that is, those who were educated in special schools – to 20 per cent. People who were clever with numbers worked out that this meant that 18 per cent of children in ordinary schools had special needs and this became a commonplace: 18 per cent of children in ordinary schools had special educational needs. It is extraordinary that this figure – 18 per cent – came to be accepted as uncritically as it was. The figure '18 per cent' even made its way into the title of a respectable book about special needs (Gipps 1987). For 18 per cent to be accepted (not 17 per cent or 19 per cent, note) as the proportion of children with special needs in ordinary schools shows a faith in the power of statistics that has probably never been rivalled in the history of serious discourse on public policy.

As Giddens (1990) puts it of the way in which empirical information comes to create the social world, rather than merely reflect it:

> Concepts . . . and the theories and empirical information linked to them, are not merely handy devices whereby agents are somehow more clearly able to understand behaviour . . . they actively constitute what that behaviour is and inform the reasons for which it is undertaken.
>
> (Giddens 1990: 42)

Giddens implies that as we 'discover' new ways of making sense of phenomena, these explanations in turn become inseparable from what those phenomena are. The empirical and epidemiological information drawn on by the Warnock Committee in 1978 (DES 1978) did not merely hold a mirror up to some reality which could be used by educators. Rather, it actively generated a 'reality' that had to be lived up to. As is shown in the example of reading difficulty (Thomas and Davis 1997), the construction of that reality means that practitioners will seek ways of conforming to it and confirming it. In this sense, the absorption of 'theoretical insights' into the day-to-day practices of schools are revealed in the categories which are used to 'mark out' pupils as being similar or different.

Clearly, the way in which difference is conceptualized is important for inclusion. Are differences crystallized into some set of problems that have to be dealt with by an institutional system (such as education) or are they important elements of diversity to be celebrated and cherished in a plural society? Should we question all, none or some of the means by which difference is marked? We review next the thinking of several sets of thinkers – Lyotard, Foucault, the Chicago School – whose ideas all contribute to this debate.

Lyotard: paralogy and terror

A thinker seldom drawn on in education's debate about the constitution of 'specialness' is Lyotard. At the centre of Lyotard's thinking is the foreground-ing of dissent or difference (*paralogy*) over sameness (*homology*). What stems from this is a form of politics that argues that every 'voice' should be treated as legitimate and worthy of respect as every other.

Lyotard's writing can be dense, anarchic and seemingly irrelevant to the 'real world' of education. However, there can be no doubt that the highly critical stance that he and others such as Foucault (of whom more later) have taken on issues such as the legitimacy of 'voice' have had their effects on contemporary thought. This is nowhere more evident than in the increasing respect currently being accorded to the voice of the child – and the voice of under-represented people generally. The intellectual lineage of the call to open a dialogue with those who have previously been unheard is traceable to these writers. In Lyotard's scheme there are no privileged speech communities or forms of knowledge that dominate or sit in judgement over others. What Lyotard is ultimately after is what he calls an open-ended system of knowledge, which allows for not only a plurality of voices to form a continuous horizon, but expects the 'inventive self' to generate new voices which are equally respected.

Achieving this involves the rejection of *grand narratives*. Such grand narra-tives are similar to the Grand Theory discussed in Chapters 1 and 2. Unified attempts to explain life, the universe and everything, grand narratives (or metanarratives) take on the form of an attempt to 'impose order and unity on the fragile, chaotic . . . character of the social' (Mouzelis 1995: 42). Sociology and psychology abound with such grand narratives: Marxism, critical theory, functionalism, structuration, behaviourism, psychoanalysis and so on. How-ever, grand narratives are not just limited to the academy: they are easily found in other areas of social life such as politics, economics and the natural sciences. Lyotard asserts that these grand narratives become what he calls 'phrase regimes' – that is, singular, unified (and nearly always simplistic) ways of describing and explaining complex social reality that privilege one group over another.

Underpinning these phrase regimes are covert or overt appeals to rational-ity, which Parker (1997) argues are a set of rules or standards by which other forms of reasoning, actions and content can be judged.[1] Phrase regimes that do not measure up to these criteria are suppressed or dismissed as irrelevant. Legitimate phrase regimes are therefore in a position to exclude or marginalize that which does not conform to these standards. It is the enforced silence of a person's or group's difference (what Lyotard calls the *Other*) that is seen as an act of gross injustice. By not being able to argue, to express one's difference and thus have the self fixed into something which it is not, is for Lyotard an act of 'terrorism'. An example of the way in which hearing the voice of chil-dren has changed of late, perhaps indirectly and belatedly in recognition of the salience of Lyotard's views, was brought to life vividly in the testimony given to the Waterhouse Inquiry into child abuse at Welsh children's homes (Waterhouse 2000). This inquiry disclosed 300 former residents who were will-ing to testify to abuse committed by 148 adults. As we noted in Chapter 3, the significant point here is that these young people did not consider it worth complaining at the time. It attests to the fact that they themselves perceived the extent to which they were considered not to be rational, believable people – not people who would be taken seriously. (See also Kendrick 1997.)

Underpinning Lyotard's thinking is a particular view of language. Rather than seeing it as a convenient system of symbols to aid communication, Lyotard takes the position that we are nothing more than linguistic construc-tions. Hence his emphasis on the normative power of certain phrase regimes. This view jettisons the notion that language is a medium that unproblematic-ally conveys meanings and ideas. What phrase regimes seek to achieve is a form of closure, to fix the self within systems of 'order and unity which would force the subject to conform to artificial limits, structures or modes of expression' (Haber 1994: 15).

Foucault: discipline, punishment and meticulous regimes of power

The kind of evidence drawn on by those who have helped shape the education system, whether the discussion is of Cyril Burt, with his use of psychometrics, or the Warnock Committee with its reliance on the supposedly hard data furnished by epidemiology, relies on notions of the subjective and objective. The rational observer, the disinterested social scientist, has sought always to minimize the effects of the subjective and to maximize the extent to which an objective truth is captured. For Foucault, subjectivity and objectivity are more problematic. They are 'achieved' through what Foucault calls regimes of power. It is our continuous and long-term exposure, coupled with a reflective engagement with certain types of practices, rules and discourses that we encounter in our day-to-day lives across institutions that produces this effect.[2] The school and the workplace are not only built around the 'grand plans' of what it means to be 'educated' or an efficient and productive 'worker', but networks of rules, regulations and norms which define us as subjects and objects. It is the continual and virtually seamless 'capillary action' of power such as rules over 'styles of dress', 'time keeping', 'curriculum planning', 'seating arrangements', 'classroom displays' – the list is almost infinite – which shape not only our understanding and experience of institutional reality, but in turn is shaped by us as we apply such rules and norms as though they were natural, logical and inevitable.

Foucault's self-styled and unorthodox historical methodology of archaeology and genealogy – the building of a picture through many and varied fragments of information – had as its subject neither the movers and shakers of history nor the unfolding of history along an evolutionary path, but rather those at the margins. His insights thus sometimes have great resonance for special education, wherein the focus is exactly here: children at the margins, who fail for whatever reason in the mainstream system. It is not so much the seismic shifts in history that Foucault documents (wars, revolutions, the rise and fall of empires), but the fragmentary and almost imperceptible surface changes or, as Foucault (1970) himself characterizes it:

> a modification and shifting of cultural interests, a redistribution of opinions and judgements . . . wrinkles traced for the first time on the enlightened face of knowledge.
>
> (Foucault 1970: 258)

What Foucault presents in his historical studies on sexuality, madness, medicine and prisons are examples of how the 'wrinkles' or certain types of ideas and practices are taken up and become more or less unquestioned elements of our contemporary received knowledge and practices – of how they become part of the 'political economy of power'. There is in Foucault's reading of history, not a sense of steady progression from the 'barbaric' to the 'civilised', but one of contingency, accident, discontinuity and rupture:

> The 'invention' of this new political anatomy must not be seen as a sudden discovery. It is rather a multiplicity of often minor processes of different origin, of scattered location which overlap . . . they were at work in secondary schools at a very early date, later in primary schools . . . they sometimes circulated very rapidly from one point to another . . . sometimes slowly and discreetly.
>
> (Foucault 1991: 138)

It is within *Discipline and Punish* (Foucault 1991) that are found some of his most useful and commonly referenced tools: docile bodies, normalizing judgements, hierarchical surveillance and the examination. According to Foucault one of the crucial moments during the eighteenth century was a profound shift in the way the human body was conceptualized. Descartes' separation of the mind (or soul) from the body opened up the potential to explore the body in an entirely new way. The body began to be viewed as a form of machine and hence as an object that could be broken down into its component parts. With this new knowledge of the body and of how it functions comes an understanding of how it can be 'manipulated, shaped, trained . . . obeys and responds' – or, in short, how the body could become docile and disciplined. For Foucault, discipline is not an overt act of 'triumphant power', rather it is quite the opposite as he saw its success as its ability to permeate almost seamlessly and unquestioningly the day-to-day workings of institutional life. It is through the mundane and banal sets of practices, the minutiae of rules and regulations 'the small acts of cunning . . . and subtle arrangements' (1991: 308) which gives discipline its potency.

Space

What made space such a potent concoction for Foucault, was the meshing of regulatory arrangements into the architectural fabric of buildings. The use of space in the form of 'enclosures' – purpose-built environments (schools, factories, hospitals) – was additionally used to contain and distribute individuals through 'partitioning' (classrooms, workshops, wards) contingent on some form of classification. Disciplinary space is also intended to be functional with layout determined by the kind of tasks that are meant to be undertaken.

In *Discipline and Punish*, Foucault wrote of the carceral city, but he could equally have written about the carceral school, not with a centre of power or a network of forces, but rather a multiple network of diverse elements: 'walls, space, institution, rules, discourse . . . a strategic distribution of elements of different natures at different levels' (1991: 307). At the centre of Foucault's 'carceral city' are 'insidious leniencies, anavowable petty cruelties, small acts of cunning, calculated methods, techniques, "sciences" that permit the fabrication of the disciplinary individual' (ibid: 308). In these – these 'rules of strategy' (ibid: 308) – are perhaps to be found the rejection, exclusion and marginalization of those that the school doesn't like. Foucault is implying, in other words, that the need for order is a cover under which occurs the inevitable activity that surrounds the gaining and maintenance of power.

Ranking by rule

For Foucault, the examinations and tests used in education do not merely describe: they also construct that which they set out to describe. The examination – and one could include here the panoply of assessment instruments devised by educational psychology – exists as part of a set of 'normalizing judgements' allowing for decisions to be made about the 'correctness' of an individual's behaviour. However, normal does not simply refer to a binary division between a right way and a wrong way to behave; more, it implies the normal distribution curve, referred to in Chapter 1. By using this as a reference point for measuring and recording it is possible to classify, rank, compare and distribute individuals relative to what is expected as per the 'rule':

> Instead of the simple division of the prohibition, as practised in penal justice, we have a distribution between a positive pole and a negative pole; all behaviour falls between good and bad marks, good and bad points.
>
> (Foucault 1991: 180)

Although the normalizing judgement has as its overriding aim the enclosure or the 'homogenization' of behaviour within these two poles, it nonetheless allows for the application of a more fine-grained set of criteria. In other words, difference or individual variation is permissible, but only within a specified region of tolerance. And behaviour that falls outside these limits forms what Foucault (1991) calls the 'external frontier of the abnormal'. This is the point that demarcates the mad, the bad and the dangerous from those who are the average. As Foucault remarks:

> The power of normalisation imposes homogeneity; but it individualises by making it possible to measure gaps, to determine levels . . . the norm introduces a useful imperative, and as a result of measurement the shading of individual differences.
>
> (Foucault 1991: 184)

As part of a disciplinary regime, normalizing judgements are applied meticulously and perpetually. As such, the objective was to make the 'slightest departures from correct behaviour subject to punishment'. However, as Foucault goes on to remark, punishment is neither the arbitrary application of force nor the invariant observance of 'a law, a programme, or a set of regulations'. On the contrary, punishment should always reflect a concern with the match between the transgressor and context. However, normalizing judgements serve a double-function in discipline. As well as being the criteria by which deviant individuals are punished for their non-conformity, it is at the same time used to determine the need for corrective measures in order to 'reduce the gaps'.

Observation and surveillance

The evaluations that are made vis-à-vis the 'normal' are not used simply to punish, but become part of the corpus of knowledge about that individual. Linked to this is Foucault's second component of the examination: *hierarchical observation*. For Foucault, observation or surveillance forms the basis of all judgements. As such, being able to 'see' what is occurring is a prerequisite to making an evaluation. Hierarchical surveillance is more than just a passive or incidental form of watching: it is 'embedded' within the rules and regulations that specify an organization's social relations.

We can, says Foucault, never escape from the permanent effects of the 'disciplinary gaze'. We are always being observed and, with that, judged. In drawing normalization and surveillance together, Honneth (1995) notes that the examination as a regulated combination of the methods of discipline is for Foucault the key institutional mechanism which views 'humans as individuated subjects'.

As Hoskins (1990) remarks, the kind of examination with which we are now so familiar in education was very much a product of the second half of the nineteenth century built around Francis Galton's work on intelligence. If we concentrate on its pedagogical application the examination appears to serve two interconnected functions. First, it serves the function of the establishment of a visibility through which individuals can be differentiated and judged.

Second, it is the guarantee of the transmission of knowledge from the teacher to the student.

None of these insights seems particularly sparkling to the contemporary eye, which has become accustomed to critique of normative judgement. Neither do Foucault's insights summarize well, since they emerge from his 'archaeological' method – a method relying for its potency on the reader's engagement with a particular incident or revelation. He is, in this sense, best read in the original. There are perhaps three highly significant insights that educators in general and special educators in particular can take from his work.

The first is about the way in which disciplinary regimes – the 'scientific' knowledge of psychology and psychiatry – have structured the way in which individuals' differences are thought about; this was discussed in Chapters 1 and 2. But difference is found, made and exaggerated not just by these schemas (represented in the administration of schooling) but also by the small routines of life: the 'petty cruelties' (Foucault 1991: 308).

The second is that difference – even the unwelcome difference of unpleasantness, resistance and dissent – says something (or should say something) to us, as we noted in Chapter 3, about the humanity of the systems we create and operate. Challenge represents energy, Foucault asserts, and it is the enabling of the expression of this kind of energy which is the essence of the success of an open society. Resistance 'should be seen not so much as a weakness or a disease, as an energy that is reviving' (Foucault 1991: 289). Foucault quotes the Fourierists of nineteenth-century France who said that the delinquents were those 'whose natural robustness rejects or disdains its [the social order's] prescriptions' (ibid: 289). The challenge is to listen to the voice of those who are different; if we don't, difference will always remain as Williams's (1992) *division* rather than *diversity*.

The third is the omnipresence of power: Foucault saw power as a silent and unconsidered force seeping through all aspects of life, high and low. Seen as such, its effects will always be present – hierarchizing, forever pushing x above y. If this is the case, new forms of domination and segregation will inevitably tend to replace the old ones that are rejected by a civilized society. While Foucault would have been the last person to offer prescriptions, there are corollaries of accepting a Foucauldian analysis and these concern awareness of the processes he reveals and determination to override them: such processes may not be eliminable, but it may be possible to minimize them in the inclusive structures schools construct.

Making a bit of a habitus of it: the work of Bourdieu

If Lyotard and Foucault are characteristic of a looser (and some would argue more obtuse) French intellectual tradition, then their contemporary Pierre Bourdieu (1930–2002), represents a more straightforward proposition. In his large corpus of work, Bourdieu's contribution to the sociology of education is as extensive as it is pervasive. He introduced an ensemble of concepts that have become a stock in trade for the 'jobbing' sociologist.

What Bourdieu offers, in his own words, is a set of 'thinking tools'. Like Foucault, he attempts to make us think differently about ourselves and the social worlds in which we live. His focus on practice, or put simply, what people 'do', shifts the emphasis away from abstractions or interiorizations. He tries to provide a set of tools and explanations that are neither rooted in the subjective lifeworlds of individuals nor in structures that exist beyond individuals' consciousness.

Over a 40-year period, Bourdieu was working on two well-established and interconnected sociological problems. The first is referred to as the 'structure-agency' question and concerns the relationship of the individual (the 'agent') to wider society (the 'structure'), and who exercises power over what. The second concerns the idea of social reproduction: Bourdieu is an immensely influential contributor to the sociological 'problem' of how any society reproduces itself and keeps stable without descending into anarchy. This question has remained at the core of social theorizing since the inception of sociology as a discipline in the mid-nineteenth century. It is through his work on education that Bourdieu attempts to provide new perspectives on reproduction, agency and structure.

Given that education sits centrally in Bourdieu's analyses, it is surprising that his work has not been used much in the analysis of special education. His analyses are particularly relevant for an explication of inclusion and exclusion, being about the processes by which inequality (albeit for him centred on 'class'), is reproduced. He developed over a 30-year period the interrelated concepts of *capital, habitus* and *field*, which he put to work in his own studies of French education.

Capital: quantities and qualities

Undoubtedly the best known of the three concepts is Bourdieu's metaphorical use of *capital*, borrowed from the world of political economy. Capital, he says, is something (for example, land, money, knowledge, power, raw materials) that can potentially be transformed into something else (status, commodities, more money, knowledge, power, etc.). Bourdieu suggested a number of forms of capital: *cultural* (attitudes and dispositions), *linguistic* (use and understanding of language), *political* (power and the capacity to make or influence decision making), *physical* (dress, body shape, adornments, etc.), *social* (networks and relationships with other individuals or communities), *economic* (financial resources such as money, land or property) and *symbolic* (e.g. academic qualifications, expert knowledge, etc.). The list is potentially endless as we can add to it other forms of capital. For example Reay (2004) in her work on working-class students' aspirations for entering higher education, introduces the idea of *emotional* capital. However, what is key about capital in Bourdieu's scheme, particularly in any analysis of the growth of special education, is that:

1 it is unequally distributed in terms of type as well as quality and quantity across individuals and communities

2 it can potentially be transformed into some other form of capital or just 'saved'.

As an oft-cited example, we go to school or university with cultural capital (attitudes towards learning) acquired in the family to gain symbolic capital (e.g. qualifications), which can be converted into economic capital (occupational income). Along the way, we may generate social capital by making friends and connections at work or school or university, which in turn can be used to generate, for example, more economic capital. The economic allusion suggests that:

1 some forms of capital are more scarce than others and thus 'attract' differential levels of value (use or exchange) in a 'marketplace'
2 individuals and communities compete among themselves for access to good schools, desirable neighbourhoods, etc. and/or the acquisition of new 'capital' such as academic qualifications and professional status.

As Harker *et al.* (1990) remark, capital can be 'exchanged, converted, reconverted to produce power and domination'.

Our continual participation in this game has the effect of reproducing forms of dominance and subordination. Any selective or segregative system, such as that afforded by special education, plays an active part in this through the hierarchies that it creates and reinforces, but its sequelae are created passively in the everyday practices that emerge within and as part of the system. So, while a separative system may be set up for the purpose of streamlining the smooth running of the mainstream system, everyday practices emerge by virtue of the apparent logic, the putative good sense of the system, which go to reinforce the dominance and subordination that already exist. Thus, for example, the examination system that Bourdieu says exists to reproduce power and domination, is taken by administrators and practitioners both to reflect and manifest 'natural', 'sensible', God-given aspects of the psychological world. It thus becomes common sense for those working in special schools to assume that their 'less able' charges have no place in an examination system and these students become therefore even more separated as they are excluded to an even greater degree from the mainstream world (see Thomas 1997a, for a discussion of the place of special school students in the examination system).

Two forms of capital that are worth discussing in more detail are the *cultural* and *social* varieties, as they have direct implications for education – special or otherwise. Cultural capital is central to Bourdieu's discussion on education. Cultural capital is a cluster of dispositions seen as being vital for successfully navigating institutionalized education. For Bourdieu, the dominant cultural understanding of being 'good' at school includes not only the possession of some degree of intellectual ability, but also a distinctive and positive attitude towards the school in general and, more importantly, its value system. As suggested by Lamont and Lareau (1988) cultural capital is 'institutionalised i.e. widely shared, high status cultural signals (attitudes, preferences, formal knowledge, behaviours, goals and credentials) used for social and cultural exclusion'.

Schools do not generate cultural capital; they merely process and legitimize it. Cultural capital originates mainly within the family and to a more limited extent the local community. As such it is inculcated through the process of primary socialization and forms part of what Bourdieu refers to the *habitus* – which we unpack later. As Kingston (2001) observes, cultural capital derives its force from the ability of gatekeepers (e.g. schools) to judge and reward those who possess it and exclude those who do not and the role of a segregative system in effecting and easing such a process of exclusion needs little explication. As with all forms of capital, cultural capital is not a resource equally distributed across all social groups, but held in greater quantities by some (for Bourdieu, the upper and middle classes) and much less so by others (the working classes).

Getting a bad habitus?

In Bourdieu's attempt to link agency and structure, the idea of *habitus* is intended to provide the personal, subjective or 'agent' dimension. Perhaps oversimplifying, habitus is who we are; we are the embodiment both physically and psychologically of the field (see later) or social world in which we belong. We are born into families and communities that are structured in certain ways: they have roles, values, taboos, prohibitions and norms that we learn through a process of primary socialization. If this process is sufficiently thorough, it is rare that we question or undermine these principles as they appear to us as real and as natural as trees or clouds. It is this taken-for-grantedness about the world and our place within it and the tacit sense of ontological security and comfort we feel when we are 'in the right place' that Bourdieu calls the *doxa*. It is from this *doxa* that one can feel that the world – the psychological world – comprises phenomena as 'natural' as intelligence: phenomena that are to be taken for granted.

But acquiring our habitus is much more than just a simple process of cultural inculcation, as it also reproduces, or more technically, instantiates, the very conditions of its own existence. In short, our habitus directs our practice and in turn this reproduces the habitus. Hence the habitus is not simply a set of ideas that exist inside our heads about ourselves and the world, but ideas which also permeate how we act in the world. Additionally, the habitus functions at the affective level, as it is involved in how we feel and how we engage with the world as an aesthetic object. Our capacity to discriminate between what is 'tasteful' and what is 'vulgar' or 'offensive' is all mediated via the habitus. There is also according to Bourdieu and Wacquant (1992) an obvious physicality to the habitus, which is highly important as it connects directly to the notion of practice.

As Shilling (2004: 477) remarks 'there are substantial inequalities in the symbolic values accorded to particular bodily forms'. The point Shilling makes concerning the relationship between physical capital and cultural and social variants is an interesting one. Far from being superficial frippery, the presentation of and the management of the self is critical in the display and articulation of habitus: accent, deportment, style of dress, body movement, linguistic register and so on are symbolic markers of the field we come from.

Jenkins (1992) argues that: '[The] power of the habitus comes from the thoughtlessness of habit and habitation, rather than consciously learned rules and principles.' Socially competent performances are produced as a matter of routine without reference to a body of codified knowledge. Hence we reproduce the social world not through any cognition, but simply through being and acting in the world. For Bourdieu, this act of reproduction occurs through *practice*, which, in turn, is layered by what he refers to as *strategies*.

Stuck in a field?

If habitus is intended to capture the subjective dimension, the notion of 'field' is the objective or structural part of Bourdieu's scheme. What Bourdieu is arguing (in a way not unlike much sociological theorizing), is that although we subjectively experience and act in the world as rational individuals (or at least we think we do), this is for the large part 'shaped' in ways over which we do not have much control. For Bourdieu, this external 'force' is referred to as the *field*, which as suggested by Wacquant (1992: 17) is made up of:

> a set of objective historical relations between positions anchored in oppo-sitions of power . . . [they are also] autonomous as it [the field] prescribes its own particular values and regulative principles [which] delimit a socially structured space in which agents struggle . . .

The concept of field, although abstract, when conjoined with capital and habitus, can be useful in trying to think through the relationship between special education, other parts of the education system and those fields (e.g. systems) beyond its boundaries. What Bourdieu is presenting is a social system that is:

1 loosely connected by a series of fields that possess boundaries of some form (institutions such as education, politics, science, the economy, culture, social class, the family, etc.), which are differentiated in some way and relatively autonomous from each other, but can function as external forces over each other
2 hierarchical in organization (i.e. fields are made up of dominant and sub-ordinate parts)
3 made up of different positions (roles e.g. teacher, student, headteachers, par-ents, postcode counters, etc.) whose relationship to each other is primarily structured via unequal power relations
4 in part shaped and constituted by historical factors and effects
5 underpinned by sets of principles (values, goals, norms, etc.) that both regulate and define the parameters of practice.

Although fields can and do interconnect (e.g. politics with law or the econ-omy with education), each is quite distinct from the other in terms of logic, structure, traditions, procedures, rituals, taboos and so on.

Wacquant (1992) argues that we also need to view the field as a 'space of conflict and competition', wherein individuals struggle to control the dominant form of capital within the field, as well as the power to define the value and form of that capital. Which, if any, is dominant: cultural, social or physical?

A Bourdieuian analysis discloses interesting insights for special education. An example lies in the use of assessment. As we have argued earlier, assessment is far from being a neutral process in the allocation of resources, but is a critical armature in the definition and constitution of 'special need': how it should be managed, appropriate (or not) modes of communication and forms of intervention linked to current or past pedagogical thinking and so on. A concept such as intelligence acquires a certain taken-for-grantedness in the habitus surrounding assessment. As part of the doxa it becomes available almost as a form of social capital in the power relations between certain professionals in a field. As Tomlinson (1982) observed, for most of the twentieth century, the history of assessment in special education can be written as principally concerned not with diagnosis or ascertainment, but with professional groups' degree of control over the operation of the system, created via the capacity to construct and reconstruct the student in their terms. With the rising power of educational psychologists as experts during the 1920s – due to the increasing credibility of psychological constructs such as intelligence in the habitus – conflict was engendered with medical practitioners, who had previously seen themselves as the only significant agents in the measurement and definition of various forms of educational 'disability'.

Significantly, Bourdieu refers to the product of pedagogic action, which is to generate in us a sense of misrecognition. That is, we accept as being natural and inevitable the way the social world is shaped and our place within it (whether as a 'winner' or 'loser' and, of course, segregative systems reinforce such acceptance), but do not in any way come to recognize it as arbitrary and only one of any number of possible configurations.

Sticky labels?

Labelling 'theory' emerged out of the Chicago School of sociology and was first used to explain how particular types of social behaviour came to be seen as deviant. Rather than treat deviancy as a product of *personal* moral deficiency or inadequate socialization which then *causes* rule infraction, which was the received wisdom within criminology (see Cohen 1985), deviancy becomes the product of societal response. The following well-known quotation from Becker (1963) summarizes the position:

> [D]eviance is not a quality of the act a person commits, but rather a consequence of the application of by others of rules and sanctions to an 'offender' . . . Deviance is not a quality that lies in the behaviour itself but the interaction between the person who commits an act and those who respond to it.
>
> (Becker 1963: 9)

From this perspective, any transgression from a norm or set of norms is not in itself deviant, it *becomes* deviant only when it elicits a particular set of responses; usually negative. The establishment of a negative or hostile reaction is a key feature, as it links to the notion of deviance as being an undesirable form of difference. This is where the notion of primary and secondary deviance become useful. Lemert (1967: 17) argues there are two stages to being labelled: primary deviance, which is the 'possession' of a set of social attributes that increases the probability of being labelled, and secondary deviance, which is 'behaviour or social roles . . . which becomes a means of defence, attack or adaptation to the overt and covert problems created by societal reaction to primary deviance'. A further distinction needs to be drawn, which is that rule breaking does not necessarily lead to a 'deviant label' (Becker 1963).

In other words, there are certain social characteristics or roles deemed to be marginal, relative to the dominant norm structure that increases the probability of being given a label and hence moving towards a deviant career. More importantly, once the label has been attached – and this has to be done via an 'agent of social control' (to use traditional sociological vernacular) – for example, a judge, doctor, teacher, educational psychologist – it becomes part of an individual's status. Consequently, all other roles that an individual plays out become submerged under this status. One of the best known examples of labelling is in Goffman's (1963) study of stigma. As a concept, stigma is highly elastic, but similar to deviance it is highly portable, context dependent and the outcome of social interactions. As Coleman (1997) notes:

> What is most poignant about Goffman's description of stigma is that it suggests that all human differences are potentially stigmatisable. As we move out of one social context where a difference is desired to another where difference is undesired we feel the effects of stigma. This conceptualisation of stigma also indicates that those possessing power can determine which human differences are desired or undesired. In part stigmas reflect value judgements.
>
> (Coleman 1997: 217)

As with the concept of deviance, stigma is not merely about the possession of an attribute to use Goffman's (1963) terms, but relationships that stem from encounters, usually face to face, with that attribute.

The notion of primary deviance is a useful concept as it suggests that *merely* possessing marginal characteristics will increase the chances of secondary deviance occurring. This should not be merely equated with the 'self-fulfilling prophecy' in that the individual simply becomes the label. This to a large extent is a vulgarization of the model which makes it overdeterministic and teleological. As Lemert (1967) argues, deviance or the 'pursuit' of a deviant career is not at all an inevitable consequence of secondary labelling. Rather, it depends on:

1 how much deviation is engaged in
2 the degree of social visibility
3 the strength and nature of societal reaction.

Labelling also draws attention to unequal power relations between the labelled and the labeller, not only in terms of possessing the authority to 'attach' the label in the first place, but through continual interventions that attempt to reinforce, stabilize and amplify it.

Turning around difference

There are perhaps two unifying features of the work of those whose ideas we have briefly outlined here:

1 an emphasis on the problematic nature of knowledge and the extent to which the very words we use shape our understanding of social systems. For Lyotard, the domination of certain kinds of 'phrase regime' is key; for Foucault, it is the importance of particular 'discourses'
2 the emphasis on the extent to which the models used to think about difference themselves change and construct the thing they set out to observe and study. Whether difference is perceived as welcome diversity or unwelcome deviance turns not so much on the accuracy of the instruments used to measure that difference, but rather on the context within which they are used. For Foucault, Bourdieu and the labelling theorists, the attribution of a positive or negative, a welcome or unwelcome ascription, is a product of the context and power relations inherent in that context.

Concluding comment

Over the twentieth century the possibility of celebrating difference was dampened by certain ways of thinking – or, putting it in the more accusatory language of Lyotard or Foucault – by 'regimes' of thought. These are at their most obvious in the large intellectual schemas, the kind of model given legitimacy by association with supposedly scientific enquiry or theoretical grounding. It was these schemas which provided an intellectual climate in which arguments for segregative school systems could flourish. It is worth noting that at the turn of the century a significant body of opinion saw neither purpose nor virtue in segregation (see Thomas *et al.* 1998 for a discussion); the reason that this body of opinion did not flourish could be said to lie in the regimes of thought which dominated the intellectual climate of the time, as we noted in Chapter 2.

It has to be said that there can be something pessimistic and depressing about the analysis of these various thinkers. Read in one way, they appear to imply that there exists running through the fabric of social life an incessant struggle for supremacy, and if this is the case the implications are unfavourable for inclusion. In Chapters 6, 7 and 8, we go on to suggest that while such analyses may indeed imply a reality that is inimical to an inclusive outlook, awareness of the processes to which they point can only be helpful for the development of policy and implementation.

Summary

Difference and identity are constructed in and through social relations. Whether difference is seen positively, as diversity, or negatively as deviance or deficit depends on the mindset of the person or group of people who observe that difference. Various thinkers – Lyotard, Foucault, Bourdieu, the labelling theorists – have helped to show how the words we use, the systems of thought and enquiry that an intellectual establishment employs, shape the interpretation of difference. One of their most important insights is that instruments of enquiry, including our very discourse, not only reveal the nature and extent of difference, but also go to construct that difference. They reveal also the imperative to seek homogeneity in institutional life and the corresponding imperative to delineate and differentiate those who differ from the norm. Their analyses, while in some ways depressing, are important for thinking about how to counteract the processes they reveal.

Notes

1 For a further discussion of rationality's place in educational inquiry see Thomas 1998.
2 In Foucault's work, discourse has a very specific meaning and is not reducible to what we would call everyday or ordinary speech acts. As Dreyfus and Rabinow (1982) point out, discourse is concerned with 'serious speech acts' – these are particular types of statement that are made by 'experts': doctors, teachers, lawyers, psychologists and so on. In short they are statements that articulate a form of truth, 'a claim to knowledge which is capable of being passed on, valued, but also open to exegesis and commentary and hence proliferation of meaning' (Dreyfus and Rabinow 1982). They can therefore be quite unstable. But Foucault's conceptualization of discourse goes beyond the mere characterization of them as utterances made by socially credible speakers. It would also be easy to suggest that they are simply the embodiment and the codification of practices and ideas, concepts, theories and so on. Although both of these elements are implicated within a discourse, in Foucault's terms they are the very devices that construct both the speaker and the objects that are spoken about. What Foucault was interested in were the kinds of rule – who could say what, about what and in what style – and how these had to be applied to produce a given discourse. Discourses do not live on their own as isolated speech acts, but inhabit a realm Foucault called 'discursive formations'. These are an enunciative network of other discourses that talk about, describe and construct similar objects. This is significant in two ways. First, and as in any system of signification, a single discourse can only become meaningful when placed alongside other discourses. In other words a form of inter-textually. Second, the importance of a single discursive element can in turn be assessed relative to others. However, taken together these formations play a crucial role in the constitution of 'domains' or, more simply, disciplines such as economics, sociology and psychology. The uneven development of these discursive formations into domains, effectively institutionalizes the very rules that govern the production of discourse. Thomas Kuhn's (1970) notion of 'normal science' is a close approximation of what Foucault was discussing.

Inclusive schools in an inclusive society? Policy, politics and paradox

So far, we have examined the ways in which children and young people have been thought about and their difficulties 'constructed' out of assumptions about deficit, weakness, disturbance or vulnerability. We turn now to the question of policy, for the changes in thinking that we have outlined and discussed do not occur in a vacuum. They exist as part of a broad range of local and national debate articulated by the public, by professionals and by politicians about the nature of the society we live in and as part of the raft of fiscal and regulatory mechanisms in a democratic system that are set in place to mould the contours of public life. These in turn exist as part of a legislative environment which imposes obligations on individuals and organizations such as schools about discrimination along the lines of race, gender or disability. Inclusion cannot, in other words, be effected simply on the basis of the way that teachers and academics conceptualize difference; it is part of a complex wider picture.

There is a notional commitment to inclusion in much policy that is being created at national government level (see DfEE 1997) and at local level in schools' policy documents (see Thomas *et al.* 1996), yet these commitments are made inside a larger political and policy context that many would interpret as antithetical to inclusion. It is this central tension that is explored in this chapter: the inconsistency, if such it is, between one set of beliefs and another. If, as Maurice Kogan (1975) once argued, policy is the authoritative, or in some instances the authoritarian allocation of values, then this assertion has great resonance for special education. To a large extent, the history and immediate trajectory of special education is bound up with the policy interventions that help shape its form and content. Whether we like it or not it is impossible to avoid policy. We can ignore it, extend it, subvert it, rewrite it, but we cannot escape it.

The social categorization of children and young adults as somehow being 'special' is constructed in and legitimized through the kind of policies that 'speak' about them. Policy is not neutral. It is very much a signifier for underlying social relations of power. The importance of policy on and for special education and inclusion is reflected by Cox's (1998) statement concerning social welfare in general:

> Every welfare programme represents a set of principles as well as a set of measures to realise these principles. It therefore follows that efforts to change the measures will have an impact on the principles . . . [U]nderstanding this relationship between ideas and policies is crucial to understanding the effect of both the fiscal and moral reforms of the welfare state.
>
> (Cox 1998: 5–6)

The nucleus of Cox's (1998) remark concerns the interplay between what he calls 'principles and measures'. Clearly, any shift or redefinition of principles will bring about a corresponding change in measures – that is to say, the instruments applied to making policy 'work'.[1]

Our intention in this chapter is to explore two themes. First, we explore the changes in values that have been taking place across state welfare policy over the past 20 years (from the New Right to New Labour). Second, we look at the way in which policy is translated and absorbed into the lifeworld of schools.

It is important to recognize at the outset that special education forms a small but relatively substantial component of the state welfare system. This, we believe, is an observation that tends to become obscured in many discussions about special education. In this sense, any change in the wider welfare regime can and does have an influence on special education. Nowhere has this been more apparent than with the introduction across the whole gamut of state welfare services in the late 1980s. This global measure, while not directly aimed at special education, nonetheless had a profound impact on issues to do with entitlement and provision. It was shown quite starkly in a number of studies that quasi-marketization, ostensibly introduced to improve the 'quality' of education, had by and large a segregatory impact (Bines 1995; Vincent *et al.* 1995).

More recently, with a growing official interest in special education there has been a shift from treating it as a marginal and problematic aspect of state-maintained schooling, to a more central component in the wider 'inclusion' project (DfEE 1997). We argue later that this interest is part of a much broader strategy to realign and reconstruct a new role and purpose for state welfare, which began in the late 1980s and accelerated in the late 1990s.

We shall argue that there is a tension between the way in which inclusion is framed across other areas of state welfare and that which 'speaks' directly to special education. The dismantling of the post-war universalistic conception of welfare and the emergence of particularism[2] as the new organizing concept in Britain has had profound implications right across all the main state welfare agencies: health and social care, social security and education. This new guiding force in state welfare, coupled with shifts towards ostensibly decentralized forms of control and governance and the reframing of client–professional relationships, have had and are still having a profound impact on provision.

Running through all this, as argued by Penna and O'Brian (1998) and Taylor (1998), is also an underlying shift from the politics of provision to the politics of identity, which is partially bound up with critiques of the inflexibility of universalism. As Cox (1998) suggests, this is further exacerbated by the displacement of welfare based on 'social rights' to a regime constructed around 'discursive rights'.[3] While this may be read in terms of empowerment and the positive acknowledgement of difference, it can equally be conceived of as a competitive struggle over the definition of needs and associated resources played out within existing institutional arrangements. In this sense, the mobilization of interest groups endlessly engaged in strategic manoeuvring becomes paramount. The corollary of this is that those individuals who are 'disenfranchised' or belong to groups which simply lack the resources to acquire resources become further disadvantaged. To say whom gets what depends on who shouts the loudest. In the context of additional provision in education this is well noted in the work of Gross (1996) and Riddell *et al.* (1994). Distributive justice is, in other words, insufficient when calculations about putative need are based on representations made by groups that, in turn, have access to varying 'social capital'. As Lee (1996) notes, unless questions about what 'need' means are thought about and resolved:

> [R]esource allocation according to need will remain, at best, a process characterised by acts of faith. At worst, it will remain characterised by the kind of shenanigans ... whereby 'need' serves as a legitimating front behind which policy-makers can pursue whatever type of allocation they wish.
>
> (Lee 1996: 131)

Principles and measures: re-conceptualizing state welfare

In unpacking Kogan's (1975) observation concerning policy and values, a useful starting point in being able to make sense of what has occurred under a new centre left government in the UK is to explore the recent past and, in particular, the legacy of what came to be known as the 'New Right'. In a rhetorical sense New Labour is attempting to redraw the welfare map and particularly so in relation to education – and there is a strong undercurrent of 'inclusion' in the messages that emerge from government. Nevertheless, there are clear continuities with its predecessors: many of the main elements of the New Right's reforms have been either left unquestioned or have been extended.

The sea change in social policy effected by New Right has had profound effects on exclusion and inclusion. The emergence of the New Right as a dominant force (most notably across the USA, New Zealand, Australia and the UK) during the 1970s and 1980s marked a significant rupture with the established post-war political orthodoxy. It marked a departure from consensus about welfare provision for those who were assumed to be disadvantaged or vulnerable to a more individualistic and meritocratic set of principles – a set of principles summarized in notions about 'benefit dependency' (see Green 1998) or, more prosaically, in Secretary of State Norman Tebbitt's advice to the unemployed to get on their bikes and go to look for work. However, it is important to note that the label 'New Right' is a somewhat clumsy notion, which masks a range of different political ideas and practices that shift from cultural context to cultural context. For analytical purposes it is generally seen as comprising two main strands of thought (see Bosanquet 1983; Hall and Jacques 1983; Kavanagh 1987; Knight 1985; Levitas 1986). First, there is the *neo-liberal* strand with its emphasis on the 'free' market with minimal state intervention and assertive and acquisitive individualism. Second, there is the *neo-conservative* strand with its accent on nationhood, duty, family and tradition.

Although both strands articulated divergent theories regarding the relationship between the state, the individual and civil society, the point of connection between the neo-liberals and the neo-conservatives was their antipathy towards the welfare state (Gamble 1986; George and Wilding 1994). It is important to note that the existence of the state was not in question: what was at issue was the nature and extent of its permeation of civil society[4] with fears that the state would curtail individual liberty through such mechanisms as regulation or taxation. For the neo-liberals, the market embodied principles of freedom and acted as a metaphor for individual liberty across other spheres of social life: education, healthcare, housing and so on.

If a process of free exchange produces the best consequences in the economy, therefore by extension this mode of interaction will generate the best consequences elsewhere. The argument against the state is deftly put by one of the most well-known exponents of the neo-liberal case: for Hayek (1976), the state is best characterized as a collective capable of distorting the process of free exchange. According to Hayek (1976: 70), the market process of allocating benefits and burdens 'can be neither just nor unjust, because the results are not intended or foreseen and depend on a multitude of circumstances not known in their totality to anybody'. The state by intervening in this process, which any organized welfare regime ultimately does, imposes a set of outcomes based on some conception of 'need' or 'justice', which undermines and curtails the spontaneous action of individuals.[5]

For the neo-conservatives, in contrast to the neo-liberals, the restraint the state places on the dynamism of the market and individual liberty is a secondary concern. For writers such as Roger Scruton (1980) of the so-called Peterhouse School (see Levitas 1986 for a critique), the pursuit of liberty as envisaged by the neo-liberals is implicated in the erosion of 'tradition' – which is worth saving. Tradition in this sense is very much constructed around such abstract and diffuse themes as 'national identity', 'allegiance', 'authority' and the 'natural order' where inequality between individuals is seen as both inevitable and desirable (Levitas 1986). There are clear implications for inclusion here. If there exists some 'natural order', whose maintenance is necessary to the coherence and stability of society, then it is invidious to impose threats to this order in calls for inclusion.

As Belsey (1986) notes, the neo-conservative prescription for the 'good society' is based on strong government, social authoritarianism, hierarchy and subordination. By contrast to the neo-liberals, the neo-conservatives' objection to the welfare state is focused on what they see as the erosion of traditional patterns of morality, authority and gender roles through the pursuit of equality via the extension of civil rights. Here, then, is an even more corrosive influence on the notion that one should act in pursuit of beliefs – about equality, valuing diversity or even a plural society. Again, welfare is seen as a distorting influence, although in this case not on the market, but the 'natural' social order. The overreliance on the state for the provision of services undermines the traditional notion of the family, church, school and workplace as the repositories of authority and submission. The state's role is pivotal in the maintenance of social order.

As such, it is seen as legitimate for the state to intrude on those areas of social life that threaten to subvert the social bond (Kavanagh 1987; Levitas 1986). The juxtaposition is of the neo-conservatives' 'order' and 'authority' to the supposed dynamism and fluidity of the neo-liberals' social order. There are points of tension and conflict here, but there are also elements of intersection. For at the centre of the New Right polemic – both neo-liberal and neo-conservative – was the argument that the state and particularly such institutions as education, health and social security, had created three interrelated concerns (Newman and Clarke 1994):

- *moral*: welfarism had generated a culture of dependency underpinned by anti-capitalist values and sentiments
- *financial*: high public expenditure and borrowing required high taxation and interest rates which 'de-incentivized' work
- *social*: the repression of individual freedom and autonomy.

As a means to overcome these impediments, New Right administrations used the power of the state to create social and economic life around a new set of core values borrowed directly from the classical economists of the nineteenth century and traditional Toryism welded together within a discourse of popular democracy (Hall and Jacques 1983). In turning their objections to welfare into a practical political project, the New Right embarked on either privatization or, at the very least, the imposition of private sector practices and structures to public life. However, despite the commitment of administrations from 1979 to 1997 to restructuring state welfare provision, it can be argued that the basic patterns of spending and provision remained relatively stable during the period of 1979 to 1987. As an indicator of this stability, spending on welfare as a percentage of gross domestic product had remained fairly constant (Hills 1998). But in structural terms there were real changes from 1988 onwards in the social, administrative and fiscal climate with the introduction of a series of changes in most areas of welfare: in education with the 1988 Education Reform Act; in the NHS and social services with the 1990 National Health Service and Community Care Act; in housing in the form of the 1988 Housing Act. Other and more recent legislation such as the 1993 Education Act can be seen as a continuation and consolidation of the original Acts, introducing measures either to extend or plug gaps within the original formulation.

These Acts have, as Clarke *et al.* (1994) argue, created a profound shift not only in terms of 'function, but also in power relations within [social and welfare agencies]'. In mapping out the key changes within welfare, Clarke *et al.* (1994) point to a number of features that are indicative of this shift during the 1980s and the 1990s:

- an emphasis on market approaches as expressed in compulsory competitive tendering; the construction of internal markets; a cultural shift to defining welfare service users as customers or citizen–consumers; the construction of surrogate markets in the form of quasi-markets
- the emergence of welfare pluralism, or mixed economies of service provision and funding that are not simply reducible to market-influenced approaches, but a complex fragmentation and 'partnership' between newly formed 'independent' agencies, commercial providers and 'not-for-profit' agencies.

Many of the features that Clarke *et al.* (1994) identify were also implicit within the restructuring of education. What is particularly significant about these points just indicated is not only the structural durability of such reforms, but their continuation and even further entrenchment under New Labour and, if one examines their provenance, their conflict with inclusive principles.

The 'new' basic pattern of organizing and managing welfare, in other words, can be seen as the major legacy of the New Right. The provisions of the 1998 School Standards and Frameworks Act could not have been introduced without its ground-clearing work.

Although it is possible to argue that the gap between many New Labour and New Right measures is small, there exist attempts to fuse those measures with socially oriented outcomes. Communitarianism represents possibly the best known of these attempts. It is the one that is most associated with centre left thinking, and is articulated as a route between the old and discredited forms of collective socialism and the more recent neo-liberal individualism. Heron and Dwyer (1999) suggest that communitarianism is concerned with moral restoration through finding a balance between 'rights and responsibilities'. In teasing out what this means Heron and Dwyer turn to two other variants on this theme: Macmurray's *interconnected communities* and Etzioni's *moral community*. Macmurray's thesis implies is that there is a moral interconnectedness between people. He asserts that freedom and responsibility go hand in hand. Therefore if I act in a manner that is mindful of others – and so does everybody else – then, in the long run, this is bound to have optimal consequences for a society. Macmurray is offering what Rousseau would recognize as a form of *social contract*.

In a similar vein, Etzioni's argument centres on the asymmetry between rights (what an individual can claim) and responsibilities (what an individual should or ought to do). In Etzioni's scenario the balance is skewed towards the rights side of the equation to the detriment of responsibilities. Community in this context comprises individuals, families and neighbourhoods, conceived of as repositories of shared values and beliefs, which, in turn, are expressed as moral precepts. In this sense, an individual's responsibilities are primarily – but not entirely – to the community rather than the state. Therefore, if all individuals act in the 'right way', that is adhere to and are motivated by this consensus, then the emergent property will be the moral community.

A new variant of these themes exists in 'stakeholding'. There is a strong element of continuity with communitarianism here, in that welfare regimes (or in Etzioni's terms 'the community') shift the responsibility for meeting needs on to the individual. In short, stakeholding is about being socially and economically included. But this is not a form of inclusion that should be seen to be synonymous with equality and notions of redistributive justice. Like communitarianism, it is built around a network of reciprocal rights and responsibilities. Therefore, if you want to be included you have to 'agree' to the conditions of membership, as Hutton (1996) expresses it, with that agreement having implications for both individual and organization (Field 1996). These models and their implications for inclusion in schools are explored further in Chapter 7.

Increasing the production of pig iron by 15 per cent – a new rationality of schooling?

The past 20 years have seen an unprecedented expansion in the range and scope of written policies on almost every aspect of schooling. In itself this is symbolic of an almost permanent revolution, as governments of different political hues across most western industrial societies grapple with social change.

Ball (1999) identifies the following dimensions to a 'new orthodoxy' in central government's thinking about education:

1 improving national economics by tightening a connection between schooling, employment, productivity and trade
2 enhancing student outcomes in employment-related skills and competencies
3 attaining more direct control over curriculum content and assessment
4 reducing costs to government
5 increasing community input to education by more direct involvement in school decision making and the pressure of market choice (Ball 1999: 199).

There is a clear inconsistency here between, on the one side, the celebration of diversity and a positive conception of difference and, on the other, an imperative to promote national economic well-being. It is interesting to note that in the thinking of the New Left education is conceived not only with a role of economic restoration, but – alongside this – cultural and moral regeneration as well. Paradoxically, central to this project is the neo-liberal conception of the market.

For the political right, the market, with its appeal to competition and related themes of efficiency, cost effectiveness, choice and accountability, was perceived as the panacea for the deficiencies of state-run education inflicted with the stasis imposed by bureaucratic–professional domination. At one level, the market represented a mechanism through which to calculate, distribute and manage resources more effectively and efficiently. On another level, it was and still is a signifier for much a much wider set of changes. Embedded within the local management of schools (LMS) was a profound change: it signified a change in the social relations, not just of schooling, but welfare in general. It redefined not only the external relations between institutions of schooling – LEAs, schools and central government agencies – but internal relations as well: between teachers, pupils and parents leading to what Ball (1994) describes as a recomposition in the 'matrix of power'.

Far from encouraging the interagency 'joined-up' working, which is often called for as an essential element of the despecialization necessary to inclusion in schools, the effect of all this was a crystallization in professional roles, including not only those in schools but those of the support services also. According to Bines (1995) there was:

> a substantial change in professional roles, activities and autonomy, legit-imated by a critique of professional effectiveness; the growth of manageri-alism as an ideological and organisational solution to perceived problems of public service management . . . a growth in central government control of service definitions and funding procedures coupled with devolution of management to individual localised service units and a diminution of local government or other regional, democratically accountable responsi-bilities for service planning and delivery.
>
> (Bines 1995: 62)

The neglect of special education procedures in the changes imposed by the thinking of the New Right was significant. The presumption was that special education would eventually meld into a new structure defined by the market for its 'customers'. However, it was recognized fairly early on that this would be far from the case. The exclusion of special education from the Education Reform Act did not mean that it was either exempt or immune from the poten-tial outcomes of the Act. As Bowe *et al.* (1992) have argued, it sharply brought special education into the newly constructed market, budgetary and curricular framework. The unthinking incorporation of special education in these pro-cedures led to some profoundly anti-inclusive outcomes in practice. For example, local management of schools was extended to special schools and the accountants Touche Ross (1990) were put in charge of the process of extension. Their train of activity in doing this was to ask those in the system, including special school heads, how they thought special education should be funded. The conclusion reached by these accountants was that special schools were often 'centres of excellence' and that they should not be allowed to wither on the vine as children moved outside the system to the mainstream. They were thus funded according to the number of *places* (whether they were filled or not) at special schools.

Because of this system, with money staying with the special school, there was little finance freed up to fund children when they were mainstreamed. The widely accepted recommendation from these accountants was, however, at variance with the body of empirical evidence in education (reviewed in Chapter 2), which has consistently indicated that special schools are no more effective than mainstream schools. There was no educational or inclusive rationale for the assumption about 'centres of excellence'; the rationale pushing the reform of management into the special school arena was identical to that driving it in the mainstream arena. It was a rationale constructed out of the imperatives of the market.

It was the introduction of the market in both these arenas that led to the fragmentation and dilution of local forms of provision for children in difficulty and this impacted equally hard against new forms of inclusive practice. Gewirtz *et al.* (1995) point to what they called the *semiotics of schooling*. They argue that as schools attempt either to consolidate or improve their local market position, their policy and provision for children with difficulties becomes displaced.

The role of the LEA that was promoted in the late 1990s from a government committed to inclusion was different from the residual–provider approach that developed between 1988 and 1997 (Loxley 1999). Its new role as seen from the perspective of central government has been mapped out in a number of policy initiatives and legislation, which have as their objective recalling the LEA from 'exile' (Audit Commission 1998; 1999; DfEE 1997; Ofsted 1999). Probably the most significant of these measures has been the introduction of LEA education development plans (EDPs).[6] In short EDPs are being advocated as a mechanism to create a more 'joined-up' approach to coordinating and supporting schools, as well as encourage a more 'efficient' use of resources within LEAs.

The paradox is that there is, on the one side, an explicitness of recent articulations of commitment to inclusion in, for example, *Excellence for all Children: Meeting Special Educational Needs* (DfEE 1997). On the other, many features of policy, which owe their ancestry to the thinking of the New Right reviewed earlier (namely, the retention of open enrolment, retention of selection under the rationale of parent choice, use of attainment targets) are antagonistic to inclusion. In policy terms this could be called 'incremental dissonance'. What is happening is the layering of new policies that have as their notional objective 'inclusion', on top of practices that have demonstrably contrary effects. An ungenerous observer might suggest that the government is trying to have its cake and eat it. Now, as in the early 1990s, there exists a tension between the demands made on schools via the quasi-market and performativity[7] and their inclusive responsibilities for those children and young adults who could not or would not adapt to this environment.

Schools and the policy process: change by osmosis?

If schools and LEAs are to be accorded the role of 'primary change agents' in bringing about inclusion, then clearly attention needs to be paid to the processes involved in introducing new policy arrangements.

Defining policy is difficult. On one level, it can be viewed in simple terms as representing normative guidelines for action; that is, it sets out how things *should* be done. Although this conception is useful to a point, as policy is concerned with defining objectives and in some instances the means through which they are attained, it is nonetheless rather generalized and largely instrumental, inadequately capturing the many ways in which policy is con-structed, interpreted and subverted. As Fulcher (1989) suggests, policy can be 'written', 'spoken' or 'enacted'. Even this, however, carries with it difficulties. Are we saying that each one of these three 'modes' constitute policies in their own right or are they merely dimensions of that which we call policy? For example, a written policy can take on both a 'spoken' or 'enacted' form or it could simply just sit at the bottom of a drawer and be ignored. Alternatively, policy can be part of an institution's 'oral' tradition – tacitly understood, but having no textual equivalent. The same can be said of 'enacted' policy, again a set of guidelines for action that have become enmeshed within an institution's culture that does not have any textual referents; new entrants through a pro-cess of osmosis become socialized into it. Alternatively, policy may have its 'roots' in a textual form from which the 'spoken' and 'enacted' modes draw, with participants working along a continuum ranging from strict conformity to complete modification. The latter appears to have been the case with most 'special educational needs' policies in schools (see Tarr and Thomas 1997).

Pointing to these differences on their own, however, is to put aside the problematic and issues of nested (and often disjointed) policies (both active and dormant) that percolate in and around institutions. This emerges clearly from the more sensitive 'implementation' studies: policy appears to be 'sedi-mented'; old policy programmes that were once 'shiny and new' now compete, merge, complement, embarrass and sit uncomfortably next to more recent initiatives.

Orthodox forms of analysis tend to separate policy formulation from policy implementation. This distinction is based on what Sabatier (cited in Fitz *et al.* 1994) characterizes as 'top down' and 'bottom up' studies. In short, 'top down' studies conceive of the policy process as being hierarchical and linear and encapsulated within a rigid division of labour between those who formulate policy and those who implement it. This perspective on the policy process is bound within a rational and bureaucratic model of individual and organiza-tional behaviour. Conversely, 'bottom up' studies take as their starting point:

> the institutions, organisations and actors considered to be most closely involved in the lives of the target group of individuals and, it is they, through their interaction with consumers, who determine the extent to which polices are rendered effective.
>
> (Fitz *et al.* 1994: 55)

The 'bottom up' approach shifts the unit of analysis away from the concerns of the primary policymakers to those who are involved in carrying out policy: the 'street level' bureaucrats and their client groups. This approach according to Fitz *et al.* (1994) began to dissolve the distinction between formulation and implementation, as it highlighted the interpretive capacity of social actors and organizations to refocus policy directives to fit the material conditions of their work. The studies of Gartner and Lipsky (1987) on the introduction of

SEN legislation in Massachusetts, and Lipsky (1980) on the role and work of 'street level' bureaucrats in public services in the USA, are classic examples of this approach in relation to special provision. The use of this framework by Vincent *et al.* (1996) in exploring the work of LEA officers is another. However, Sabatier (cited in Fitz *et al.* 1994) highlights three potential problems with it. First, there is a tendency to overstate the extent of resistance, whether conscious or not, that can be applied at the local level over the centre's policy intent. Second, this work is 'present orientated' and neglects the effects or influence of prior policy developments on participants. Third, an overriding emphasis on participants' perceptions and actions may lead to a neglect of how social, cultural, legal and economic factors structure their perceptions and actions. A fourth point that needs to be added relates to the degree of latitude that is conferred on social actors, whatever their role and status, by a given policy. The relative tightness or looseness of policy specifications will also structure the 'discourse of the possible'.

This separation between formulation and implementation is clearly problematic, as it rests on certain assumptions concerning the making and the execution of policy (Fitz *et al.* 1994). It implies a distinct and observable cut-off point between the two activities. Although it is logically possible to conceive of a point of origin, Fulcher (1989) suggests that policy needs to be conceived as a continual process, wherein formulation and implementation take place at all levels within the education system. Furthermore, the introduction of new policy is not a discrete act, as it connects and interacts with existing policy and practice.

Ball (1994) offers a richer insight by suggesting that we need to look at policy from two different, but complementary perspectives. The first perspective Ball refers to is 'policy as text'. Our day-to-day encounters with policy are usually in the form of policy as a physical text, which we sometimes naively comprehend as constituting a coherent and single authoritative voice: the QCA, the DfEE, Ofsted and so on. Ball argues that the 'finished' document needs to be seen as:

> The product of compromises at varying stages (at points of initial influence, in the micropolitics of legislative formulation, in the parliamentary process and in the politics and micropolitics of interest group articulation). They are typically the cannibalised products of multiple (but circumscribed) influences and agendas. There is ad hocery, negotiation and serendipity within the state, within the formulation process.
>
> (Ball 1994: 18)

Policy is not, in other words, the virtuous outcome of some consensual democratic process. Rather it is the outcome of struggle and contestation, of a continually shifting political process, which not only decides *what* ideas are permissible, but *who* should articulate them. Added to this, Ball remarks that different policies, albeit emanating from a supposedly unified set of political values, can be quite divergent. An example lies in the meshing of and tensions between the neo-liberal and neo-conservative strands of the Thatcher governments. Inclusion provides a contemporary case study in this process: there are a complex set of tensions around central commitments to inclusion while maintaining policy emphases on parental preference, selection and the raising of standards measured using narrow academic criteria.

In this sense, policy becomes merely a textual repository of a multitude of voices or as Ball puts it: 'representations which are encoded in complex ways (via struggles, compromises, authoritative public interpretations and reinterpretations)' (Ball 1994: 16). The notion of 'encoding' leads to the inevitable act of 'decoding', which takes place in those arenas that are the very object of policy intervention. If encoding is fraught with political intrigue, then decoding is no less problematic. Ball argues that as readers of policy, we approach the text in the same manner as we would any other complex system of symbols – novels, poems, paintings or films. That is, we bring to bear our own particular interpretive frameworks. In this sense, there is no equivalence of meaning between a policy and its actualization within an organization; it is 'recreated' and 'interpreted' by practitioners in the light of their own personal and institutional contexts. Or as Bowe *et al.* (1992) argue:

> Practitioners do not confront policy texts as naive readers, they come with histories, with experiences, with values and purposes of their own . . . parts of texts will be rejected, selected out, ignored, deliberately misunderstood . . . furthermore, yet again, interpretation will be a matter of struggle. Different interpretations will be in contest, as they relate to different interests.
>
> (Bowe and Ball with Gold 1992: 22)

In much the same way that the process of encoding is struggled over, so too is decoding. In this context, there can never be a single objective and definitive reading, only a struggle between sets of readings. The outcome of this contest, where one reading predominates over another, is structured by such internal factors as individual or sub-group status, commitment, resources experience, gender, position within the school or LEA hierarchy and all encased within the usual micropolitical jostling. In addition to this, we can also argue that the 'victorious' reading cannot be treated as absolute, but more of a temporary settlement. In much the same way that political manoeuvring within the central state can be characterized as being as unstable and fluid, then we should see the school in much the same light. Drawing on Foucault's conceptualization of power, Ball (1994) acknowledges that, while policy texts 'posit the restructuring, redistribution and disruption of power relations', this cannot be seen as a *direct* consequence of policy text. In Ball's (1994) terms, policy *enters* into pre-existing power relations within the school – it does not alter them from the outside.

If this is the case, if the 'reading' of a policy is inextricably bound with a consensual feeling of what is right, then the impact of an inclusive policy on its own is likely to be minimal. Schools were 'advised' by government (DfE 1994b) to say in their special educational needs policies what strategies they had adopted to include all children, but if there is little appetite to do this, the policy will exist merely as an articulation of the possible.

Concluding comment

The political shifts and movements of the last quarter of the twentieth century were felt not just in Britain but across the developed world as the thinking of the right made its impact on public services of all kinds. The reverberations of that thinking are still felt, even in the policies of more inclusively minded administrations. Their continuing echoes present dilemmas for public servants who believe in inclusion, since inclusive commitments sit uneasily against a policy agenda whose consequences are undeniably segregative and exclusive.

In the *Realpolitik* that presents itself, those who are committed to inclusion must surely seek to change that which can be changed. In schools, policy can stress not only ideals, but practices also (see Thomas *et al.* 1996) – and those practices can be of the kind noted in Chapters 3 and 4. In other words, school staffs can commit themselves to creating fairer, more humane environments at school, to dismissing the obfuscatory nonsense of certain kinds of policy that seek merely to deflect criticism or seek merely to demonstrate (but only demonstrate) that something is being done. Local administrators and politicians can commit themselves to examining the nuts and bolts of financing mechanisms that exist alongside the expansive and generous phrases of an inclusion policy. They can, for example, implement the kind of recommendation in the government's Green Paper (DfEE 1997), which suggested that all children could be registered on the roll of a mainstream school, whether or not they attend special schools.

Others with an interest in the form education takes, whether they be school governors, academics, or teachers undertaking professional development courses, can be vigilant in the search for new forms of social arrangement that promise more inclusive environments at school and in society. In Chapter 7, we examine some of these – ideas such as Marquand's (1996) notion of moral activism and Rieser and Mason's (1992) 'intentional building of community'. As Parsons (1999) has noted, part of the reason for the fact that exclusions are at such a high level in Britain is that education in the UK is too often a 'thing apart' and children's difficulties at school are made to remain an educational problem, outside wider policy. Parsons remarks on the contrast, for example, between the UK and Denmark – with Danish school campuses sharing a site with dentists' and doctors' surgeries – or Sweden, where school, library and village centre are integrated. The kind of planning necessary for this kind of development is possible alongside policy that still, for whatever reasons, stresses the imperatives of choice and selection. Admittedly, the larger policy diminishes the effects of the local changes, but it does not eliminate them. One hopes that inclusive developments in local and international exemplars will influence the thinking of government, whose Secretary of State for Education and Employment could at the beginning of the new millennium assert:

> This government has given a clear commitment that we will be guided not by dogma but by an open-minded approach to understanding what works and why. This is central to our agenda for modernising government: using

information and knowledge much more effectively and creatively at the heart of policy making and policy delivery.

(Blunkett 2000: 12)

If this commitment to 'what works' is backed up by funds and by regulation, for example on mechanisms of finance, there is every reason to believe that change leading to inclusion can be effected.

Summary

Can policy effect inclusion in schools? Up to a point. The problem is that layers of policy are sometimes incompatible – one conflicts with another. In this chapter, those different layers of policy – and more importantly the different intellectual stables from which they emerge – are explored. There are those of the New Right, with its emphasis on individualism, the free market, tradition and the family; and there are those of the new centre left, which stresses the importance of community and 'stakeholder welfare'. We argue that there are attempts in much recent policy to fuse both kinds of thinking and that expressions about the need for a plural, tolerant, inclusive education system sometimes sit uneasily with policy that fore-grounds the benefits of choice, selection and the comparison of schools on the basis of their pupils' attainment. While proclamations from politicians about bene-fits of inclusion are to be welcomed, the effects of exhortation will be counteracted by policy whose effects are to promote competition. All this is taken in a context of the problematics of policy in education: 'policy' implies a set of directions to be followed. In education, however, the directions are interpreted by everyone from civil servants to local administrators to teachers and intent is attenuated and compromised as directives, instructions and ideas move from one person to another. In conclusion, pragmatism is called for: progress toward inclusion can emerge from many and various changes at local and school level.

Notes

1 In this sense, we need to see 'instruments' as traversing a wide range of modes and forms of activity: fiscal, expert systems, administrative networks, legal infrastructures and so on. It is also important to note that there is not a straightforward correspond-ence between principles and measures. Policy principles by their very nature are abstract statements about what *ought to be* and therefore capable of being 'imple-mented' only through a variety of *measures*.

2 According to Thompson and Hoggett (1996) universalism is based on the principle that an independent measure is used to adjudicate between different cases. For example access to state-run healthcare is not contingent on personal circumstances, apart from being ill. The same is true in relation to state schooling: universal criteria apply. Conversely, particularism is based on the notion that differences have to be recognized. For example, to be able to attend a higher education institute is con-ditional on specific entry requirements. Being able to attend a fee-paying school is conditional on parental income. But as Thompson and Hoggett (1996: 34) argue, although universalism and particularism start at different positions they both end up at the same place. Universalism works by 'providing a fair standard by which to treat

particular cases, and, on the other, particularism derives its moral force from an under-lying universalism'. Although they make a case for a positive notion of particularism, as it is currently deployed it carries with it highly negative connotations.

3 The concept of social rights is traditionally associated with T.H. Marshall (1965) who saw their development as part of the natural evolution of liberal–progressive societies. He saw such rights as being complementary to civil rights (equal representation before the law) and political rights (the equal right to vote, organize, participate in govern-ment). Social rights are concerned with equal access to education, healthcare, finan-cial support if unemployed. Although in principle each citizen has an equal right to all of these, access and/or entitlement is mediated via the use of specific rules to deter-mine eligibility and equality of treatment. In this sense, rule-governed patterns of allocation conform to the notion of distributive justice in that what people get is based on the fair and unbiased assessment of their needs. However, as Cox (1998: 10) observes, the very rules (the codification of social rights) that were used to ensure equitable treatment are now seen as being 'too uniform and insensitive to individual needs'.

4 The term 'civil society' has traditionally been used to designate the separation between the state and other social institutions or more specifically non-governmental organizations such as the family, the economy, the legal system, education and so on. Although this is superficially useful, it does however collapse when we begin to con-sider the extent to which the state in one form or another has permeated most of the preceding examination over the past 100 years. In fact, it would be very difficult to find any institution that was completely 'untouched' by the state.

5 A significant point to make about Hayek is that any notion of distributive justice is anathema to him. Hayek's concept of society is vehemently libertarian and the col-lectivization of anything – unless it is through the spontaneous action of individuals – undermines this form of liberty. Thus, the thing that so many of us – so misguidedly, as Hayek would point out – call 'society', is in reality nothing more than the sum total of the consequences of individual actions. Hayek's definition of social justice rests on the notion that 'redistribution' takes place by the actions by certain members of society. For him, any notion of justice is ill conceived because it implies an agreed standard of need or worth. And seeing society as nothing more than a collection of individuals, it is perfectly reasonable to assert that each individual will have a different opinion about who deserves what and why. For Hayek, a free society – one that is based on individual liberty and a market system – does not generate a consensus about what is a fair distribution of wealth and property – except for what occurs within the market, which is deemed neutral in both its nature and its results. This simple notion has important ramifications for any notion about inclusion, for if one accepts it there can be no meaningful collective action in its support.

6 There are two main functions of an education development plan. First, to impose nationally some degree of coherence on the role of the LEA which since 1988 had been in a state of organizational anomie. As such, all EDPs, which have to be approved by the Secretary of State for the DfEE, by law have to address four main functions: school improvement, special educational provision, access and strategic management. Second, to reverse fragmentation at the local level, which in turn would allow for a more 'unified' approach to meeting DfEE-imposed performance targets and policy objectives.

7 Performativity is a concept that was first used by Lyotard (1984). It denotes the use of outcome-related measures of performance to improve accountability and hence con-trol. Usually this is framed by reference to quantitative indicators judged against some pre-defined targets. (Attachable to this is the increasing use of qualitative measures

that may be enumerated. This is common practice by Ofsted in compiling their national and LEA reports.) We do not have to look very far to find examples of performativity in education. The most obvious are the school performance 'league tables' that contain data on a school-by-school basis relating to pupil attainment on standardized assessment tests at age 11 and GCSE/A level examinations. Another example is the recent introduction of DfEE-imposed targets on LEAs for increasing school performance in English and mathematics and GCSE/A levels. However, performativity is not just about the external imposition of targets on organizations, but the meshing of these demands with the way in which teaching and learning is organized. In other words, meeting targets becomes just as 'natural' and routine as taking the morning register. Furthermore, performativity is intended to permeate the very notion of teacher professionalism. In this sense, it becomes part of what makes a 'good teacher'.

Constructing inclusion

On the one side . . . inequality harms by pampering; on the
other by vulgarising and depressing. A system founded on it
is against nature, and in the long run, breaks down.
(Matthew Arnold, quoted in R.H. Tawney 1964: 33)

In this chapter an argument is made for the case that various ideas, owing
more to thinking in politics and economics than to that in psychology or
sociology, have recently converged to provide a compelling case for inclusion.
These ideas, originating in notions about social justice and human rights, provide shape to contemporary thinking about the environments in which education is framed. These ideas have arisen across the world over the last quarter
of a century and are of diverse provenance: the social democracy of northwest
Europe (and particularly Scandinavia); communist local government in Italy;
civil rights agenda in North America; and, more recently, social justice as a
theme across the world.

It is all these streams of thought that have led the way in changing the face
of special education during the last part of the twentieth century. The fact that
this is the case sparks a debate, as we noted earlier in this book, about the
proper place of disciplines such as psychology, medicine and sociology –
which have traditionally guided special educational practice – in formulating
ideas about the future of education. It sparks a debate also about the nature of
the interaction between values and what has been called 'evidence' in shaping
policy. It has been taken to be common sense, even axiomatic, in policy thinking that certain kinds of evidence should guide policy. But recent critiques,
which were discussed in Chapters 1 and 2, have indicated that the nature of
the 'evidence' has depended greatly on the theoretical superstructure out of
which that evidence emerges. The supposedly concrete evidential structure on
which we make decisions about policy and practice in special education has
proven to be frailer than had been imagined. If this is the case, then we may
have less reason to view as in some way inferior other sources of guidance for
judgements about the future direction and nature of educational institutions
and systems.

One conclusion that could be drawn from this is that there should perhaps be more reliance on values in guiding the shape and nature of state-run education. But such a conclusion would provoke fierce opposition, for values have long had a bad press in a world that prides itself on its rationality. Indeed, the term *value judgement* is in itself often a derogatory one. Some sorting out is necessary here, then, since an assessment of the place of values in guiding the direction of special education (which is particularly susceptible to well-meaning, but often mistaken efforts to change) is necessary. To avoid an unhelpful decline into a moral relativism, however, questions about values, rights, ethics and justice all need to be considered together with developing ideas about community and social justice. In this chapter, therefore, we move on from the challenge we made in earlier chapters that the discipline base of special education lies in the old *'ologies'*. We argue, on the platform of this earlier discussion, that since the supposed evidence generated by these disciplines has been idiosyncratic, misleading – and often simply wrong – emerging frameworks of social justice should unapologetically now provide the stimulus for thinking about the shape of education for a new century.

The linking of education and social justice is, of course, not new. It is no coincidence that those pioneer educators who have spoken the clearest and simplest truths about teaching and learning (and this was discussed in Chapter 1) have also had much to say about the articulation of education, politics and social justice and the importance of the interconnections among these. Jean-Jacques Rousseau's eighteenth-century advocacy of learning through experience, his view that expression rather than repression was necessary to produce a well-balanced, freethinking child were bound up with his notion that the expression of free will was an essential antidote to the absolutism of church and state.[1] Rousseau's ideas rested in turn in those of John Locke, the seventeenth-century English empiricist philosopher who rejected the educational methods of his time in *Some Thoughts Concerning Education* (Locke 1964), calling for learning to be enjoyable and based on interest. His notions of social contract, also borrowed by Rousseau, likewise linked education with a freethinking people and the notion that sovereignty could be entrusted to the people and should properly reside with those people.

To believe, then, that the kind of society we create emerges from the kind of education we provide has a long intellectual pedigree. The quest for comprehensive education and now inclusive education are part of that tradition, one that sees benefits to all emerging from the practices adopted in education. In other words, there are gains in greater comprehensiveness not just for the small minority who would formerly have gone to special schools, but there are, perhaps more importantly, reciprocal benefits – benefits for all.

Against inclusion?

If values are to form the foundation for inclusive policy, there will be problems in practical terms. As we were completing the writing of the first edition of this volume, the results of a major appraisal of teachers' perspectives on special education and 'special educational needs' was published by Croll and Moses (2000). Table 7.1 shows some of their results with respect to 294 teachers' and 48 headteachers' views on the future of special schools.

The bottom row of Table 7.1 makes depressing reading for those who are committed to the idea of inclusion, for it implies that very few people at the chalkface seem to be won over by the arguments being put for it. One is tempted to wonder why there is such resistance in the face of the evidence about the limited effectiveness of special schools, in the face of much uncertainty about the significance of 'within-child' factors in the provenance of children's difficulties at school and in the face of an increasingly inclusive political environment and a correspondingly anti-discriminatory legislative environment.

But there is some comfort to be taken in the statistics of Croll and Moses, for it appears that there *is* a shifting mindset about what 'specialness' in children means. Croll and Moses find that the number of teachers attributing 'learning difficulty' to 'within-child' factors dropped from 70 per cent in 1981 to 48 per cent in 1998, while those who responded 'don't know' when asked for explanations for learning difficulty rose from 9 per cent to 21 per cent. Whether this higher 'don't know' figure represents a manifestation of Haldane's (1965) 'duty of doubt' (of which we wrote in Chapter 2) is uncertain, but it does undeniably mark a major shift along the continuum of uncertainty. People who are doing the job of teaching and managing in schools are less confident now, it seems, about the robustness of explanations that locate learning difficulties unproblematically in the child. Even more encouraging (although it may not seem such at first sight) is the way in which responses differ to different kinds of supposed difficulty. While 67 per cent of heads felt that special schools were needed for 'children with emotional and behavioural difficulties', only 35 per cent saw the same need for those with severe learning difficulties, with fewer still seeing the need for children with physical disability (25 per cent). None at all thought special schools were necessary for children with sensory difficulty.

Why is this encouraging? Surely, it might be said – with troublesome children at the apex of perceived need for special school – it points to heads' cynical wish to get rid of these children and include only those who will present no disruption to the calm routine of the classroom. The encouraging feature of this is that the expedience revealed by the heads' responses at least may demonstrate a loosening of faith in the supposed benefits of special pedagogy. Heads seem to be saying here that it is possible and proper to include

Table 7.1   Views on the future of special schools (from Croll and Moses 2000)

	Headteachers (%)	Teachers (%)
[There is] a continuing role for special schools	100	98
More children should attend special schools	54	33
Fewer children should attend special schools	8	6

children, that it is in the best interests of the children concerned, but that where this causes disruption in their schools it is not acceptable.

The logic of this is incontestable, for heads have schools to manage. The hope which it reveals is that opposition to inclusion has moved from the principled to the pragmatic. Where once practitioners might apparently have said that special school is the right place for certain children because it was assumed that the best menu of help was available to those children there, now it appears from the sliding scale (with EBD at the top and sensory disability at the bottom) that the opposition is primarily on practical grounds. The message is not, 'We can't teach certain children' but rather 'We can't manage or cope with certain children.'

This version of opposition leads to a specific avenue of debate and one that is relatively simple to address, for it is about the shifting of resources rather than the winning of hearts and minds. It is an avenue of debate that focuses on funding and on the mechanics of the delivery of support. It leads to questions about how to liberate the substantial resources locked into a continuing special school system. It is worth examining this for a moment to see the mechanical nature of the issue. The issue is that with the current system of funding of special schools by numbers of places (rather than numbers of children), the fixed costs of those special schools that still exist do not diminish when a child moves out to the mainstream. Thus there is no liberation of resources to make inclusion of the moved child satisfactory. This problem is well documented in the UK by the Audit Commission (Audit Commission/HMI 1992). Under this system, while six-figure sums of money go to pay for children at some residential special schools, those sums do not accompany those children if they move back to the mainstream. Neither are they available as a resource when the mainstream school is in the process of referring a child in the first place: there is no offering of choices such as: 'This child will go to a residential special school which will cost £100,000 per year. Alternatively, the £100,000 is available to spend on inclusive support in your school.' There is similar resistance to this kind of flexibility in the USA, where Hehir (in conversation with Miller 1996) points out that despite legislative commitment to inclusion in many states, money does not follow children as they move to inclusive placements (see also Hehir 1997). The solution, he suggests, is for states to review and change their special education financing formulae, as Dessent (1987) suggested more than a decade ago for the UK.

If changes of this kind do occur in such a way that proper support arrangements are enabled, other benefits demonstrably ensue: the inner London borough of Newham (see Jordan and Goodey 1996), for example, has the lowest proportion of children attending special schools in the country yet also boasts the lowest proportion of children excluded from schools in London (see Abdelnoor 1999).

While it is certainly not straightforward making this kind of change, neither is it impossible. It involves a technical programme of action – or what the Fabians (who were at the forefront of pushing forward social justice in the UK early in the twentieth century) used to call 'gas and water socialism' (see McBriar 1966). We shall return to the need for this technical debate, a debate about fiscal levers and legislative change, in a moment. The conspicuous need for technical considerations about how to enable inclusion throws more sharply into relief the various and different arenas of debate which surround the issue. There are, we would venture, at least three such arenas:

- principles behind inclusion
- evidence for the success or otherwise of inclusive practice
- mechanics; i.e. the technical changes needed to make inclusion happen.

These are in some sort of order. Mechanics follow decisions about practice, which are, in turn, based on principles and evidence. But much opposition to inclusion rests in the supposed inconsistency between principles and evidence and in the taking of principles and values to be equivalent to 'ideology'. We shall deal with each of these.

Inconsistency

Some commentators have seen a tension between principles and evidence. Croll and Moses (1998: 21) claim that: 'There is clearly a potential tension between arguments for types of provision which rest both on fundamental value positions and also on empirical evidence.' In a similar vein, Hornby (1999) takes one of the writers of the present volume to task for noting in one place that inclusion is right but in another that it is difficult to do. Inconsistency is the alleged problem. For both sets of commentators, to want to hold both to principles and evidence is an untenable position to take. Like oil and water, the two are unmixable. But the argument is surely more complex; as one of us has noted elsewhere (Thomas and Tarr 1999) in responding to Croll and Moses:

> Why should we not want to understand the effects of a policy decision which comes out of our values? If an unsegregated school system is in line with our values *and* it can be shown to be as good as or better than segregation (in terms, for instance, of outcome measures for all pupils), we will surely cheer. A problem might arise if our values said 'do x' but our research evidence said 'x will produce some outcomes which you would not in the absence of x wish for'. We would then have to decide whether 'x' was so central to our beliefs about what is right that we would be willing to put up with unwelcome consequences. Or, more likely, we would look for ways of doing 'x' while mitigating its unwelcome effects.
>
> There is no 'tension' [Croll and Moses 1998: 21] here 'between arguments for types of provision which rest both on fundamental value positions and also on empirical evidence'. Rather, it is a perennial characteristic of policy that our guiding values may produce many consequences. If all the consequences which follow from our adopting policies related to our values are positive, all is well and good. However, it may well be the case that some of the consequences are not positive . . . Certainly, such consequences may cause one to assess one's original value-based decision against its effects, which in turn will be weighed by reference to other values.

That this process should be explicit is surely correct. That it characterises complex policy decisions, with value weighed against value, and effect-of-value-decision against effect-of-value-decision is surely uncontentious.

(Thomas and Tarr 1999: 25)

If this argument is valid – if it is illegitimate, as we argue, to talk of a 'tension' in wanting both to follow principles and look at evidence – what in fact does the evidence say? Some of the evidence about the ineffectiveness of special education was reviewed in Chapter 2. It is not the purpose of this chapter to review the evidence in detail and a fuller discussion appears in Thomas *et al.* (1998). But it is probably worth noting what Hegarty (1993) has said following a major international review of the literature for the Organisation for Economic Cooperation and Development (OECD). Failing to find a clear-cut advantage for segregation or integration (partly because of the methodological problems of comparing non-comparable groups), he concludes: 'While [the inadequacies of comparative research] means that any inferences drawn must be tentative, the absence of a clear-cut balance of advantage supports integration' (Hegarty 1993: 198). He seems to be saying that unless evidence relating to children's progress and happiness at school is unequivocally unsupportive of inclusion, then the principles we have used to guide the current trend toward inclusion should continue. Both principles and evidence do have a part to play in determining policy.

Ideology and rhetoric?

To want to espouse the worth of values and principles is not to be 'ideological' in one's views about or arguments for inclusion. This is an important matter to address, for criticism of inclusion often pivots on the notion that its proponents are motivated in large part by ideology rather than evidence (see, for example, Croll and Moses 1998; Wilson 1999). This criticism of 'ideology' and 'rhetoric' ('rhetoric' about inclusion is another favourite target in the censure of the inclusive position – see Hornby 1999) has assumed some weight and it is important to pay some attention to it. The basic premise (one that we do not share) of those who hold to this position is that there are two kinds of argument. On the one side, there are evidence-based, rational, arguments rooted in logic. Wilson (1999: 110) clearly believes his reasoning belongs to this charmed cluster, since he begins his article with the extraordinary sentence: 'In this article I am concerned with logic, not ideology.' On the other side, it is implied, there are arguments (if, indeed, the word 'argument' is not assumed to do too much justice to the position) that are sentimental, politicized, sloppy, value laden and unscientific. In short, the latter are ideological.

We reject the proposition that it is a simple matter to divide arguments in this way; we would in fact go so far as to say that the distinctions drawn between the arguments are specious. This is so not just because the word 'ideology' is so supersaturated with meanings that it is impossible to know what the critic who uses the word is suggesting.[2] More importantly, it is because 'ideology' is replete with covert assumptions about the correctness and

rationality of the critic of the supposed ideologue and the hopeless senti-
mentality and/or prejudice of ideologues themselves. To quote from Eagleton
(1991: 2): 'Nobody would claim that their own thinking was ideological, just as
nobody would habitually refer to themselves as Fatso. Ideology, like halitosis,
is in this sense what the other person has.' Burbules (1992) puts it similarly:
'Assertions that a system of belief and value *is* ideological already presume a
superior vantage point from which [the beliefs of the other] can be disclosed
and criticised.' In a similar vein, Bourdieu says that he avoids the word 'ideology' because it 'seems to convey a sort of discredit. To describe a statement as
ideological is very often an insult, so that this ascription itself becomes an
instrument of symbolic domination' (Bourdieu and Eagleton 1994: 266).

People who attack another's position as 'ideological', in other words, often
fail to recognize the 'locatedness' of their own position and are mystified, as
Cicourel (1993) suggests, by anyone drawing attention to this. As Burbules
(1992: 7) notes in the same context: 'When one labels a position as "ideological", one already has made certain implicit decisions about how it is to be
disclosed and criticised.'

Burbules continues: 'Characterising belief systems as ideologies is, in common usage, a handy way of attributing to them a host of implied failings –
political contentiousness, manipulative use of language, partisan ranting,
sloppiness, inaccuracy, or downright falsehood' (ibid: 8).

To posit that other people's views are ideological is in other words, a little
like trying to deny the status and worth their position. Implied in the label in
the case of its use in the debate on inclusion is the acceptance of the imprimatur of epistemological clarity which the revered '*ology*' (usually psych*ology*)
proffers and the denial of any sort of knowledge or opinion not located in that
canon.[3]

Unrealistic Utopianism?

And if the argument is that 'ideological' is about the politics of Grand Theory,[4]
a good case can be made for the proposition that the philosophical roots out of
which pressure for inclusion emerges are in fact very distinct from the Grand
Theoretical speculations from which most of the derogatory intimations of
'ideology' emerge. A powerful argument can be made for the case that the
social justice stream of thought in which inclusion is located comes more from
Fabianism than from Marxism.[5] With Fabianism's emphasis on the eclectic
rather than the synthetic, concentrating on practical detailed reforms and the
rejection of grandiose theoretical speculations, it is surely the antithesis of the
commonly held view about what ideology is. The Fabians 'sedulously avoided'
(McBriar 1966: 99) Utopianism. The purpose of education, Sidney Webb said
in 1903 in the *Fabian News*, is to develop 'the most civilised body of citizens . . .
in the interests of the community as a whole, developing each to the "margin
of cultivation" ' (cited in McBriar 1966: 208). To make such a assertion could
be called ideological because it is rooted in values. However, to give it such a
label would tell us as much (or more) about the beliefs and understandings of
the person doing the labelling than of the supposed ideologue.

These, as much as the canons and maxims of the supposed 'ideologue', need examining in any evaluation of the justice of a position. One should surely be wary of social scientists who claim to follow some superior route to know-ledge: who claim that their thinking is therein deliciously supple and their conclusions therefore valid, while your thinking is ideological and your con-clusions invalid. As the philosopher of science Georges Canguilhem (1994: 41) reminds us, science (when one looks at the history of almost any advance) cannot be defined much more satisfactorily than the 'elimination of the false by the true' – or, perhaps less baldly, in Ziman's (1991) terms the elimination of less reliable by more reliable knowledge. It is far too easy to overlay some smooth methodology, some unvarying canon of received procedures, assumed to be guiding the sensible scientist. There is no epistemological or method-ological Excalibur freeing one set of social scientists from the contamination of belief, understanding, prejudice – or even, dare one say it, political position.[6] As Giddens (1994: 29) puts it: 'All forms of knowledge, no matter how general they appear to be, are saturated by practice.' Drawing from Oakeshott and Hans-Georg Gadamer he makes the case that there is often the assumption by those who presume themselves to be rational that they have somehow cor-nered the market on sensible discussion and 'answers' and particularly answers coming from tradition or embedded practice. This tendency, as we have seen with intimations of 'ideology' and 'rhetoric' about inclusion, is particularly true of education, where the assumption of the superiority of a particular kind of knowledge is commonplace. In education, where practice is so central, there is no way in which practice, belief or value can in some clinical way be dis-sected out of a more disinterested kind of knowledge. The latter will always remain illusory.

Being a 'moral activist' about inclusion

Often, discussion about appropriate kinds of schooling has, as we noted in Chapter 1, rested in critiques of the education system that locate phenomena such as special education in the 'social order'. Abberley (1987), an exponent of this view, has suggested that 'The main and consistent beneficiary [of exclu-sion] must be identified as the present social order, or more accurately, capitalism.'

There are many ways in which one can have differences with this analysis and these are touched on in Chapter 1. But to suggest that this analysis does not provide an accurate or exhaustive account of the growth of special educa-tion is not to deny the significance of any analysis that takes as its starting point notions of social justice.

And, as we noted in Chapters 5 and 6, there has been much discussion recently that takes an examination of social justice outside the parameters set by Marxist thinking. Rorty (1998), for example, insists that the latter is unsatisfactory: that greater social justice is achieved not by generalized appeals for social reform, but by using democratic institutions and procedures to con-ciliate needs and widen consensus. Consensus is the key and is linked with

Giddens's (1994) notion of 'dialogic democracy'. Rorty interestingly links Foucault's analysis of the construction of normality, so central to the notion of inclusion, with the much earlier analysis of Dewey[7] and uses it to argue for looking through a pragmatic lens on democratic change:

> [Some] do not agree with Dewey and Foucault that the subject is a social construction, and that discursive practices go all the way down. They think that moral idealism depends on moral universalism – on an appeal to universally shared demands, built into human nature, or to the nature of social practice.
>
> (Rorty 1998: 35)

It is ironic that such universalistic demands sometimes draw on Foucault, who so comprehensively declaimed grand explanatory systems. It is ironic that they seek to create some mélange called theory, out of which will be effected 'inexplicable, magical transformations' wherein iniquities are punished by what Rorty calls 'an angelic power' (ibid: 102). Rorty identifies such demands with a new academic Left, who:

> step back from their country and, as they say, 'theorise' it. It leads them to do what Henry Adams[8] did: to give cultural politics preference over real politics, and to mock the very idea that democratic institutions might once again be made to serve social justice. It leads them to prefer knowledge to hope.
>
> (Rorty 1998: 36)

Rorty mourns the loss of hope – the loss of a sense of fraternity and solidarity that at one time characterized the contribution of the academy and the traditional left to American life. He mourns, with the emergence of the new theorizing academy in America, a loss of emphasis on a sense of justice, which for a time supplanted that country's unashamed rhetoric of individual rights. The emphasis on social justice he sees as now having very nearly evaporated in the thinking of the academy as the imperatives of theorization take the place of those of change.

Rorty's call for a return to the equivalent of the Fabians' 'gas and water' of social justice is important for inclusive education on two counts. First, it is important because inclusive education offers one way of putting into practice ideals about social justice. Second, it is important because it is in itself an instrument for enabling and engendering a more liberal polity – a more tolerant, civilized and plural society. It can help enable respect for others and concern for their welfare. It thus moves outside and beyond neo-Marxist conceptualizations that explain the exclusion of certain groups and minorities with theoretical constructs such as oppression and which force certain kinds of categorization and agglomeration (of people with disabilities, people who present difficult behaviour, ethnic minorities) alienating those newly formed groups and minorities not only from the majority but also from others who may be excluded.

The latter conceptualizations force what Marquand (1996) calls a 'passive-hedonist' collectivism – one that merely pushes for the righting of the

oppression of individual groups. It leads him to eschew any simple dichot-
omy of individualism and collectivism and to insist that finer distinctions
be drawn between different *kinds* of individualism and different *kinds* of
collectivism:

> Individualism can be passive and hedonist, or active and moralist. So can
> collectivism. Individual liberty can be valued, in other words, because it
> allows individuals to satisfy freely-chosen desires, to live as they please so
> long as they do not prevent others from doing the same. Or it can be valued
> because it enables them to lead purposeful, self-reliant and strenuous
> lives, because it encourages them to take responsibility for their actions
> and, in doing so, to develop their moral potential to the full. By the same
> token, collective action and collective provision may be seen as instru-
> ments for maximising morally-neutral satisfaction, or as the underpin-
> nings of personal and cultural growth, of engagement with the common
> life of the society and so of self-development and self fulfilment.
>
> (Marquand 1996: 21)

Marquand proceeds to contrast the socialism of two British political academics: he points out that while Anthony Crosland's[9] collectivism was essentially
passive hedonistic, R.H. Tawney's[10] was moral activist. The argument is almost
that passive hedonists, whether of an individual or collectivist bent, have
more in common than moral activists, whatever their predilections to individualism or collectivism. It is as though the moral activist dimension binds
certain kinds of thinking and this is important for education, for there is an
extent to which injunctions to be more equal or to be fairer are insufficient
without this moral dimension.

A good example as far as inclusion is concerned comes in interpreting the
generally accepted axiom of John Rawls (1971) about the just distribution of
resources. Rawls argued for the elimination of inequality through the redistribution of resources in his *Theory of Justice*, saying that, in general, there should
be an equal distribution of social resources, but that there should be a bias
in this distribution in favour of those who are 'disadvantaged'. The axiom
is: to each according to their need. This, however, is insufficient without a
moral activist dimension and the point becomes crystal clear in discussion of
special education and inclusion. Rizvi and Lingard (1996) make the point that
redistribution by itself is insufficient to achieve equity. The thesis they pro-
pound is that redistributive logic on its own obscures and thereby perpetuates
injustices in existing institutional organization. For emphasizing redistribution could mean merely shifting resources into special education and this
would not achieve the kind of changes necessary for social justice; as Lee
(1996: 130) puts it: 'It is possible to construct equities that are associated with
dis-welfare.'[11] Roaf and Bines (1989) make an allied point: that an emphasis on
needs in special education detracts from a proper consideration of the *rights* of
those who are being educated. Interestingly, Armstrong *et al.* (2000), writing
on inclusion in France, reveal a country with seemingly more interest in social
justice and participation than the slogan of inclusion. In the more intelligent
and reflective social and political climate in which education appears to be

discussed in France, it transpires, for example, that use of the drug Ritalin for 'ADHD'[12] is illegal. Discussion about these issues in France, in contrast to that in the UK and the USA, seems to be as much about rights as about putative needs (and the relevance and status of such supposed 'needs' was discussed in Chapter 3).

It is this emphasis on rights that the moral activist stance encourages and it is central to thinking on inclusion. Following Marquand's reasoning, it is insufficient merely to appeal abstractly to some kind of Rawlsian justice for this may lead merely to formulaic, unguided attempts at redistribution. A respected American commentator on social justice, Nancy Fraser (1996), like Marquand, tries to move outside simple redistributive logic and sees in our 'postsocialist age' what she calls a *redistribution–recognition dilemma* to questions of social justice. While she does not examine special schools or pedagogy, her conclusions are germane for education, for she notes that while redistribution focuses solely on resources (and this is clearly relevant) other kinds of injustice in contemporary society have become almost more important than economic injustice.

This is surely so in special education, where no claim could seriously be made that positive economic discrimination is not given to children at special schools, particularly in the USA, where 15 times as much is spent on a special school pupil as on a mainstream pupil. In fact, in some US school districts one-quarter of the budget is spent on special education (see OECD 1994; Wang *et al.* 1995). The economic redistribution argument is not in other words sufficient on its own: it is the way in which it is spent that is more important. But Fraser's argument moves beyond even this. It avers that more insidious and arguably equally powerful forms of injustice take the place of resource injustice. They arise from *non-recognition*, that is to say being rendered invisible by dominant cultural practice and from *disrespect* – through routine malignment or disparagement. To illustrate her point, Fraser draws on the work of Charles Taylor (1992), who suggests that non-recognition or mis-recognition can imprison someone:

> in a false, distorted, reduced mode of being. Beyond simple lack of respect, it can inflict a grievous wound, saddling people with crippling self-hatred. Due recognition is not just a courtesy but a vital human need.
>
> (Taylor 1992: 25)

It is thus only through seeing injustice through the lenses of non-recognition and disrespect that redistribution makes any sense in the contemporary world. Without these additional dimensions, redistribution may remain hollow, leaving in place practices that demean and disempower people. It is this demeaning and disempowering to which so many who have passed through the special school system have referred (e.g. Rieser and Mason 1992).

Non-recognition and disrespect arise from the way that segregative systems handle existing inequalities between children, inequalities arising both from what children can do with their bodies or from their 'cultural capital'.[13] The key question is whether a segregated school system exaggerates or attenuates such inequalities. As R.H. Tawney put it:

[W]hile [people's] natural endowments differ profoundly, it is the mark of a civilised society to aim at eliminating such inequalities as have their source, not in individual differences, but in its own organisation, and that individual differences, which are a source of social energy, are more likely to ripen and find expression if social inequalities are, as far as practicable, diminished.

(Tawney 1964: 57)

For inequalities to be thus diminished, recognition and respect have to be at the forefront of our minds in planning schools. For equality to exist in more than name children have to have opportunities to do the same as other children: to share the same spaces as other children and to speak the same language as other children. Taking Bourdieu's (1984) notion of 'symbolic capital' as a thinking tool[14] here, there is surely a sense in which different language and symbol systems develop in different kinds of school. If children do not have the 'right' language because they have attended a special school, they will be unable to exchange this 'symbolic capital' for other kinds of capital. Exclusion from the wider culture is the consequence. In Fraser's and Taylor's terms (earlier), the result is not only invisibility in the wider culture – their homes, neighbourhoods and eventual workplaces – but also a 'distorted, reduced mode of being'. Carson (1992) explores how the devaluation, non-recognition and disrespect of which Fraser and Taylor speak emerge from the practices of the school system; they emerge from rejection, segregation, congregation, discontinuity of life experiences and blame. Eliminating inequality is thus about more than providing money and better resources: it is about providing the seedbed for recognition and respect by providing chances to be included – to share in the common wealth of the school and its culture.

It is worth pausing here to note some other consequences of inequality. To return to the quotation from Matthew Arnold given at the beginning of this chapter, there are two sides to inequality and his warnings of the consequences of inequality seem clear in the context of schools. Not only does inequality harm by 'depressing' (the reduced mode of being spoken of by Taylor) and by a socialization into long-term dependency as Oliver (1995) points out, it also harms by 'pampering'. This pampering emerges out of the wholly unrepresentative situation that mainstream schools encounter when their rolls are shorn of a significant minority of pupils. The 'pampering' of mainstream schools has its effects in a more academic curriculum (as Postman 1995 has indicated), in less flexible pastoral systems and in a more regimented and less humane environment.

But to return to the main point: eliminating inequality happens not just through redistribution. Moral activism is necessary. The hopeful account provided by Marquand's moral activism shares some similarities with Etzioni's (1993) communitarianism, which urges in schools something similar to the 'humane environment' argued for at the end of Chapter 3. Communitarianism places schools at the centre of a project to renew trust in the values of respect, dignity, tolerance and democracy through the example of staff and through an organization that evinces and displays these values in the way that students are treated. It is worth noting here that Golby (1997: 126) argues that communitarianism 'trivialises the practical issues' faced by schools when they are placed by Etzioni and others at the centre of a project to restore civic virtue and tolerance. He concludes pessimistically that 'Schools are more a result of the moral anarchy they are supposed by communitarians to combat than a solution to it' (ibid: 137). Drawing on Hall's (1977) notion of the school as 'beached institution' – that is, an institution out of harmony with what is locally valued – he rejects the proposition that much can practically be done to have an impact on such large concerns as students' respect for others and their tolerance and understanding. He does not mention inclusion, but it would seem to offer one way of enabling children to see others more humanely and to have more respect for difference. This was certainly the case in the Somerset Inclusion Project (Thomas *et al.* 1998), where a central finding was of palpably increased tolerance and understanding, not only among students but also among staff, in schools which included children with disabilities. Inclusion brings with it recognition: a minority of children is no longer rendered invisible to the majority in the main school system.

To include a 'recognition' element in one's thinking about justice is rather like the moral element called for by Marquand. The distinctions drawn by Marquand are similar to those made by Clarke (1978), who talks of 'moral' and 'mechanical' reformers. The point the latter makes is that a moral dimension, like the introduction of a comprehensive, inclusive education system, is essential for the lasting development of civic pride and social justice. The mechanical reformer (such as Crosland) is one who believes that change can come about reasonably unproblematically through top-down provision and imposition: there is here a central role for public expenditure on education, social security and welfare. But the problem is that the changes effected by this kind of investment, as Plant (1996) points out, are likely to disintegrate very quickly:

> [I]f one attempts to pursue a political strategy that does not draw deeply on values held by the population at large, it may well collapse very quickly once it is challenged by a belief system which is more confident about its salience to the values of the society in which the reform is sought. It is really quite amazing that a political settlement so influenced by social democracy could have collapsed as quickly and as comprehensively as it did after 1979,[15] and one of the explanations of this may well be that it was a form of mechanical or indirect politics.
>
> (Plant 1996: 174)

Inclusive systems – and these are systems that seek to include all children, whatever the provenance of their difficulty at school, whether it be poverty, cultural origin or disability – must surely help to create the morally active and politically aware populace which Marquand and Plant are seeking: the 'dialogic democracy' of Giddens (1994: 117–24). Young people who leave school having seen and experienced those who are different and those with difficulties included in the common life of the school will be more likely to form part of a society with a conscience. The message of these political scientists transposed to education is that without young people who are sensitive to difference or for whom there has been no example in school of willingness to accept, there can be no expectation of solid or lasting improvement in social justice. We shall all be subject in our civic life to the vagaries and shifts in the 'belief system', changes in thought fashion.

How, then, does one achieve the moral activist collectivism of Marquand? Part of the answer must lie in the very structures operating in our schools and in the administrative systems that surround them. Instead of simply assuming that hearts and minds will be won by more generous public funding of schools, there needs to be a commitment to introducing inclusive systems (and some of these are reviewed in Thomas and Vaughan 2004 and Thomas *et al.* 1998). Another part of the answer lies in the example provided by the schools themselves, as part of a virtuous circle. In inclusive schools, in which students see with their own eyes children of all kinds and from all backgrounds valued, there will be the powerful example of a moral stance. Children from a range of backgrounds and who may or may not have conspicuous difficulties are seen to be treated equally. Without this example, there is forever the example that expedience forces exclusion – and there is every chance that children will remember this model.

Inclusion thus has a dynamic and practical part to play in developing 'moral activism'. There is no point expecting magical transformations in practice or some kind of collectivist *Zeitgeist* to spring from an unguided redistribution of resources. Redistributive justice on its own carries with it the possibility of reversal by those with a different social priorities and it engenders no possibility of lasting improvements in social justice. Equally importantly, it enables no adequate resolution of notions about the difficult agenda of action that should follow any redistribution.

Inclusion is about more than 'special needs'

In the context of all this it is important to step back and to stress again that inclusion is about more than merely the integration of children from special schools into mainstream schools. And it is about more than 'special educational needs' emerging from learning difficulties or disability. The superseding of 'integration' by 'inclusion' is more than merely renomenclature. 'Inclusion' was a word that was usually used to describe the process of the assimilation of children with learning difficulties, sensory impairments or physical disabilities to mainstream schools. In fact, the use of the term 'special educational needs' usually specifically excluded other children – for example, children whose first language was not English – following the specific exclusion of these children from the definitions of the 1981 Education Act.

The central idea motivating most sympathetic commentators on inclusion, by contrast, is that children who are at a disadvantage for any reason are not excluded from mainstream education. This represents a redefining and modernizing of the term 'special needs', which is surely more consistent with the spirit of the Warnock Report (DES 1978). The Warnock Committee talked about a fluid definition of special need, whereby categories would be abolished and a child's needs would be defined as and when they arose. (It is interesting that having talked about a continuum of need, the committee then went on, some might say inconsistently, to define special needs purely in terms of the constructs of learning difficulty and disability by which it had traditionally been defined.)

Taken to its logical conclusion, inclusion is about comprehensive education, equality and collective belonging. The latter is linked by Tawney (1964), as we have noted, with the question of inequality in a civilized society. His reasoning is relevant when thinking about the organization of education, for many of the features of a segregative education represent what Gordon and Green (1975: 73) called 'an affluent society's excuses for inequality'. These kinds of feature, with assumptions of deficit and all the attendant paraphernalia of special pedagogy and its 'remedial' and segregative methods, exaggerate existing differences. Tawney did not deny that people are born different. But this should not be used as an excuse for a system that throws a spotlight onto those differences. He asserted that a truly civilized society strives to reduce the inequalities that arise from any 'givens' and from its own organization. The organization of society's institutions – such as schools – should lighten and reduce those inequalities that arise from birth or circumstance, rather than exaggerate them.

Children's difficulties at school do not arise solely from putative 'learning difficulties' but may arise from a range of factors related to disability, language, family income, cultural origin, gender or ethnic origin and it increasingly seems clear that it is inappropriate to differentiate among these as far as inclusivity is concerned. This is especially so as recent evidence still attests to the interdependency of supposedly discrete 'factors' such as race and special needs. Artiles (2003) and Lipsky and Gartner (1996) review research showing that black students are far more likely to be labelled 'retarded' in the USA (equivalent to the British 'moderate learning difficulties') than are white students – who are more likely to be categorized as 'learning disabled'. As the American social commentator Iris Marion Young (1990: 45) makes clear, the mere existence of supposed groups forces us to categorize – and the categories encourage a particular mindset about a group, while in reality the 'groups' in question are 'cross-cutting, fluid and shifting'. Assumptions about disadvantage and oppression rest on these categorizations where, in fact, they may be unwarranted. Meekosha and Jacubowicz (1996) also note there is no discrete class of people who are disabled. In fact, they argue, people with disabilities are as heterogeneous as people in general and the agglomeration of all disabilities alienates disabled people from other minorities; it perhaps forces the kind of passive hedonism referred to by Marquand. And the stressing of a minority status emphasizes the presumed weakness and vulnerability of the group in question rather than the inadequacies of the supposedly supportive system.

The notion of inclusion therefore does not set boundaries (as the notion of integration did) around particular kinds of supposed disability. Instead, it is about providing a framework within which all children – regardless of ability, gender, language, ethnic or cultural origin – can be valued equally, treated with respect and provided with real opportunities at school. There is the danger, as

Slee (1998: 131) has put it, that: 'Terms such as "special educational needs", "integration", "normalisation", "mainstreaming", "exceptional learners" and "inclusion" . . . merge into a loose vocabulary.' That is to say, the terms are bundled together to represent a single agenda concerning putative learning difficulties and disability. But inclusion should have a far broader yet more distinct meaning, moving from what Roaf (1988: 7) has called an 'obsession with individual learning difficulties' to an agenda of *rights*.

Porter (1995) provides a summary of differences between what he calls the traditional approach (which may include 'integration') and an inclusionary approach. The main distinctions he draws are summarized in Table 7.2.

While this analysis, made in 1995, is satisfactory for describing an inclusionary approach insofar as it applies to classroom activity, it perhaps puts too little emphasis on the active promotion of acceptance, respect and equal opportunity that are central to inclusion in the moral activist sense described earlier.

In addition, while it eschews the importance of specialist knowledge and special pedagogy, it possibly stresses insufficiently the wider environment in which learning occurs – what in Chapter 3 we called a shift from a therapeutic approach (30 years ago) to a whole-school approach (10 years ago) to a humane environment approach, it is to be hoped, for the future. While examining children's learning and teachers' strategies are clearly important, such an examination should not detract from the need to examine the effects that the social and physical environment of the school is having on its participants as learners. In Chapter 3, the focus of this was on the ways in which the environment, systems and operation of the school affect its participants' behaviour. (This included attention to some pretty mundane and non-professional matters – for example, that there are plentiful drinking fountains and that they are maintained regularly; staggering playtimes and school start and end times in large schools; ensuring fair queuing systems at lunch.) There are clearly other ways, however, in which uncomplicated thought about the operation of the school can have inclusive benefits – uncomplicated thought that owes no allegiance to any theoretical school or to any special pedagogy. The young people of Educable (2000), for example, provide a list of recommendations for

Table 7.2   Porter's (1995) comparison of traditional and inclusionary approaches

Traditional approach (which may include integration)	Inclusionary approach
Focus on student	Focus on classroom
Assessment of student by specialist	Examine teaching/learning factors
Diagnostic/prescriptive outcomes	Collaborative problem solving
Student programme	Strategies for teachers
Placement in appropriate programme	Adaptive and supportive regular classroom environment

better schools, following a wide range of interviews with disabled peers. These include:

- Common rooms, for each year, should be available in secondary schools to help young people mix with each other.
- Rest rooms should be available in schools for young people whose medical condition or disability causes them to become tired.

Such ideas, from children and young people themselves, derive a distinctiveness from this very fact. These original suggestions emerge from the fact that the young people have been encouraged to say what they would want and what would be important to them in a school which claimed to be inclusive. The freshness and common sense in these suggestions derive in large measure from the fact that they are uncluttered by the constructs, dreams and jargon of professional educators. Many of the notionally participative structures set up under, for example, new 'education action zones' in the UK, are created in the spirit of professionals acting in the 'best interests' (Newell 1988: 200) of the child and family. Even though the new structures are intended to empower, it may be that children, young people and families fail to engage with those structures. The refreshing fact about the Educable research is that, taking as a starting point their desire for inclusion in mainstream schools, young people themselves have sought ways of increasing and improving their participation.

The need to stress these participatory aspects of inclusion are writ large in an international context. Booth (1999) describes his work in countries 'of the South', where participation is denied for a number of reasons: poverty; war; environmental degradation; abuse and violence; HIV and AIDS; the spoken language being different from the language of instruction; pregnancy and childcare. He points out that the 'special needs version' of inclusive education is doubly irrelevant for learners in these countries, where the pressing and overriding need is for participation.

Moral activism, inclusion and realism

If all this is the case and if there is a case for a moral activist dimension to policy and practice, how is it to be effected? How are we to avoid empty rhetoric about equality and hollow exhortations to widen participation? There are no recipes here, although there are case studies that promise the hope of success in similar ventures. There are case studies of inclusive services taking the place of special schools (e.g. Thomas *et al.* 1998); of local authorities closing special schools and providing instead inclusive services (Jordan and Goodey 1996), and of heads of special schools effectively moving into their neighbourhood schools (e.g. CSIE 1992; Wilson 1990). The Centre for Studies on Inclusive Education has in the context of practical help for mainstream schools recently published its *Index for Inclusion* (CSIE 2000), which is a set of materials and guidelines that take schools through a process of inclusive school development. It is encouraging that the government has supported the use of this document, by paying for its introduction into all schools in England. Equally encouraging is the government's provision of £15m from its Standards Fund for 100 local inclusion projects across the country.

And in the UK government's discussion paper on the future of special provision (DfEE 1997) a number of suggestions were made for promoting inclusion. The government suggests that:

- special schools should have targets for numbers of children whom they successfully reintegrate
- mainstream schools that reach high standards in improving their provision for a wide range of special needs be awarded a 'kitemark'
- special schools should become more like services, providing resources and expertise to local mainstream schools
- all children should be registered on the roll of a mainstream school. This, if the money for the child also went to the mainstream school, would encourage creative thinking about inclusive solutions.

Welcome as all these suggestions and developments are, one wonders – as we noted in Chapter 6 – about the likely success of exhortation and demonstration projects without structural change. At roughly the same time that the government's support for the *Index for Inclusion* was trailed in a press release, a short letter appeared in the *Times Educational Supplement*, under the banner 'False sympathy for inclusion'. From a group of teachers, it said:

As learning support staff in a multi-racial school we support the principles of inclusion and of raising academic standards.

We feel strongly that unrealistic target-setting, an over-prescriptive curriculum and league tables are not sympathetic to the principle of inclusion. They negatively affect the status of children with special educational needs or those for whom English is an additional language.

We have seen such children become 'unwanted' because they affect the league tables in a negative direction and we have evidence of schools refusing to take such children before national tests.
Maggie Chambers plus 12 other signatories
(*Times Educational Supplement* 2000: 23)

Continuing pressure to be at the same time competitive *and* inclusive looks, these 13 teachers are saying, remarkably like tokenism. Pressures of all kinds – to be successful in examinations, to meet silly targets – lead schools to reject rather than accept children who are likely to drive down results. Hence the recent dramatic rises in numbers of excluded children (see Parsons 1999).

This sentiment expressed by these teachers is often heard in schools and it recalls the work of Croll and Moses discussed earlier in this chapter – work which appeared to indicate a willingness among teachers to support inclusion in the right circumstances, but which indicated also that the circumstances were not currently right. The concern has to be that 'inclusion' is merely a headline, a slogan contradicted by other policy and unsupported by structural, financial and legislative superstructure. It is the last to which Rorty (1998: 105) referred when he said, echoing Dewey, that 'piecemeal reform' is necessary – reform of those dull processes of regulation, resourcing and legislation that compete feebly against theorization for academic status, yet have incomparably more impact. It is commitment to such a philosophy of getting the infrastructure right that led the Italian government eventually to accompany its principled programme of special school closure with an injunction on authorities to make appropriate provision. Following National Law 118 in Italy, which mandated integration, there followed a period of *integrazione selvaggia* – wild integration (Johnson 1993), during which adequate resourcing was not available. The ensuing crisis led to the necessary ground-level changes being made. These included:

- legislation (Law 517) establishing that each integrated class should have no more than two children having special needs and must not exceed 20 pupils
- support teachers must be provided at a minimum ratio of one for every four disabled students
- training for support teachers was improved with the introduction of a *polyvalente* course, lasting 1300 hours
- the government established a 'Permanent National Observation Centre for Integration' whose role it was to monitor the operation of the legislation and promote research projects.

(adapted from Johnson 1993: 469; see also Rieser and Mason 1992)

Financing is a key instrument in enabling the move to inclusion and it needs to be continually borne in mind. Despite its importance little work has been done to explicate its impact on the move to inclusion.[16]

The impact of finance, however, is more subtle than a simple focus on the formulae of resource distribution would reveal. Students of economics study a process called 'cost externalization'. It is a term used by economists to describe a process wherein manufacturers and producers shunt their costs of production elsewhere. The costs they might incur in producing goods or services are thereby paid by someone else. The freight carrier, for example, uses lorry transport because it is cheaper than rail transport. But the costs imposed by making that choice – in diesel fumes that cause asthma that has to be treated, in vibration damage to buildings that have to be repaired or in amenities or environment destroyed or despoiled for the construction of new roads – are not incurred by the freight carrier. They are not incurred because it is possible, given weak or non-existent fiscal and regulatory mechanisms, to move them to others: it is possible to *externalize* the cost.

A suggestion that is now emerging more and more frequently, in association with what is sometimes called 'the stakeholder economy' is that commercial institutions should pay the price – literally – for adhering to practices that are now felt to be inappropriate or antisocial. Businesses must be obliged to take account of the hidden costs of their less acceptable practices – costs of restricted opportunity for employees, of pollution of the environment, or whatever. At the moment they create damage for which they do not have to pay. While the economist Kay (1996) makes this point in the context of large companies and their obligations to their employees and their customers, the lessons learned from this analysis are surely valid also in schools. The social costs of segregation, many disabled people have argued, are high: the cost of exclusion and segregation is the alienation of people who would otherwise have been able and willing to take a much fuller part in society. Yet high-excluding schools and high-segregating LEAs have not had to bear these costs of social exclusion.

Plender (1997) takes this further, attributing to the school, and institutions like it, more of an active role in a stakeholding society. He suggests that in such a society, the role of state and individual are downplayed while the role of intermediate institutions (such as schools) is reinforced. In an inclusive society, entrustment of public funds to governors and headteachers must be accompanied by an obligation to find ways of making inclusion happen.

Concluding comment

A lot changed in the political climate of the last decade of the twentieth century. The individually oriented ethic of the 1980s was largely displaced – although echoes of it linger in the fondness of governments for performativity, selection and competition among schools. With that ethic's allegiance to meritocracy and competition, it had owed much to the free market liberalism of thinkers like Friedrich Hayek ([1949] 1998). The political rhetoric then was of competition and mocked the notion that what was dismissed as 'honest convictions and good intentions' (Hayek [1949] 1998: 15) could effect any sort of real betterment in social conditions. That tradition provided ample rhetorical justification for continuing segregative forms of provision in education, whether in special or selective schools.

In the new ethic that took shape around the mid-1990s, talk of an 'inclusive society' and a 'stakeholder society' came to replace the earlier ethic of competition and winner-takes-all. We have reviewed here new ideas like David Marquand's 'moral activism', and Nancy Fraser's 'recognition' as important ingredients for thinking about such an inclusive society. There has in this been a determination to find ways of making inclusion about more than merely the 'honest conviction and good intention' about which Hayek wrote. If schools are to celebrate diversity and promote fraternity and equality of opportunity, there have to be ways of operationalizing such ideals. This chapter has reviewed some of these – a combination of various pragmatic, down-to-earth measures at both school and administrative level, measures to do with financing and organization that are not hard to implement, given the will.

Changes have been possible in thinking about inclusion in education not only because of the broader change in social climate, but also (and perhaps more significantly), because of changes in the way that 'difficulty' is conceptualized; there seems far less willingness now to locate the difficulties which children may experience at school unproblematically *in* the children themselves – whether the 'in-ness' be about children's learning or behaviour or about their social background, family income, gender or race.

In the next few years there is likely to be an extension of the changes that took place at the end of the twentieth century, with an increasing recognition of the interconnectedness of the issues surrounding inclusion. Increasingly, these interconnected issues, some of which are discussed in Chapter 8, will be dealt with outside the professional and disciplinary boundaries once set:[17] outside what Illich (1975: 77) called 'professional fiefdoms' and outside the notion of special pedagogy. Our choice of the word 'pedagogy', rather than 'schooling' is deliberate, for the message of the first four chapters of this book is that it is not special *schooling* that is the sole issue. Just as important as the place children go to school is the set of expectations invested in the practices that surround special education.

Summary

Inclusion is about an extension of the comprehensive ideal in education. Seen as such, it is less concerned with children's supposed needs (and much commentary in any case increasingly challenges the status of the thinking behind 'need') and more with their rights. There is, however, criticism of inclusion and this criticism highlights the rights orientation of inclusive dialogue, asserting that it is ideological, rhetorical or Utopian. Its validity, however, is defended here. It is defended not only on the grounds that the tenets of inclusion – tolerance, pluralism, equity – are goals to be striven for unapologetically, but also on the grounds that the alternative, namely an education system geared around some menu of specialized and definitively effective pedagogies for different 'problems', is one that will seemingly forever elude us. An argument is made for the case that the inclusive society sought by a new centrist politics demands an active response in education. Such a response, while patchy, clearly already exists in schools and in many cases antedates the stimulus provided by recent political changes. It is argued that further moves in this direction depend on an active espousal of certain ideas by educators, to do not only with financing and redistribution, but also to do with recognition, respect and listening to the voices of those who have been through special education.

Notes

1 There is debate about the extent to which Rousseau's ideas are linked in *Émile* and the *Contract*. Colletti (1974: 147–8) says that 'In Rousseau morality does not govern politics, but politics itself is the solution to the moral problem . . . while *Émile* is devoted to the education of the individual in the "old" society, the true education offered to the "new citizen" of the *Contract* lies in participation in public life itself.'
2 Eagleton, in his book *Ideology* (1991: 1–2), in fact, identifies no fewer than 16 meanings for the word: ideology can mean various things from 'the process of production of meanings, signs and values in social life', to 'a body of ideas characteristic of a particular social group or class' to 'ideas which help to legitimate a dominant political power' to 'systematically distorted communication' – and a dozen others. Indeed, the meanings have become so diffuse as to render the word meaningless. As he points out 'any word which covers everything . . . dwindles to an empty sound' (ibid: 7).
3 This is discussed further by Thomas and Glenny (2002).
4 Wright Mills (1970) described the overarching, explain-all speculations of socio-historical analysis as 'Grand Theory'. He suggested that such theory (in particular in

the philosophies of Compte, Marx, Spencer and Weber) creates a 'trans-historical strait-jacket' into which the evidence of history is coerced.

5 Such non-Utopian communitarian thought was not, of course, unique to Europe. See Rorty's (1998: 50) discussion of the 'American leftism' based on Croly, Ely and Addams which evolved at the turn of the century and which 'helped substitute a rhetoric of fraternity and national solidarity for a rhetoric of individual rights'.

6 See Thomas (1998) for a fuller discussion of the issue.

7 Indeed, Rorty (1991: 193) suggests that 'Foucault can be read as an up-to-date version of John Dewey'.

8 Henry Brooks Adams was an American historian, philosopher of history, and cultural critic. He edited *The North American Review* and wrote *History of the United States of America During the Administrations of Thomas Jefferson and James Madison* (1891) and *Degradation of the Democratic Dogma* (1919) which provides a 'dynamic theory of history'. Rorty notes that 'William James thought that Adams's diagnosis of the First Gilded Age as a symptom of irreversible moral and political decline was merely perverse. James's pragmatist theory of truth was in part a reaction against the sort of detached spectatorship which Adams affected' (ibid: 9).

9 Anthony Crosland was a post-war Labour politician who wrote *The Future of Socialism* (1964). This was a pivotal work in developing the thinking of the British Labour Party after the war, predicting growing affluence and consequent decline in Marxist class struggle. He noted that: 'Total abstinence and a good filing system are not now the right signposts to the socialist Utopia.' While clearly a progressive, it is the emphasis on the significance of affluence that puts him among Marquand's 'passive hedonists'.

10 The author of *Equality*, R.H. Tawney is of enormous significance in the British socialist movement. Blackburn (1999: 107) suggests that he is 'alongside G.D.H. Cole and Harold Laski . . . one of the most important contributors to British socialist thought this century'. He favoured moderate (some would say too moderate), workable policies over radical ideas.

11 Lee (1996: 48) further problematizes the whole notion of equity, saying that users of the word should define what they mean or 'confusion and conflict' will be the result. He notes: 'Authors often refer to equity as an essentially contested concept, but in so doing they are usually only offering a platitude. The complexity and problematic nature of the notion is usually inadequately explored; not many stop to analyse the concept itself; most just use equity, typically uncritically' (ibid: 48). Of the various kinds of equity outlined by Lee, the one most closely approximating to the use here is 'social justice'.

12 ADHD is an abbreviation for Attention Deficit Hyperactivity Disorder and the drug Ritalin has controversially been much used in its 'treatment'. The identification of this supposed 'disorder' and the willingness of both medics and educators to want to 'treat' it with drugs provides a case study example of the readiness ever to seek a clinical, even physiological, root for children's problems. In a recent volume on ADHD, the author unselfconsciously attributes heterogeneous symptoms to the same disorder for the following reason: 'ADHD is primarily a condition of brain dysfunction, probably involving difficulties at multiple sites in the brain, helping to explain the wide variation in symptoms and differing responses to medication' (Kewley 1999).

13 Bourdieu used the term 'cultural capital' to refer to the accumulated resources and insignia which can be 'cashed in' for society's goods and services (see, for example, Bourdieu 1984; Bourdieu and Passeron 1977).

14 Bourdieu insisted that he did not theorize; rather, he used 'thinking tools': 'Let me say outright and very forcefully that I never "theorise", if by that we mean engage in

the kind of conceptual gobbledygook ... that is good for textbooks and which, through an extraordinary misconstrual of the logic of science, passes for Theory in much of Anglo-American social science ... There is no doubt a theory in my work, or, better, a set of *thinking tools* visible through the results they yield, but it is not built as such ... It is a temporary construct which takes shape for and by empirical work' (Bourdieu, in Wacquant 1989, cited in Jenkins 1992: 67).

15 It was in 1979 that the UK Conservative government led by Margaret Thatcher took power.

16 Lee (1990; 1996) found great variation in the funding made to different kinds of facilities in different local authorities. Allan *et al.* (1995) in Scotland made similar findings, where per-pupil costs in MLD facilities were found to range from £3100 to £7700. Other research on this theme (for example, that of Bullock and Thomas 1997; Levacic 1995; Lunt and Evans 1994 and Thomas 1990), addresses the relevant issue in relation to additional educational needs (AEN) and, for example, the use made by LEAs of proxy indicators such as free school meals as distribution criteria. All of it indicates that much rationalization in the use of resources could be undertaken to promote inclusion.

17 There are already many examples of projects involving interagency work (for example Arnold *et al.* 1993; Kendrick *et al.* 1996; Roaf and Lloyd 1995) and the government has recently established some interesting experiments in enabling access and participation to learning outside the walls of the school (DfEE 1998b).

Inclusive education for the twenty-first century: histories of help; hopes for respect

In Chapter 7, we discussed some of the rationale for inclusive education and the move from an emphasis on needs to one on rights. This shift was at the core of the changes in thinking that occurred during the 1990s and the first few years of the twenty-first century. We argue in this chapter for ideas about inclusion now to move forward once more, to fold around a range of matters concerning the interconnections among learning, community, identity and belonging. We argue in this final chapter for an inclusion conceived with many surfaces – disability, certainly, and social justice no less – but, more importantly, other facets of life at school: community, social capital, equality, respect, affirmation and happiness.

Why is a yet broader ambit to the idea of inclusive education needed now?

The changes that occurred during the 1990s came from uncertainty about the status of conceptualizations of disability and other kinds of difficulty, fore-grounding their social and discursive construction. Accompanying the uncertainty that characterized the questioning of concepts of disability was a recognition that inclusive education ought to be about more than the educa-tion of those who formerly would have attended special schools or been in receipt of special programmes. So, inclusive education came to mean the inclu-sion of all learners, paying attention to any features of a student's experience that may create difficulties at school. The refiguring in thinking about inclusive education was profound and contained both constructive and deconstructive elements, as we have noted so far in this book. In the constructive tradition, arguments have rested in the positive value of a plural, equitable system rooted in human rights, while in the deconstructive tradition arguments have centred on the harmful consequences that may emerge from separate systems and pedagogies. Both traditions have argued for an end to separate education systems.

But there have persisted into the twenty-first century strong voices – recently, for example, Kauffman and Hallahan (2005) and Warnock (BBC 2005a) – arguing for the benefits of continuing separate education and specialized pedagogies. Their arguments have rested principally on the impracticability of inclusion, its ideological or values-based provenance and the pedagogic and social benefits of special education. Counterarguments to this genre of reasoning have been advanced on epistemological grounds (e.g. Gallagher 2004; Reid and Valle 2005), on outcomes-based grounds (e.g. Hegarty 1993; Zigmond 2003) and on social justice and rights-based grounds (e.g. Artiles 2003; Rustemier 2002).

Valid as these counterarguments are, we argue – and this is the main platform of this chapter – that a yet stronger case needs to be made for inclusion. In part, this is necessary more comprehensively to engage with the critics of inclusion. More importantly, however, it is necessary to link with present-day ideas about thinking, learning and pedagogy and to escape the furrows of twentieth-century thinking on exceptionality. It is necessary also as a response to a new world of increasing diversity, fragmenting order and a widening gap between rich and poor within and between nations as globalization accelerates. It is about envisioning a new, inclusive education for contemporary life: one that is equal to the opportunities and challenges of new kinds of living, new kinds of modernity.

By making this more general case, we intend to broaden the theoretical foundation on which the continuing development of inclusive education is able to stand. The case we make goes beyond arguments for desegregation, human rights and social justice, crucial though these are to the case for inclusion, and it extends to more universal benefits of inclusive schooling. The argument is organized around three connected themes:

- The first theme concerns the benefits that emerge from recognizing and rejecting the influence of the diagnostic and restorative history of special education – an influence that continues to contaminate current thinking in inclusive education. Special education and its view of exceptionality drew on a psychology of learning that is wrong for today's education, a psychology that is in fact wholly contrary to contemporary understandings about learning. Although inclusive education could draw its insights about learning and development less specifically from those erstwhile sources and more eclectically from the broader social sciences and humanities – which have much to say about learning – it usually fails to. We make an argument for a more serious engagement with the newer understandings, particularly those that tell us that learning takes place in communities. Thus conceived, failure to learn rests not so much in the absence of ability as in the absence of identity in community.
- Second, and following from the first theme, arguments for inclusion have to be built on knowledge of the damaging consequences of inequality, relative poverty and contrastive judgement in schools. Our discussion here rests around knowledge about 'gradient effects': it leads to a new 'psychology of difference' that is emerging via the work of economists such as Amartya

Sen and epidemiologists such as Michael Marmot in their explication of more nuanced understandings of the effects of poverty and difference. It examines the mechanisms by which such a psychology of difference may work in educational communities.

- Third, we build our argument for inclusive education on knowledge about the benefits of social connection, communities of learning and social capital. Our discussion here intermixes ideas from progressive education and socio-cultural theory and it finds links with those ideas in work from the broader social sciences, such as the recent work of political scientist Robert Putnam and economist Richard Layard. We make these arguments in the context of the strengths and limitations of rights-based argument around inclusive education.

Histories of diagnosis and disconnection versus new understandings of learning

Thinking about the future, as this chapter presumes to, demands reflection. To anticipate the shape of an inclusive education in the twenty-first century, one needs to understand its contemporary status as a product of its history, of the discourses that shaped its development during the twentieth century. In this context, it is first important to note that inclusive education is undeniably the child of special education. While inclusive educators would surely recoil from any charge that their work displays any sign of throwback to the field's roots in special education, it is clear that inclusive education embodies a mindset whose lineage is visibly traceable to its forebear's. It thus concerns itself predominantly with the right to integration in the least restricted environment of what are taken to be 'exceptional' students (see, for example, the discussion of Hehir and Latus 1992 and the wording of legislation[1] that guarantees the social and academic integration of disabled or exceptional citizens). Slee points out that such thinking has maintained a 'misconception that disabled children are to be the sole beneficiaries of inclusion' (Slee 2001: 120).

The recent thawing of rigid demarcation lines about exceptionality has done little to refigure thought about direction: little, in other words, about the viewing of the field as being about remedy, putting right, change, even if the focus in doing that has latterly moved from student to school.[2]

Knowing this lineage to exist between special and inclusive education, what forces have shaped the growth and decline of this field? Shifting currents – in politics, in the academy, in what can loosely be called the *Zeitgeist* – were behind the varying fortunes of special education in the twentieth century and it was out of these currents that came the field's waxing and waning.

The key move of *Zeitgeist*, at least as far as the waning of special education and the beginnings of the rise of inclusion are concerned, was one of a slow and painful shift away from separation as a taken-for-given feature of organized social life. As Arthur Miller remarked in his Prologue to *The Crucible* 'all organization is and must be grounded on the idea of exclusion and prohibition' and this impulse to exclude (and the panic that accompanies attempts to dilute separative systems, as noted in *The Crucible*) has been at the root of segregative systems of education. As Bauman (1995: 180) puts it: 'Rules of admission are effective only in as far as they are complemented by the sanctions of expulsion, banishment, cashiering . . . sending down.' He goes on to note that ordinary education has been maintained only by the presence of ' "corrective institutions" awaiting the failures and the recalcitrant'.

If Miller and Bauman are right, exclusion will find an omnipresence in our institutions. Yet there have undeniably been changes of late to attitudes to exclusion. What changes can one discern in the drive to exclude that culminated in a reversal in the last quarter of the twentieth century – a reversal that involved understanding and promoting the benefits of inclusion?

The separative disposition borne of the eugenics about which we spoke in Chapter 2 was eventually extinguished, but, sadly, educators had little part in its extinction. (Indeed, under the influence of psychologists such as Terman and Burt, the 1950s saw some of the largest expansions in special education in the century.) Rather, it was the *Zeitgeist* that came eventually to succeed the Second World War that dispensed with the segregative logic and a set of tacit reappraisals and reformulations emerged to replace the discourses that had before dominated. After that war, the respectability of eugenics evaporated and no one any longer dared to advocate that segregation was in anyone's best interest. People began to recognize that separation in any sphere of life is for the convenience of the majority, marginalizing, disenfranchising and often oppressing the separated minority. Key texts such as Erving Goffman's *Asylums* ([1961] 1968) reinforced the move away from separation, as Goffman irreverently suggested that separative institutions acted as society's 'storage dumps' (Goffman [1961] 1968: 73). In the early 1950s, Chief Justice Warren put it neatly for the opinion of the Supreme Court in the celebrated case of Brown v. Board of Education (US Supreme Court 1954): 'We conclude that, in the field of public education, the doctrine of "separate but equal" has no place. Separate educational facilities are inherently unequal.' This was a conclusion reached because separation 'generates a feeling of inferiority as to [students'] status in the community that may affect their hearts and minds in a way unlikely ever to be undone'.[3]

Brown was an important marker, but public recognition of the reasoning embodied in the Brown judgment reached its climax in the USA in the civil rights movement of the 1960s, a movement concerned mainly with 'race' that gave confidence in its wake to other groups that had felt discrimination, segregation and oppression. Also, as we noted in Chapter 7, in Europe there were political movements ranging from the social democracy of Scandinavia to the collectivist local government of Italy (see Johnson 1993) that demanded new action to outlaw separation, discrimination and segregation. Across the world, new legislation began to be enacted to counter discrimination. A new tide had demanded a closure on segregation and separation in all spheres of life, including education.

New psychologies of learning and a new modernity

At the same time, other ideas swelled together during the 1950s and 1960s and their confluence made for the liberalization and progressivization of the education system internationally. Stimulated by figures such as John Holt and Lawrence Cremin in the USA and Jean Piaget in Europe, there was a re-awakening of interest in progressive educational thinkers such as Dewey, Montessori and Froebel. In a fascinating analysis, Gardner *et al.* (1996: 29) describe how 'developmental and educational traditions' came together, with an interest in children as constructors of their own learning in meaningful contexts.

And the change in climate came also from other, broader shifts: from a new mistrust in science as a provider of answers to social questions; from a decline in respect for authority and a new wariness about its interests and motives; from caution about the status of professional knowledge, and from a powerful consumerism, on the back of which students and their parents felt able to challenge the decisions of authorities and professionals.

The point of this brief retrospective is to set in context the development of special and inclusive education as cultural and political phenomena: products of the general discourses – as much as the educational discourses – of the twentieth century. These new discourses continue to evolve and, as they accelerate with the speed of contemporary life, they must be understood, accommodated and planned for. One must understand, for example, that the end of the twentieth century and the beginning of the twenty-first saw hastening fragmentation, decreasing trust and a move to what the sociologist Zygmunt Bauman (2000) has called 'liquid modernity': an era in which variety, ambiguity, nomadic behaviour and declining trust interplay; an era in which there is burgeoning uncertainty about the confident answers of the past.

Understandings and analyses of these changes are crucial. Part of inclusive education's difficulty in broadening its purview has been the compartmentalization of the academic endeavour that guides educational enquiry, with knowledge being codified according to the constructs of psychology, sociology and, less often, philosophy. These codifications rarely intermix. Inclusive education now needs more eclectic academic analyses, drawing and interweaving more extensively from the human sciences: from economics, anthropology, sociology, healthcare, ethics, politics and international studies. Debate must stop separating the pedagogic from the social – it must help to prevent, in other words, the fate Lawrence Cremin (1961) predicted public education would always meet in the USA: 'In other countries at times of great social upheaval, they have a revolution. In the United States, they add a new course to the curriculum.'

Cremin's warning was that simplistic disaggregations of the social from the educational must be rejected. But 50 years on, as commercial and cultural globalization gather speed, the error of the USA is now the error of the world: the 'new course to the curriculum' solution has gone forth and multiplied internationally (see Wolf 2001). In this, one needs also therefore to make a plea for an international consciousness about inclusive education and its place in contemporary discourse (see Sayed 2002), for many countries of the south appear to be imposing on themselves a form of cultural imperialism as they make presumptions about the appropriateness for them of what they take to be the cutting-edge inclusive education of the west. Such a delusion is almost bound to continue if the isolation of the west's academy remains as marked as it is, with Americans in particular 'dangerously uninformed about international matters', as Fiske puts it (2005: 2).[4]

The reciprocated ignorance is damaging: the argument of this chapter is that inclusive education is meaningful only when embedded in understandings about community and society, only when seen as both reflective of, and creative of, inclusion in society. Here, far from needing to draw on western experience, certain parts of the developing world – for example Costa Rica, Sri Lanka and the Indian state of Kerala – can stand instead as exemplars to the west, much as certain parts of the developing world were identified by Paulo Freire (1972) a third of a century ago as exemplars for moves to improved literacy. We discuss these cases in more detail later in this chapter.

Progressive education versus diagnosis and disability

Simultaneous with the social and political movements that have diverted education from segregation and moved it towards inclusion have been a portfolio of significant studies that have led to a questioning of where the separative instinct of special education has directed us. For this instinct has sacrificed considerations about educational purpose and community – the kinds of consideration for which Dewey (1938) and other progressive educators pleaded throughout the twentieth century – and have substituted for these considerations diagnostic, separative and help-based solutions to failure to learn at school. Special education emerged with a superconstruct, disability, enfolding performance in learning, behaving and doing at school, complete with its own taxonomy of mild, moderate and severe manifestations, each with its own battery of putative syndromes.[5] And it developed a range of mechanical and technical remedies to the difficulties that children have supposedly confronted in respect of their learning, behaving and doing and we examined some of these in Chapters 1 and 2.

What has been borne of this diagnostic and remedial preoccupation? As we tried to show in earlier chapters, it has been less fruitful than one would have hoped. More than this, however, the deliberate distancing from wider social, cultural and educational considerations in the employment of such an approach led to unanticipated problems, as we indicated was the case with Direct Instruction. The lesson seems to be that the specific focus on deficits detracted from thought about what education is about and what it is for. If more thought had been given to how children become rounded people as part of a learning community, less credence may have been paid to the fixes that Direct Instruction and its like promised.

What the failure of the programmatic, remedial 'solutions' we discussed in Chapters 1 and 2 appears to show is that it is not diagnosis and help that are important but rather the provision of the right conditions for learning in like-minded communities. This idea should not be new to educators of the late twentieth century. The ideas of Dewey, developed independently of the Soviet psychologies of Leontiev (1978) and Vygotsky (1934/1986; 1978), both paved the way for a mushrooming interest as the century progressed in what has been called 'sociocultural theory' – what Blackler (1995) has called encultured knowledge or what Smith (1998) has more uncomplicatedly called learning in clubs. Developments continue in such ideas about the nature of learning at school and beyond (e.g. Engeström 2004; Lave and Wenger 1991; Scardamalia and Bereiter 1999), developments that share an emphasis on the centrality of meaning, narrative, apprenticeship – in short, the context and culture for learning. The message is simple: if context is wrong, learning doesn't happen.

But these developments seem to have appeared only as a blurry apparition to special education and, sadly, special education's myopia has in part been inherited by what has gone under the name of inclusive education. Special education and its offspring in inclusive education have glanced up against these ideas and bounced off, with their resilient and palatable constructs of identification, failure, disability and help emerging with hardly a scratch from the encounter. This is despite much straightforward empirical work on learning difficulty that has supported the sociocultural turn and ought to have caused some hefty self-reflective doubts about the validity of such 'difficulty' or 'disability'. We noted examples of such work in Chapter 2. For example, there is the work of Rueda and Mehan (1986), which showed that it was social interchanges that made or broke learning for children at school. Children who were labelled 'learning disabled' in fact managed to do all the things they weren't supposed to be able to do – checking, monitoring, evaluating and so on – but this was in everyday rather than scholastic activity. Rueda and Mehan conclude that the kinds of learning skill required of children at school are in fact context bound – triggered by the student's immediate social circumstances.

Hart (1996) provides similar insights on the deficit and disability perspective on failure to learn at school. Analysing the actual spelling mistakes of her own students, she rejects any idea of learning disability. One of her students, Adrian, made mistakes such as 'afared' for 'afraid', and 'wrouasem' for 'awesome'. Hart describes how she moved from assumptions about 'considerable difficulty' to the realization that Adrian's constructions represented considerable intellectual accomplishment. Far from being 'difficulties' they were the 'astonishing achievements of someone who is successfully negotiating his way through a highly complex process of hypothesis testing and generalization in relation to the workings of the writing system' (Hart 1996: 82). Alongside the insights provided by these idiographic accounts, there is also the highly detailed empirical evidence amassed by researchers such as Coles (1978; 1987; 2003) (and see also Senf 1987).

Students may switch off from school, from learning. This is why they fail. In boredom, isolation or fear other systems will kick in (as we all know from personal experience) and prevent learning (or at least prevent the achievement of the objectives that are set at school). John Holt (1964), in his inspirational vignettes of classroom failure, described these processes with great acuity. He showed, merely through appeal to our own experiences as teachers and learners, that children who find difficulty with their work at school may encounter such difficulty for a plethora of reasons, but they need the same for learning as any other child: interest, self-respect, confidence, freedom from worry, a warm and patient teacher. In short, they need inclusion in a welcoming learning community. Special education's legacy is the persisting belief that this isn't sufficient; that one needs all kinds of special procedures to help one understand and help these 'exceptional' children. The persistent return is to those elusive 'learning disabilities' despite the power of more recent insights.

It is understandable why these views should have prospered. The promises made by special, compensatory, and now, inclusive education are the bread of life for policymakers (see Power 1997; Vickers 1965). Policymakers need (and are naturally and optimistically drawn to) programmatic response that promises restoration and revival. Spend-and-cure exerts a magnetic influence on them, despite the evidence going back decades that this kind of decon-textualized, programmatic 'help' may not only be of little or no value, but may actively be doing damage – to learning and to social assimilation (Christoplos and Renz 1969; Midwinter 1977; Schweinhart and Weikart 1997; Weatherley and Lipsky 1977; and see Offord *et al.* 1999 for a discussion of the effects of intervention more generally).

Separate pedagogies built on ideas of ability and exceptionality

The interests of the earliest special educators in diagnosing and teaching separately had major consequences for the field as it detached itself and drifted away from mainstream education, to develop its own discrete ecology. And the ecology has to an extent been retained by inclusive educators – in a separa-tion of thinking, if no more – from mainstream educators. That ecology was formed in the early psychologies of Wundt and Thorndike in their searches for laws about basic learning that stripped out concern for context, language and interest – stripped out, in other words, everything that makes human learning unique. It was rooted in the psychology of William James, who tried (and failed) to boost his 'memory muscle' by doing memory exercises. It was rooted in the work of the early psychometricians, who sought 'scientific' ways of identifying difference. It had established itself in a state of self-exile from the mainstream, where it relied on a psychology that particularized and com-partmentalized learning and said that failure to learn represented some kind of disability.

The central construct on which such psychology and the pedagogy of exceptionality was built was that of ability. And it is from the construct of ability, of course, that the idea of learning disability found its origins. McClelland (1973), writing more than 30 years ago and referring to the 1958 Social Science Research Council Committee on Early Identification of Talent (McClelland *et al.* 1958), noted, even then, that powerful criticisms of the notion of intelligence, general ability and the testing movement were not new. The committee had, as long ago as the 1950s, recorded clear theoretical and empirical objections to the validity of the notion of ability. There is no doubt that the understandings recorded there and, subsequently, dented educators' faith in intelligence measurement and particularly IQ, but they had less evident influence on underlying beliefs about ability per se.

The deep-seated beliefs of which McClelland was critical posit a simple relationship between something largely constitutional, namely ability or intelligence, and its consequence, namely attainment. Ability leads to attainment. Lack of ability leads to lack of attainment. Simple. The assumptions here have, of course, been acutely critiqued by Ericsson and Delaney (1999), Gould (1981) and Howe (1990) among many others and recently large-scale international analyses of trends in intelligence have demonstrated again how tenuous the notion of constitutional ability is: Dickens and Flynn (2001) have shown how gains of more than a whole standard deviation in IQ occurred between 1952 and 1982 in cohorts of 18 year olds, revealing the significance of large-scale environmental effects over and above those of supposed constitutional difference. Wahlstein (1997) interestingly discusses the plasticity of IQ in findings such as this and the reasons for the significance of environment for the development of IQs.

Despite such analyses (as McClelland might have predicted) the resilient beliefs about which the US committee on talent were critical nearly 50 years ago still abound today (see, for example, Spencer's 2004 discussion, and the claims of Herrnstein and Murray 1994). These beliefs about ability have had, and continue to have, a disproportionately weighty influence in special education and, latterly, inclusive education. The reason for the persistence in these views about ability lies in the field's reliance on a particular psychology of learning. The field has been embedded in a psychology that was on a different train line from twentieth-century discussions about learning. The route on which the rest of education has been travelling has been described well by Olson and Bruner (1996: 11), whose thrust is that our own species shows an 'astonishingly strong' predisposition to culture and a sensitivity and eagerness to follow the 'folkways' of people around them. Or, as Premack and Premack (1996: 303) put it, in calling for an anthropology of pedagogy to replace the sterile, meaning-deprived psychology of learning that dominated much of twentieth-century psychology: 'Humans have pedagogy while animals do not.'

Inclusive educators, while acknowledging and disavowing the mistakes of their predecessors in special education, often still share their worldview – not so much eschewing the insights of the new 'cultural' psychology as somehow not seeing it. Inclusive and special educators share a concern for seeing what's wrong, putting right, for bringing to order, for correcting, albeit that the focus has conspicuously moved from the student to the school in the reappraisals that have led to the shift toward inclusive education. The school-centred focus, however, often happens within identical curricular and learning frames. The assumption may now be that the school rather than the student has gone wrong, but this is still within a framework of exceptionality, special need, disability, disadvantage – and, of course, the antidote: help. The language of need out of which ideas are built about learning 'disability' or problem behaviour therefore induces procedural responses within static institutional and curricular parameters. It mechanically induces a set of actions from the school and its support services, but these are more like minor reflexive spasms than changes of direction. They are bureaucratic shows of willing built within pedagogic walls that remain sturdily in place – despite the periodic buffeting from the ideas of progressive educators. Skrtic (1991: 165) calls these procedural and professional responses and reflexes 'symbols and ceremonies', since they do nothing to alter the central direction of response of the school in its attitude to teaching and learning.

Perhaps worse, however, these symbols and ceremonies distract attention from discussion about what is expected of education. Indeed, the presence of a special facility, whatever it be labelled – 'inclusive education', 'special education', 'compensatory education', 'learning support' or something else – detracts from an intelligent reappraisal of the natures of learning and pedagogy for all.

Where, among inclusive educators, are calls for a turn toward progressive education, to the direction of context and culture, to the arguments posed by Dewey, Vygotsky and Holt? While there has been serious engagement with the 'effective schools' movement, this has not been matched by engagement with the new 'cultural pedagogy'. Inclusive education has to become more than a synonym for special systems in mainstream schools, more than a peripheral dimension to mainstream education. The argument so far in this book is that children's success or failure at school is due less to 'learning disabilities' and more to an array of factors around which acceptance and inclusion are constructed. Recent critiques have foregrounded the place of the school as a social institution in 'constructing' learning difficulty, but have not often offered insights into general processes underlying this. Notable examples of exceptions exist in Artiles (2003), Benjamin (2003), Ferguson *et al.* (1992) and Tomlinson (1985) in examining factors such as race or gender in the process of construction.

These analyses are crucial and we agree that this process of construction is indeed made by race, gender and other discretely identifiable issues. The question to be answered is how these characteristics – race, disability, gender, etc. – influence individuals' learning in the school. How is difficulty in learning constructed out of these and other characteristics? We posit that difficulty is constructed out of disruptions in learning caused by discomfort, alienation, fear, hostility, mistrust and that if schools are not vigilant they can be breeding grounds for such phenomena. Once such phenomena have done their work in generating difference, the school can make contrastive judgements that exaggerate the differences (and we examine this and a 'psychology of difference' in the next section). With the convenient attribution of difficulty in learning to certain stereotypes, it is easy to downplay the influence of the broad disruptions to which we are pointing.

This is particularly so where government edict across the world in the name of 'standards' forces such alienation and mistrust. The celebrated children's author Philip Pullman (2005) has noted anxiously that formalization of language teaching in the National Curriculum means that children aged 7 to 11 years have to be taught 'the grammatical functions of words [and] the grammar of complex sentences, including clauses, phrases and connectives'. Pullman's comment on this: 'Think of the age of those children and weep.'

It is such experiences that led John Holt (1977) to describe schools as 'prisons', bereft of any hope for enabling the kind of creativity or learning necessary for life in the real world. Continuing in this tradition, Frank Smith (1995; 1998), paints a picture of many student experiences at school being 'fruitless and punishing' (Smith 1998: 1), asserting that learning at school must be based on meaningful experiences through immersion in communities of learning and practice or being part of a club. The idea of the 'club' is crucial to learning in the kind of inclusive community that we are suggesting here. Stripping away the jargon of contemporary educational discourse on learning, Smith makes it clear that it is acceptance, self-respect and doing things together in a meaningful, comfortable setting that is essential to real learning. We should worry less about teaching, Smith argues, with its mechanical 'solutions' to failure to learn that inevitably miss the mark. We should pay more attention to experiences of social learning and doing. This, of course, is in the Vygotskian ([1934] 1986) tradition of social learning and it is to this that we shall tie ideas on community in the final section of this chapter.

The conclusion one can come to on the basis of the arguments and evidence so far presented is that the supposed 'learning disabilities' from which many children were presumed to have suffered represented the effects of certain kinds of difference – not lack of intelligence or disability. They represent what one might call a closure on learning, wherein self-appraisal occurring via comparison of oneself with others brings on detachment and an identity of failure. So doing, it invokes the alienation that breeds the boredom, disinterest and anxiety that inhibit learning.

Why has such understanding not been assimilated by the inclusive education community? It has been realized since the 1920s and Gordon's (1923) studies of canal boat children in the UK, or Wheeler's (1970) similar studies of, and findings about, 'mountain children' in the USA, that it was cultural milieu rather than any inborn characteristic that determined a child's success at school. As Leyden (1978) has pointed out, it was the endemic constructs of special education (and latterly inclusive education) that promulgated the belief that it was ability (and disability) – not poverty, difference or life experience – that was the principal force at play in determining such success or failure. Sadly, such beliefs about ability are still not only extant but thriving, propagated often by powerful vested interests (see Claxton 2005 for a lively discussion of beliefs about ability and Coles 2000; 2003 for an exposé of some of the vested interests).

Recent epidemiological work confirms these narratives about failure. The work of Blane *et al.* (1996), looking at the link between school performance and deprivation showed that the relationship is so close that the two variables appear to be simply alternative measures of the same thing. In the same vein, Singer and Ryff (1997) counter the hereditarian Bell Curve arguments of Herrnstein and Murray (1994) by showing how ethnic and class inequalities related to differences in education, money and power define exposure to adversity and, in turn, how a person wins or loses.

If identity, poverty and difference are so important, what has the research of recent years told of their significance in causing failure at school? This recent research has given a more sophisticated and nuanced picture of poverty's effects and one that stresses inequalities rather than absolute deficiencies: inequalities in status, in opportunity and in experience as well as in capital. It appears that inequality creates a complex of factors around one's identity and self-respect that in some way deconstruct one's ability to thrive in a community of learning. It is to this issue of inequality that we now turn in a search for the implications for inclusive education – as evinced both in educational policy and classroom practice.

Inequality, relative poverty and contrastive judgement

In the previous section, we discussed the inertness of traditional ways of thinking about exceptionality. In this section, we review some recent discussion about the effects of inequality, especially work that gives some clue to the mechanism of poverty's influence. This work enables a comparative lens to be put to the question of inclusion. Emphasizing the very great reductions in absolute material deprivation of late, especially in the west, it points to the effects on identity that relative poverty and difference bring and thus suggests a causal connection between the ways that children feel about themselves at school and what in the previous section we called 'closure on learning'.

There are all kinds of influences at school that may affect one's identity and these influences, if our argument so far is valid, are more important for success at school than more straightforwardly pedagogic or curricular matters. We go on to suggest that promoting inclusiveness – promoting, in other words, the kind of environment that positively affects self-worth – is at the heart of the reduction of failure. In this section, we shall argue that inclusivity can be promoted both at school and at wider community levels and that both efforts operate, as it were, reciprocally: inclusive schools are likely to produce better achievement, more cohesive communities and healthier people and more inclusive communities are likely to produce better schools.

Gradient effects – clues to a 'psychology of difference'

Keating and Hertzman (1999: 3), in summarizing a range of epidemiological research, talk of a 'gradient effect', by which they mean the extent to which social differences exist between members of a population. They discuss the importance of this effect in generating contentment (or otherwise), with the important point being that the greater the difference existing between members of a population, the greater the unease, mistrust and discontent existing there. They put it thus: 'Particularly striking is the discovery of a strong associa-tion between the health of a population and the size of the social distance between members of the population. We have come to describe this as "the gradient effect".'

Many commentators in the fields of political science and economics have tapped into these understandings, stressing the mechanism by which differ-ence appears to cause difficulty. That mechanism exists in the sequelae of contrast and it represents, if you like, a new 'psychology of difference'. When contrasts exist beyond a certain point and if the structures in a society make no attempt to ameliorate the extent of those contrasts, alienation, hostility and mistrust are experienced. Layard (2003), for example, suggests that content-ment and inclusion are related more to comparisons between income, rather than absolute amounts of income. He notes: 'To a large extent we want things and experiences because other people have them' (2003: 14). Hirsch (1977) argued similarly that beyond a certain level of comfort, all consumption is positional, with the consequence that people are trapped in self-defeating cycles of desire and dissatisfaction. Easterlin (1974), Dennis (1997), Sen (1992) and Vickers (1965) have made similar arguments and all rest essentially in the gradient effect.

Keating and Hertzman make the point that the gradient effect has its con-sequences in education as well as health: 'This gradient effect [obtains] not only for physical and mental health but also for a wide range of other devel-opmental outcomes, from behavioural adjustment, to literacy, to mathematics achievement.' Chiu and Khoo (2005) confirm the existence of the phenome-non in education on a range of measures of achievement: students' achieve-ment is worse in countries with larger distribution inequalities and students in countries with greater 'privileged student bias' have lower overall achievement. Countries distributing funding more equally (such as Finland, Hong Kong and South Korea) perform best on a range of achievement outcomes.[6]

It is important to re-emphasize that the significant ingredient in notions of gradient lies in inequality: it is about the differences that exist and their magnitude and visibility. It is these differences that have impact on a whole range of outcomes and Willms (1999a) reports important findings about the significance of gradient for education. Willms examined associations between parent education and child literacy in different OECD countries – including Sweden, the Netherlands, Canada, the USA and Poland – and in different US states. He found that where parents themselves were highly educated (measured by number of years in education), literacy levels of their offspring differed least, so children with highly educated parents performed equally well in each country. But for less educated parents, advantage went to the Swedes and Dutch, with Americans and Poles performing worst. Findings are similar inside the USA, with children of less educated parents in southern states performing worse than equivalent children in northern states.

After reviewing more studies about school effects (e.g. Ho and Willms 1996) Willms suggests why this might be so – why, in other words, the children of less educated parents do better in Sweden, for example, than in the USA. One of the central conclusions is about gradient: 'When students are segregated, either between classes or tracks within schools or between schools within a community, students . . . from disadvantaged backgrounds do worse' (Willms 1999b: 85). He notes that such segregation may come from many and varied directions: from special programmes for 'gifted' children to phenomena such as charter or magnet schools. By contrast, he notes approvingly that attempts have been made in some areas for school restructuring that moves away from such segregative measures to initiatives for curricular restructuring, parental participation and site-based governance. He also suggests that the beneficial influences operating in low-gradient places may be in the way parents are encouraged to relate to the school in governance and as volunteers, a point made also by Vincent (2000). The World Bank (1999) has brought together a range of statistics that support Willms's case: when parents and local citizens are actively involved, says the Bank, 'Teachers are more committed, students achieve higher test scores, and better use is made of school facilities in those communities where parents and citizens take an active interest in children's educational well-being.'

If these analyses are correct, the relationship between the gradient effect and inclusive education is crucial and it is two way. In societies with greater inequality and less inclusion, there is lower achievement at school and there are more casualties of the school system, as Keating and Hertzman and others have shown. But also, from the work of Willms one sees that there is evidence that greater inclusion (or, by contrast, segregation) in the education system itself influences the gradient effect. The effect is, in other words, reciprocal and manipulable. There is therefore hope of influencing the effect not only in national policy but also in local practice, and such influencing should form a central plank of twenty-first century inclusive education.

The latter conclusion is supported by the work of medical epidemiologist Michael Marmot (2004: 187). From reviewing a broad body of work, he has indicated that an inclusive society will depend in part on an inclusive education and it will result in the better contentedness, health and welfare of its inhabitants.

The comparative and epidemiological work referred to so far has been in the west, but it is important to note also that there is evidence for the gradient effect operating internationally as well as within rich nations. There is, for example, the work of Caldwell (1986), who examined the correlation between gross national product per head and infant mortality. A high correlation was expected and revealed. However, by focusing on the exceptions – countries (or states within countries) with lower rates of infant mortality than would be predicted from their level of income, notably the Indian state of Kerala – Caldwell came to a more interesting finding as far as inclusion is concerned. It is this to which we now turn.

Benefits of being valued and included

The best predictor of such exceptional performance, Caldwell noted, was the level of women's education. It is not difficult to see why there may be a causal relation between mothers' education and an outcome such as low infant mortality. Yet in Kerala, good health is not confined to infants. Life expectancy, too, is far better in Kerala than in other regions of India. The conclusion to be arrived at is that the women's education may be causally important not just because women may know more about, say, nutrition and development for babies, but also because women are valued and included – something more intangible but nonetheless seemingly just as significant. Thus, the provision of education for all seems to be operating at two levels: it is providing for individual knowledge, but it is also symbolic of society's affirmation of once-marginalized groups and its endorsement of those groups' participation and inclusion (see also Cremin 2007; Noddings 2005). So in some way this provision seems to be endowing added value. Perhaps this value-added comes in the form of a boost for identity, status, belonging and self-belief. Inclusion, and the status it brings, breeds not only health but also the conditions for learning and growth to occur.

Amartya Sen (1999: 45–8) describes the process operating in Kerala as a 'support-led' approach to improvement in life conditions: 'The support-led process does not operate through fast economic growth, but works through a program of skilful social support of health care, education and other relevant social arrangements.' He points out that despite their very low levels of income, the people of Kerala and Sri Lanka enjoy far higher levels of life expectancy than do the much richer populations of Brazil and South Africa.

Comparison: the root of judgements about ability, difficulty and disability

Ideas about relative status, identity, belonging and self-belief appear to us to have currency far beyond the ambit of econometric discussion and making for a new psychology of difference. These ideas – the new psychology of difference – provide an armature around which play a host of new possibilities for understanding children's difficulties at school. One can suggest that the alienation and exclusion experienced by students are constructed largely out of comparison – the comparison of each student herself or himself with others and the institutional endorsement of such comparison by teachers and other professionals. The point to be made is that it is not so much absolute standards of ability that are important for assessing learning 'disability', as perceptions concerning relative status.

The resilience of notions of ability despite the force of empirical evidence and rational argument to contradict them was noted in the first section of this chapter. Here, we go further to suggest that their seemingly irreversible crystal-lization in the public mind can be explained in terms of their value in comparative assessment. Inside the assessing systems of schools there are, in fact, few objective standards and in their absence there remains for judgement of difficulty or success little more than the comparison of one student with another. It is on such comparisons – no more and no less – that notions of ability rest and are perpetuated.

Comparison is at the core of ability assessment. The notions of ability and disability in special and inclusive education were elevated by the supposedly scientific study and measurement of intelligence, measurement that reified the comparative elements of judgement about ability. Measurement in times past when the instinct to separate seemed uncontentious thus provided a rational basis for segregation. Worryingly, however, in our notionally inclusive educational world it still provides a process for enabling and legitimizing the differentiation, hierarchization, comparison and judgement of students. Perceptions of 'difficulty' or 'disability' are thus constructed around and within discourses of comparison – around normality and abnormality, success and failure, the functional and the dysfunctional; they do not take place in some inert empirical universe.

The same comparative processes that operate in judgements about ability have also occurred, and still occur, with behaviour 'disturbance'. Where difficult behaviour is concerned – in contrast to learning difficulty – there has been a long tradition of study into processes of labelling and exclusion and their origins in comparison – of the effects of placing students in hierarchies. Much of this understanding originated in the analyses of Cohen (1955) and Matza (1964), who were unsatisfied with pre-existing theory that proposed more materially related explanations for delinquency. Instead, Cohen looked to status, comparison and identity to account for delinquent acts. He described a process of status denial that tacitly exists in schools and in wider society for certain young males who lack the means to acquire socially approved forms of status. These young men thus experienced what he called 'status frustration', collectively reacting against standards to which they could not measure up. Crucially, however, they still strove for status and worked to define their own forms of status. Hargreaves (1967), Willis (1977) and subsequent labelling theorists have described similar phenomena, as has Delpit (1988) in her analysis of the ways in which power relations affect the identity of minority groups at school. In a range of recent studies, Steele and his colleagues (e.g. Cohen *et al.* 1999) have shown that what they call 'stereotype threat' – simply recognizing that others could judge you based on a cultural stereotype – can have serious effects on identity and learning.

How do hierarchies and status affect identity in such a way that ability to learn and even health are dramatically affected? Marmot (2004) puts the mechanism down to the complex set of relations that exist among inequality, hierarchy, cooperation and control over one's own life. He suggests: 'There is a large body of literature [referring to Sapolsky 1999] supporting the importance of these five characteristics – control, predictability, degree of support, threat to status, and presence of outlets – that modulate the impact of a psychologically threatening stimulus' (2004: 114). This last, the threatening stimulus, is conspicuously found in the judgemental environment, with its contrasts and comparisons, created in much of today's state-regulated education. The need is to give back respect, identity and control to those inhabiting the institutions that we create for them or to ask serious questions about the suitability of those institutions for a large minority of young people and we touch on this latter point later.

How might comparisons be amplified or attenuated by the school? There are school-related answers that we have noted already. But there are surely ways that one can proceed that go beyond strategic algorithms to more broad-ranging policy change. Among these considerations – one that is discussed by Willms (1999b) – is the construction of 'social capital' and it is this to which we now turn.

Social connection, communities of learning, social capital for learning and inclusion

Social capital

Although a range of social commentators (e.g. Bourdieu 1983; Coleman 1988; Hanifan 1916; 1920) have used the term social capital, it is Putnam (1995; 2000) whose analyses have set debate alight. Putnam discusses (2000: 19) social capital as the connectedness among people, the 'social networks and the norms of reciprocity and trustworthiness that arise from them'. Reviewing research relating to social capital in 35 countries, Putnam (1995: 73) had noted that across those nations, social trust and civic engagement were strongly correlated, with a general trend to decline in such phenomena. He notes a widespread decline in social participation in the USA, from voting in elections to trusting people on the street.

Putnam's analyses were not the first to bring this decline in trust and engagement to the fore. In 1969 the celebrated developmental psychologist Urie Bronfenbrenner testified to a US congressional committee about evidence of a breakdown in ways of 'making human beings human' (Bronfenbrenner 1969: 1838). There existed, he said, evidence of increasing alienation, apathy, rebellion, delinquency and violence. Thirty years later he again noted increases: 'Today they have reached a critical stage that is much more difficult to reverse . . . [with] growing chaos in the lives of children and youth' (Bronfenbrenner *et al.* 1996: viii–ix).

Putnam and Bronfenbrenner were both discussing forms of exclusion. The interesting feature of Putnam's discussion is the light it shines on new kinds of exclusivity and inclusivity. He distinguishes between bonding (that is to say, exclusive) and bridging (inclusive) social capital, each of which can be seen in forms of school organization. Bonding will reinforce particular reciprocities, exclusive identities, conformity, small-mindedness, solidarity and exclusion – called the 'dark side' of community by Noddings (1996: 258) – while bridging social capital will be more outward looking:

> Bridging networks, by contrast [to bonding ones], are better for linkage to external assets and for information diffusion . . . and can generate broader identities and reciprocity, whereas bonding social capital bolsters our narrower selves . . . Bonding social capital constitutes a kind of sociological superglue, whereas bridging social capital provides a sociological WD40.
>
> (Putnam 2000: 22–3)

One can see how bridging and bonding could be encouraged or discouraged by the school (see also Linehan and McCarthy 2001; Winkelmann 1991).

Bridging could be promoted by 'WD40' activities such as Circle Time, by the encouragement of sharing and cooperative activities, for example the 'jigsaw groups' of Aaronson and Bridgeman (1979), the 'reciprocal teaching' of Palincsar *et al.* (1993) or the 'peer mediation' described by Cremin (2002; 2007). One might go further to posit that more fundamental within-school norms and beliefs lie behind such encouragement and connectedness – beliefs in equal potential, in respect and recognition for all. The less desirable 'bonding' would be encouraged through 'house' formation, organized competition, token economies, etc. The active and explicit fostering of community in the school is discussed in a range of contexts and recent developments (see, for example, Bennacer 2000; Berry 2006; Carreiro King 2003; Cornelius and Herrenkohl 2004; Lucas and Thomas 2000; Parsons *et al.* 2006).

Declines in trust and reciprocity – the fragmentation which Bauman (2000) discusses – are patently occurring. However, fragmentation is clearly not what people want: in a mobile and increasingly disconnected society, people are seeking connections to community and to narratives through the history of that community and the school's place in this is manifest. In the UK, around one-third of the adult population is registered on the website Friends Reunited, which links people together on the basis of their old school (see BBC 2005b). A school in the centre of London, Elliot School, is the UK school with the highest number of its ex-students on the website. Victor Burgess, the head of Elliot School puts this down to what he sees as a change in the way that schools are coming to be seen. New communities, he suggests, are forming where others have broken up or are changing. In the new communities contact is intercultural, interclass and interracial. It happens more in cities precisely because social life is so fragmented and mobile there. There is thus a deliberate seeking of community, where people are looking for history, and trying to build narratives about community. They are doing this via the medium of school.

Crucially, the establishment of identity through such links is bound up with the ability to learn. Lave and Wenger (1991: 84) see:

> participation in a community of practice as central for increasing understanding and identity . . . Whether activity or language is the central issue, the important point concerning learning is one of access to practice as resource for learning, rather than to instruction. Issues of motivation, identity, and language deserve further discussion.

The important link here, as we come to the concluding part of this chapter are the connections between motivation, identity and learning. Learning, and the putative 'failure' of learning, come down to social processes that arise in the course of doing things socially. If one is involved, included, feeling on an equal par, one will learn. If not, one won't – and this tallies keenly with Paulo Freire's (1972) insistence that education is to be found in the lived experience of participants, where people work with each other rather than on one another. School rarely provides a place for that lived experience in the sense that Freire meant and this raises again for educators the virtually ignored potential of the workplace as another community of learning. It should inspire in twenty-first-century inclusive policy a reappraisal of the place of the workplace in learning and what we mean in practice by communities of learning.

Human rights

It is important briefly to discuss the human rights dimension to arguments for inclusion.

Much discussion of inclusive education rests in the foregrounding of human rights. Yet, as many have commented (e.g. Fish 1994), a major weakness of such an approach is that rights are never commensurable: my rights may conflict with your rights and there is no way of weighing up the relative value of our claims. Economist Richard Layard (2005) has recently discussed a solution to the dilemmas that emerge from rights-based thinking, taking his inspiration from the utilitarianism of Jeremy Bentham. He suggests – and here his argument has strong connections with the arguments of Putnam and Marmot – that dimensions of contentment and fulfilment having their roots in participation, social connection and relationships with others should take precedence over rights in determining social policy. He notes that a rights discourse predisposes its users to individualistic concerns, and that 'intense individualism has failed to make us happier'. He asserts that a re-emphasis on the tenets of utilitarianism – the contentment and happiness of all, or 'the utility principle' – will be realized only in a society in which all are respected and included (see also Kitayama and Marcus 2000).

Clearly the school is crucial in this process of encouraging respect for all and Layard's discussion forces an elevation of its importance over that of individual rights, which has been the recent preoccupation of many inclusive educators. While the contemporary discussion of rights has been essential in stressing the entitlements of marginalized and disenfranchised students, it has simultaneously forced a predication of the significance of community for every student's benefit.

Respect and affirmation

Self-respect and the affirmation of one's place in a community of learners seem to be the *sine qua non* of success, in whatever terms, at school. Recently, I (GT) observed an incident in a classroom that demonstrated this to me quite forcibly. The teacher had the Year 3 children around her, sitting on the floor in a big group. 'Who can think of a word beginning with "s"?' Hands shot up. 'Yes, Joey,' said the teacher. 'Circus,' said Joey. Half-suppressed whoops of enthusiasm from the children greeted the error while hands were thrust even harder into the air: it looked as if shoulders would be dislocated. Joey was gently corrected and the teacher moved to another child. But when chosen, instead of answering, Matthew said nothing. His lungs deflated, his arm dropped and he reddened. His whole body and persona seemed punctured. 'Don't put your hand up if you don't know the answer, Matthew,' the teacher said, and moved on again. My gaze, when it returned to Matthew, saw a child alone and deflated – ready, it seemed, to lose confidence in himself as a learner.

Anyone who knows classrooms will have witnessed such scenes. Loss of affirmation, identity and respect can make for emotion akin to grief. They may be young children and almost desperate in their eagerness to please or they may be older students who seek peers' approval through clowning or aggression. Whichever, respect is vital for worth, inclusion, belonging.

The identity and respect that are so vital are made by the school's ability to promote community, connectedness, humanity, settledness, trust and the argument in this concluding section is for these as principally important features of a more comprehensive notion of inclusion.

As we noted in Chapter 7, Taylor (1992) has pointed to such phenomena and Fraser (1996) has interestingly linked a contemporary lack of absolute poverty in societies of the west to new kinds of injustice, which themselves are rooted in status. In raising the issue of status – and the significance of the hierarchy in its establishment – she takes the analysis to the level of the organization and the institution in legitimating comparative assessments. Moving away from what she describes as a Rawlsian logic of redistributive justice she notes that it is now recognition that is more important than redistribution, as absolute levels of physical well-being rise. Exactly the same is true for education: when, for example, absolute levels of attainment rise, it is recognition and identity that become most important for children's success.

Non-recognition and disrespect arise from the way that comparisons are not merely untempered by the processes of education, but are actively encouraged by its discourses and processes. Non-recognition and disrespect arise from the way that schools handle existing inequalities between children. Dash's (1998) recent narrative of the urban underclass in Washington DC illustrates the point that Fraser makes – that self-confidence, pride, dignity and an obsession with respect (summarized in the idea of 'cool') are crucial for those who have been consistently dismissed or excluded by the education system and by wider society.

The key issue is whether schools exaggerate or attenuate inequalities between their students and the contrasts that potentially follow, as Sennett (2003) has argued. Drawing on his own upbringing in Chicago's infamous Cabrini Green housing project, Sennett suggests that practices that highlight differences in personal ability will result in the erosion of civic solidarity and community. For inequalities thus to be diminished, recognition and respect have to be at the front of our minds in planning what goes on in schools. If contrastive judgement is as significant a player in the construction of difficulty and exclusion as we are suggesting it to be, providing for inclusion is about making a seedbed for recognition and respect by systematically minimizing such judgement.

The alternative to a respect-based system is one based on what a range of commentators have seen as degrading forms of compassion and forms of labelling such as 'learning disability' or 'special needs' that are intended to be kindly but which act as what Corbett (1996) has called 'sugar-coated poison'. Sennett (2003) agrees, in perceiving what he calls 'degrading' forms of compassion, compassion that is, as Midwinter (1977) and Skrtic (1991) have pointed out, amplified by professional and institutional responses to children's difficulty – responses that inhibit structural change in schools and demobilize community response.

None of this is to espouse an illusion that some students will not find less facility with schoolwork than others. Neither is it to suggest that processes of self and institutional comparison are not to be expected. One central suggestion is, however, being made: that notions such as ability and disturbance should continually be interrogated by a community of practitioners, researchers and academics in education. Difference where it exists can be celebrated, just as we try to find ways of neutralizing and suppressing elements of institutional habit, organization and policy that casually employ instruments of comparison without a view to the consequences for children's self-respect as members of learning communities at school and at work.

How should we proceed?

Inclusive education needs to take a radical turn from its twentieth-century course. The twenty-first century needs inclusive educators – all educators – to focus on the nature of learning in schools and why learning so readily closes down there. Inclusive educators must uncouple from the resolutely deficit-oriented history of exceptionality and mesh instead with contemporary currents of thinking on the ways in which children learn or fail to learn.

We have talked here of two psychologies of learning with which we feel inclusive educators are failing to engage. First, there are new models of learning that stress the centrality of community, with an emphasis on meaning, narrative, apprenticeship – in short, the context and culture for learning. And, second, there is what we have called a new 'psychology of difference' (emerging in a so far quite uncoordinated way from a variety of social sciences) that tells of a strong connection between what students feel about themselves in communities and how they learn. What both of these largely untapped streams of thought bring home is that the focus has now to be on communities of learning and how students are constructed as members of such communities through processes of comparison and judgement.

Bringing the lessons of these new models into its consciousness promises important benefits for inclusive education in the contemporary world. If, in this world – the new modernity about which Bauman (1995) has written – there are increases in the number of situations in which one feels lost, confused and disempowered, school can surely act as a counterculture. Those who work in education can take action at national, regional and local levels to change the policies, discourses and habits of school managers, education administrators and legislators. Our argument thus for a broader theoretical base for inclusive education is made in the hope of inducing pedagogical and organizational changes in education, changes that will foster community, participation and respect for all.

How can this be done in practice? It is perhaps easiest to begin with what should not be done and here it seems clear that to continue to proffer programmatic initiatives – involving ascertainment, evaluation and solution – is inappropriate. Such programmatic initiative, following the contours of much twentieth-century thinking about exceptionality, views inclusion as being about things to be put right, either in individual or school-related terms. As a strategy for tackling failure at school it has been less than successful.

What, then, should be done? First, we can **reject simplistic explanations of failure** in the deficit syndromes of special education and move to the scholar practitioner model of Reid and Valle (2005). Reid and Valle make the point that basic forms of knowledge – personal, tacit knowledge – that teachers possess must be reinstated over those that trace their lineage to the kinds of scientistic thinking examined in Chapters 1 and 2 of this book. They say that teachers need to approach their work as *scholar practitioners* and that they need to pick up again the tools of critical enquiry – 'observation, conferencing, and interviewing; generating anecdotal records; taking and analyzing field notes; constructing sociograms, analyzing student work and portfolios'. We can reject simplistic explanations of failure also from the recent teacher-blaming narratives propagated by central governments. Thomson (2002), for example, after a study of Australian schools in 'rustbelt' districts, is disdainful of such explanations and moves beyond to the lives of the individuals concerned and the communities in which they live. Central to her analysis is the reciprocity involved in the health of the school and the community and the ways in which communities nest one within another. As one primary school head said in Thomson's study: 'When the secondary school closed, bus routes went', pointing to the symbiosis involved in school and community activity and the cycle of decline involved when either party is hit.

We can look also at the **content of some of our educational enterprises** and the emotions that they induce in most students. We can consider Holt's (1977) injunction to restructure education such that it ceases to become what he suggested was a place cut off from ordinary life where work was done under pressure of bribe, threat, greed and fear. Noddings (2005) suggests radical changes to the curriculum that involve teaching mutually supportive interaction by helping students to develop 'response-ability'. Echoing John Dewey, Lawrence Cremin and Paulo Freire, she makes a case for education to return to 'aims talk'. One notes the need for this internationally as the sometimes disastrous consequences of copycat educational policy become evident in the countries of the south imitating the policy of the west (see Harber 2004).

The school and the community can be seen as **equal partners** in education – in establishing communities of learning and practice – and on this assumption educators could begin to re-examine some of the shibboleths of a century of educational policy, policy that has seen school-leaving ages inexorably rise across the world and a proliferation of certificated learning accompanied by false suppositions (see Wolf 2001) about the benefits of institutional schooling. With community and school seen in partnership, young people – especially the 40–50 per cent whom the system most conspicuously fails – could be freer to make seamless movements between the one and the other through, for example, organized systems of apprenticeships and mentorships developed by school and work community in tandem. The world of work should not be seen as a place in which learning stops.

We can note what **gradient effects** tell us about school organization and the unwelcome consequences that analysts tell us come from deliberate differentiation or segregation of any kind, whether that differentiation originates in special action for 'gifted' children or from innovations such as 'magnet' schools. We can **encourage parental participation and student voice** as ways of promoting effective communities of learning. We can look for ways in which routine comparison may be minimized inside the school, for in many cases the school exaggerates the effects of student comparison of self with others and leads to alienation and closure on learning. In the classroom, we can employ Putnam's nice analogy of 'WD40' action to promote bridging – **action that encourages cooperation, sharing, debate** and the involvement of all.

Last, and at the largest level, teachers, researchers and academics can engage with and **challenge local and national policy** that acts to exaggerate difference. Rarely is concerted action taken against local or national legislatures to challenge unjust or inappropriate measures, instituted by politicians on populist platforms such as 'improving standards'. Teachers may feel powerless in these arenas but DeMoss (2003: 61) reviews evidence which – in the USA, at least – shows that such action can help to decrease disparities, whether or not plaintiffs directly succeed in their claims. She notes: 'States seem to respond to the pressures that litigation places on them to take a closer look at the ways they fund education.'

Inclusive education is meaningful only when embedded in understandings about community and society and these understandings go well beyond inclusive education's current and historical preoccupations. If certain children become marginalized from schooling and experience what we have called a 'closure on learning', the mechanisms of closure need to be examined closely. Those mechanisms, this chapter has argued, are about loss of identity and respect in a community of learning. While affirmative action is essential to help prevent the alienation of certain groups of children from school, it is not enough.

Summary

Inclusive educators should now, twenty years after the beginnings of inclusive education, take stock of progress and move on, for radical reappraisal of theory and practice is now possible. We argue that inclusive educators often continue to pay allegiance to the traditions of special education, relying on views about exceptionality that ought to have been exiled on the emergence of recent models of learning that stress the importance of identity in a community. Most learning disability, learning difficulty and much challenging behaviour in school in fact represents what we here call 'closure on learning' in such a community rather than any distinctive disability. Alongside the lessons from these contemporary models of learning, there exists new discourse on the consequences of difference that throws fresh light on the factors that disadvantage students at school – there is a new 'psychology of difference' emerging from work in varied social scientific fields that gives insights on the mechanisms by which inequality, relative poverty and contrastive judgement construct learning difficulties. Inclusive education needs to take account of these new understandings – to appreciate the ways in which difference leads to alienation from community, which in turn leads to closure on learning. Recognizing the importance of community for learning, inclusive educators can now shift their gaze to the ways in which the school abstains from encouraging community structure and in fact does much through its routines (for example, of assessment and comparison) inadvertently to damage communities of learning. The future contribution of the inclusive educator pivots around the ability to retreat from histories of diagnosis and help and to begin looking at the ways in which schools enable community and encourage students' belief in themselves as members of such community – belief in themselves as learners.

Notes

1 This is legislation such as the Individual with Disabilities Act (IDEA, PL101-476), in the USA, and the Education Acts of 1993 and 2001 in the UK, all of which explicitly talk about the integration in the context of disability.

2 The shift of focus sometimes seems only notional as official figures (US Department of Education 1998) show that the number of children with 'learning disabilities' rose from 757,213 in 1978 to 1,745,871 in 1982 to 2,748,497 in 1997–8.

3 It is significant that this happened when it did, just after the Second World War. Note that there had been six such attempts to desegregate beforehand.

4 Although internally the USA has great heterogeneity in its cultures and languages, ignorance of other cultures seems rife (Fiske 2005), with one-quarter of college-bound high school students not knowing the name of the ocean that separates the United States from Asia (Center for International Understanding 2005: 2).

5 It is worth looking, for example, at Beech and Singleton (1997) where developmental dyslexia is divided not only into developmental surface dyslexia and developmental phonological dyslexia but also into dyseidectic, dysphoneidectic and dysphonetic dyslexias – and even, believe it or not, mixed dysphonetic-dyseidectic dyslexia-alexia.

6 In the USA funding per student varies widely – by a factor of 25, as a result of local and national variations and alumni variation (Rothstein 2000).

References

Aaronson, E. and Bridgeman, D. (1979) 'Jigsaw groups and the desegregated classroom: in pursuit of common goals', *Personality and Social Psychology Bulletin*, 5: 438–46.

Abberley, P. (1987) 'The concept of oppression and the development of a social theory of disability', *Disability, Handicap and Society*, 2(1): 5–19.

Abdelnoor, A. (1999) *Preventing Exclusions*. London: Heinemann.

Alexander, R. (1984) *Primary Teaching*. London: Holt.

Allan, J., Brown, S. and Riddell, S. (1995) SEN Provision in Mainstream and Special Schools in Scotland: Final Report to the Scottish Office Education Department. Stirling: University of Stirling.

Anderson, L.W. and Pellicer, L.O. (1990) 'Synthesis of research on compensatory and remedial education', *Educational Leadership*, 48(1): 10–16.

Andreski, S. (1972) *Social Sciences as Sorcery*. London: André Deutsch.

Archer, M.S. (1979) *The Social Origins of Educational Systems*. London: Sage.

Armstrong, D., Armstrong, F. and Barton, L. (1998) 'From theory to practice: special education and the social relations of academic production', in C. Clark, A. Dyson and A. Millward (eds) *Theorising Special Education*. London: Routledge.

Armstrong, F., Belmont, B. and Verillon, A. (2000) ' "Vive la difference?" exploring context, policy and change in special education in France: developing cross-cultural collaboration', in F. Armstrong, D. Armstrong and L. Barton (eds) *Inclusive Education: Policy Contexts and Comparative Perspectives*. London: David Fulton.

Arnold, P., Bochel, H., Brodhurst, S. and Page, D. (1993) *Community Care: The Housing Dimension*. York: Joseph Rowntree Foundation.

Arter, J.A. and Jenkins, J.R. (1979) 'Differential diagnosis – prescriptive teaching: a critical appraisal', *Review of Educational Research*, 49(4): 517–55.

Artiles, A.J. (2003) 'Special education's changing identity: paradoxes and dilemmas in views of culture and space', *Harvard Educational Review*, 73: 164–202.

Audit Commission (1998) 'Changing partners: a discussion paper on the role of the local education authority', London: Audit Commission for Local Authorities and the National Health Service in England and Wales.

Audit Commission (1999) 'Held in trust: the LEA of the future', London: Audit Commission for Local Authorities and the National Health Service in England and Wales.

Audit Commission/HMI (1992) *Getting in on the Act: Provision for Pupils with Special Educational Needs, the National Picture*. London: HMSO.

Axelrod, R. (1984) *The Evolution of Cooperation*. London: Basic Books.

Baker, E.T., Wang, M.C. and Walberg, H.J. (1995) 'The effects of inclusion on learning', *Educational Leadership*, 52(4): 33–5.

Ball, S.J. (1994) *Education Reform: A Critical and Post-structuralist Approach*. Buckingham: Open University Press.

Ball, S.J. (1999) 'Labour, learning and the economy: a "policy sociology" perspective', *Cambridge Journal of Education*, 29(2): 195–206.

Barker, R.G. (1968) *Ecological Psychology*. Stanford, CA: Stanford University Press.

Barnes, C., Mercer, G. and Shakespeare, T. (1999) *Exploring Disability: A Sociological Introduction*. Oxford: Polity Press.

Barrett, W. (1978) *The Illusion of Technique*. New York: Anchor-Doubleday.

Bauman, Z. (1995) *Life in Fragments*. Oxford: Blackwell.

Bauman, Z. (2000) *Liquid Modernity*. Cambridge: Polity Press.

BBC (2005a) 'Special needs policy "distortion" '. www.news.bbc.co.uk/1/hi/education/4665401.stm

BBC   (2005b)   www.bbc.co.uk/radio4/today/listenagain/ram/today5_oldboys_20041115.ram

Becker, H. (1963) *Outsiders: Studies in the Sociology of Deviance*. Chicago, IL: Chicago University Press.

Beech, J.R. and Singleton, C. (1997) *The Psychological Assessment of Reading*. London: Routledge.

Belsey, A. (1986) 'The New Right, social order and civil liberties', in R. Levitas (ed.) *The Ideology of the New Right*. Cambridge: Polity Press.

Benjamin, S. (2003) *The Micropolitics of Inclusive Education*. Maidenhead: Open University Press.

Bennacer, H. (2000) 'How the socioecological characteristics of the classroom affect academic achievement', *European Journal of Psychology of Education*, 15, 173–1.

Berlin, I. (1979) 'The divorce between the sciences and the humanities', in I. Berlin, *Against the Current*. London: Hogarth Press.

Berry, R.A.B. (2006) 'Inclusion, power and community: teachers and students interpret the language of community in an inclusion classroom', *American Educational Research Journal*, 43(3): 489–529.

Bines, H. (1995) 'Special educational needs in the market place', *Journal of Educational Policy*, 10(2): 157–71.

Birch, H.G., Richardson, S.A., Baird, D., Horobin, G. and Illsley, R. (1970) *Mental Subnormality in the Community: A Clinical and Epidemiological Survey*. Baltimore, MD: Williams & Wilkins.

Blackburn, S.C. (1999) 'A very moderate socialist indeed? R.H. Tawney and minimum wages', *Twentieth Century British History*, 10(2): 107–36.

Blackler, F. (1995) 'Knowledge, knowledge work and organizations: an overview and interpretation', *Organization Studies*, 6, 1021–46.

Blane, D., White, I. and Morris, J.N. (1996) 'Education, social circumstances and mortality', in D. Blane, E. Brunner and R. Wilkinson (eds) *Health and Social Organization: Towards a Health Policy for the 21st Century*. London: Routledge.

Blaser, M.J. (1996) 'The bacteria behind ulcers', *Scientific American*, 274(2): 92–8.

Blunkett, D. (2000) 'Influence or irrelevance: can social science improve government?', *Research Intelligence*, 71, March: 12–21.

Booth, T. (1999) 'Viewing inclusion from a distance: gaining perspective from comparative study', *Support for Learning*, 14(4): 164–8.

Bosanquet, N. (1983) *After the New Right*. London: Heinemann.

Bourdieu, P. (1983) 'Forms of capital', in J.C. Richards (ed.) *Handbook of Theory and Research for the Sociology of Education*. New York: Greenwood Press.

Bourdieu, P. (1984) *Distinction*. London: Routledge & Kegan Paul.

Bourdieu, P. and Eagleton, T. (1994) 'Doxa and common life: an interview', in S. Zizek (ed.) *Mapping Ideology*. London: Verso.

Bourdieu, P. and Passeron, J.-C. (1977) *Reproduction in Society, Education and Culture*. London: Sage.

Bourdieu, P. and Wacquant, L. (1992) *An Invitation to Reflexive Sociology*. Cambridge: Polity Press.

Bowe, R. and Ball, S. with Gold, A. (1992) *Reforming Education and Changing Schools*. London: Routledge.

Bronfenbrenner, U. (1969) Statement at hearings before the Committee on Ways and Means, House of Representatives, 91st Congress. Washington, DC: US Government Printing Office.

Bronfenbrenner, U. (1979) *The Ecology of Human Development*. Cambridge, MA: Harvard University Press.

Bronfenbrenner, U., McClelland, P., Wethington, E., Moen, P.M. and Ceci, S.J. (1996) *The State of Americans: This Generation and the Next*. New York: Free Press.

Brown, A.L. and Campione, J.C. (1986) 'Psychological theory and the study of learning disabilities', *American Psychologist*, 41: 1059–68.

Bruner, J. (1966) 'After John Dewey, what?', in R.D. Archambault (ed.) *Dewey on Education*. New York: Random House.

Bryant, P.E. (1984) 'Piaget, teachers and psychologists', *Oxford Review of Education*, 10(3): 251–9.

Bullock, A. and Thomas, H. (1997) *Schools at the Centre? A Study of Decentralisation*. London: Routledge.

Burbules, N.C. (1992) 'Forms of ideology-critique: a pedagogical perspective', *International Journal of Qualitative Studies in Education*, 5(1): 7–17.

Burt, C. (1962) *Mental and Scholastic Tests*. London: Staples Press.

Caldwell, J.C. (1986) 'Routes to low mortality in poor countries', *Population and Development Review*, 2: 171–220.

Canguilhem, G. (1994) 'The various models', in F. Delaporte (ed.) *A Vital Rationalist: Selected Writings from Georges Canguilhem*. New York: Zone Books.

Carreiro King, I. (2003) 'Examining middle school inclusion classrooms through the lens of learner-centered principles', *Theory into Practice*, 42: 151–8.

Carson, S. (1992) 'Normalisation, needs and schools', *Educational Psychology in Practice*, 7(4): 216–22.

Center for International Understanding (2005) *North Carolina in the World: A Plan to Increase Student Knowledge and Skills about the World*. Raleigh, NC: Office of the State Board of Education.

Chambers, J.H. (1992) *Empiricist Research on Teaching: A Philosophical and Practical Critique of its Scientific Pretensions*. Dordrecht: Kluwer Academic Publishers.

Chazan, M., Laing, A.F. and Davies, D. (1994) *Emotional and Behavioural Difficulties in Middle Childhood*. London: Falmer.

Checkland, P. (1981) *Systems Thinking, Systems Practice*. Chichester: John Wiley & Sons.

Chiu, M.M. and Khoo, L. (2005) 'Effects of resources, inequality, and privilege bias on achievement: country, school, and student level analyses', *American Educational Research Journal*, 42: 575–603.

Christoplos, F. and Renz, P. (1969) 'A critical examination of special education programs', *Journal of Special Education*, 3(4): 371–80.

Cicourel, A.V. (1993) 'Aspects of structural and processual theories of knowledge', in C. Calhoun, E. LiPuma and M. Postone (eds) *Bourdieu: Critical Perspectives*. Cambridge: Polity Press.

Cicourel, A.V. and Kitsuse, J.I. (1968) 'The social organisation of the high school and deviant adolescent careers', in E. Rubington and M.S. Weinberg (eds) *Deviance: The Interactionist Perspective; Text and Readings in the Sociology of Deviance*. London: Macmillan.

Cioffi, F. (1975) 'Freud and the idea of a pseudo-science', in R. Borger and F. Cioffi, *Explanation in the Behavioural Sciences: Confrontations*. Cambridge: Cambridge University Press.

Clark, C., Dyson, A. and Millward, A. (1998) 'Theorising special education: time to move on?', in C. Clark, A. Dyson and A. Millward (eds) *Theorising Special Education*. London: Routledge.

Clarke, B. (1997) 'What comprehensive schools do better', in R. Pring and G. Walford (eds) *Affirming the Comprehensive Ideal*. London: Falmer.

Clarke, J., Cochrane, A. and MacLaughlin, E. (1994) 'Introduction', in J. Clarke, A. Cochrane and E. MacLaughlin (eds) *Managing Social Policy*. London: Sage.

Clarke, P. (1978) *Liberals and Social Democrats*. Cambridge: Cambridge University Press.

Claxton, G. (1985) 'Educational psychology: what is it trying to prove?', in G. Claxton, W. Swann, P. Salmon, V. Walkerdine, B. Jacobsen and J. White, *Psychology and Schooling: What's the Matter?* London: Bedford Way Papers.

Claxton, G. (2005) 'Wrong way, right way – an alternative view of educating gifted and talented pupils', *Gifted and Talented*, 9: 27–9.

Clough, P. (1995) 'Problems of identity and method in the investigation of special educational needs', in P. Clough and L. Barton (eds) *Making Difficulties: Research and the Construction of SEN*. London: PCP.

Cohen, A.K. (1955) *Delinquent Boys*. New York: Free Press.

Cohen, G., Steele, C.M. and Ross, L.D. (1999) 'The mentor's dilemma: providing critical feedback across the racial divide', *Personality and Social Psychology Bulletin*, 25: 1302–18.

Cohen, S. (1985) *Visions of Social Control: Crime, Punishment and Classification*. Cambridge: Polity Press.

Coleman, J.S. (1988) 'Social capital in the creation of human capital', *American Journal of Sociology*, 94 (Supplement), S95–S120.

Coleman, L.M. (1997) 'Stigma: an enigma demystified', in L.J. Davis (ed.) *The Disability Studies Reader*. London: Routledge.

Coles, G. (1978) 'The Learning-Disabilities Test Battery: empirical and social issues', *Harvard Educational Review*, 48: 313–40.

Coles, G. (1987) *The Learning Mystique*. New York: Pantheon Books.

Coles, G. (2000) *Misreading Reading: The Bad Science that Hurts Children*. Portsmouth, NH: Heinemann.

Coles, G. (2003) *Reading the Naked Truth: Literacy, Legislation and Lies*. Portsmouth, NH: Heinemann.

Colletti, L. (1974) *From Rousseau to Lenin: Studies in Ideology and Society*. New York: Monthly Review Press.

Corbett, J. (1996) *Bad-mouthing*. London: Falmer.

Cornelius, L.L. and Herrenkohl, L. (2004) 'Power in the classroom: how the classroom environment shapes students' relationships with each other and with concepts', *Cognition and Instruction*, 22: 467–98.

Cox, R.H. (1998) 'The consequences of welfare reform: how conceptions of social rights are changing', *Journal of Social Policy*, 27(1): 1–16.

Cremin, H. (2002) 'Pupils resolving disputes: successful peer mediation schemes share their secrets', *Support for Learning*, 17(3): 138–44.

Cremin, H. (2007) *Peer Mediation: Citizenship and Social Inclusion Revisited*. Maidenhead: Open University Press (in press).

Cremin, L.A. (1961) *The Transformation of the School: Progressivism in American Education*. New York: Vintage.

Crews, F. (1997) *The Memory Wars: Freud's Legacy in Dispute*. London: Granta.

Croll, P. and Moses, D. (1998) 'Pragmatism, ideology and educational change: the case of special educational needs', *British Journal of Educational Studies*, 46(1): 11–25.

Croll, P. and Moses, D. (2000) *Special Needs in the Primary School*. London: Cassell.

Crosland, A. (1964) *The Future of Socialism*. London: Cape.

CSIE (1992) *Bishopswood: Good Practice Transferred*. Bristol: Centre for Studies on Inclusive Education.

CSIE (2000) *Index for Inclusion*. Bristol: Centre for Studies on Inclusive Education.

Damasio, A.R. (1994) *Descartes' Error: Emotion, Reason and the Human Brain*. New York: G.P. Putnam's Sons.

Dash, L. (1998) *Rosa Lee*. London: Profile Books.

Davies, N. (1998) 'The man who fought for the abused and was gagged', *The Guardian*, 3 June: 8–9.

Delpit, L.D. (1988) 'The silenced dialogue: power and pedagogy in educating other people's children', *Harvard Educational Review*, 58: 280–98.

DeMoss, K. (2003) 'Who's accountable to the Constitution? Thirty years of judicial politics in state education finance litigation', *Peabody Journal of Education*, 78: 44–65.

Dennett, D.C. (1993) *Consciousness Explained*. London: Penguin.

Dennett, D.C. (1996) *Kinds of Minds: Towards an Understanding of Consciousness*. London: Phoenix.

Dennis, N. (1997) *The Invention of Permanent Poverty*. London: IEA.

Derrida, J. (1978) *Writing and Difference*. London: Routledge & Kegan Paul.

DES (Department of Education and Science) (1967) *Children and their Primary Schools (Plowden Report)*. London: HMSO.

DES (Department of Education and Science) (1978) Special Educational Needs: Report of the Committee of Enquiry into the Education of Handicapped Children and Young People, Cmnd 7212. London: HMSO.

DES (Department of Education and Science) (1989a) A Survey of Provision for Pupils with Emotional/Behavioural Difficulties in Maintained Special Schools and Units: A Report by HM Inspectors. London: HMSO.

DES (Department of Education and Science) (1989b) Special Schools for Pupils with Emotional and Behavioural Difficulties, Circular 23/89. London: HMSO.

DES (Department of Education and Science) (1989c) *Discipline in Schools (Elton Report)*. London: HMSO.

Dessent, T. (1987) *Making the Ordinary School Special*. London: Falmer.

DeVault, M.L., Harnischfeger, A. and Wiley, D.E. (1977) *Curricula, Personnel Resources and Grouping Strategies*. St Ann, MO: ML-GROUP for Policy Studies in Education, Central Midwestern Regional Lab.

Dewey, J. (1920) *Reconstruction in Philosophy*. New York: Holt.

Dewey, J. (1938) *Experience and Education*. New York: Kappa Delta Pi.

Dewey, J. (1982) 'Reconstruction in philosophy', in *The Middle Works of John Dewey*, Vol. 12. Carbondale, IL: Southern Illinois University Press.

DfE (Department for Education) (1994a) *The Code of Practice on the Identification and Assessment of Special Educational Needs*. London: HMSO.

DfE (Department for Education) (1994b) The Organisation of Special Educational Provision, Circular 6/94. London: DfE.

DfEE (Department for Education and Employment) (1995) *Special Educational Needs in England, 1995*. London: HMSO.

DfEE (Department for Education and Employment) (1997) *Excellence for All Children: Meeting Special Educational Needs*. London: DfEE.

DfEE (Department for Education and Employment) (1998a) www.coi.gov.uk/coi/depts/GDE/coi6201e.ok

DfEE (Department for Education and Employment) (1998b) *Extending Opportunity: A National Framework for Study Support*. London: DfEE.

DfES (Department for Education and Skills) (2000) 'SEN Code of Practice on the Identification and Assessment of Pupils with Special Educational Needs and SEN Thresholds'. www.dfes.gov.uk/publications/guidanceonthelaw/dfeepub/jul00/020700/

DfES (Department for Education and Skills) (2003) 'Children with emotional and behavioural difficulties'. www.standards.dfes.gov.uk/primary/casestudies/inclusion/banda/831947/

DfES (Department for Education and Skills) (2004) 'Permanent exclusions from schools and exclusion appeals in England 2002/2003'. www.dfes.gov.uk/rsgateway/DB/SFR/s000465/index.shtml

DfES (Department for Education and Skills) (2006) 'Permanent and fixed period exclusions from schools and exclusion appeals in England, 2004/05'. www.dfes.gov.uk/rsgateway/DB/SFR/s000662/SFR24–2006.pdf

Dickens, W.T. and Flynn, J.R. (2001) 'Heritability estimates versus large environmental effects: the IQ paradox resolved', *Psychological Review*, 108: 346–69.

Dorn, S., Fuchs, D. and Fuchs, L.S. (1996) 'A historical perspective on special education reform', *Theory into Practice*, 35(1): 12–19.

Doyle, W. (1977) 'The uses of non-verbal behaviours: toward an ecological view of classrooms', *Merrill-Falmer Quarterly*, 23(3): 179–92.

Dreyfus, H.L. and Rabinow, P. (1982) *Michel Foucault: Beyond Structuralism and Hermeneutics*. New York: Harvester Wheatsheaf.

Dunn, L.M. (1968) 'Special education for the mildly mentally retarded – is much of it justifiable?', *Exceptional Children*, September: 5–22.

Eagleton, T. (1991) *Ideology*. London: Verso.

Easterlin, R.A. (1974) 'Does economic growth improve the human lot? Some empirical evidence', in P. David and M. Reder (eds) *Nations and Households in Economic Growth*. New York: Academic Press.

Edmonds, R. (1979) 'Effective schools for the urban poor', *Educational Leadership*, 37(1): 15–23.

Educable (2000) *No Choice: No Change*. Belfast: Save the Children.

Elkind, D. (1967) 'Piaget's conservation problems', *Child Development*, 38: 15–27.

Engeström, Y. (2004) ' "New forms of learning in co-configuration work". Seminar presented to LSE Dept of Information Systems, 22 January'. www.is.lse.ac.uk/events/ESRCseminars/engestrom.pdf

Ericsson, K.A. and Charness, N. (1994) 'Expert performance: its structure and acquisition', *American Psychologist*, 49(7): 725–47.

Ericsson, K.A. and Delaney, P.F. (1999) 'Long-term working memory as an alternative to capacity models of working memory in everyday skilled performance', in A. Miyake and P. Shah (eds) *Models of Working Memory: Mechanisms of Active Maintenance and Executive Control*. Cambridge: Cambridge University Press.

Etzioni, A. (1993) *The Spirit of Community*. New York: Simon & Schuster.

Farnham-Diggory, S. (1992) *The Learning-Disabled Child*. Cambridge, MA: Harvard University Press.

Ferguson, P.M., Ferguson, D.L. and Taylor S.J. (eds) (1992) *Interpreting Disability: A Qualitative Reader*. New York: Teachers' College Press.

Feyerabend, P. (1993) *Against Method*, 3rd edn. London: Verso/New Left Books.

Field, F. (1996) *Stakeholder Welfare*. London: IEA Health and Welfare Unit.

Fienberg, S.E. and Resnick, D.P. (1997) 'Re-examining the Bell Curve', in B. Devlin, S.E. Fienberg, D.P. Resnick and K. Roeder (eds) *Intelligence, Genes and Success: Scientists Respond to the Bell Curve*. New York: Springer-Verlag.

Fish, S. (1989) *Doing What Comes Naturally*. Oxford: Clarendon Press.

Fish, S. (1994) *There's No Such Thing as Free Speech*. Oxford: Oxford University Press.

Fiske, E.B. (2005) *States Prepare for the Global Age*. New York: Asia Society.

Fitz, J., Halpin, D. and Power, S. (1994) 'Implementation research and education policy: practice and prospects', *British Journal of Educational Studies*, 42(1): 53–69.

Foucault, M. (1970) *The Order of Things: An Archaeology of the Human Sciences*. London: Tavistock.

Foucault, M. (1980a) 'Two lectures', in C. Gordon (ed.) *Power/Knowledge: Selected Interviews and Other Writings 1972–1977 – Michel Foucault*. London: Harvester Wheatsheaf.

Foucault, M. (1980b) 'Prison talk', in C. Gordon (ed.) *Power/Knowledge: Selected Interviews and Other Writings 1972–1977 – Michel Foucault*. London: Harvester Wheatsheaf.

Foucault, M. (1991) *Discipline and Punish* (trans. A. Sheridan). London: Penguin.

Foucault, M. (1994) 'Critical theory/intellectual history', in M. Kelly (ed.) *Critique and Power: Recasting the Foucault/Habermas Debate*. Cambridge, MA: MIT Press.

Fraser, N. (1996) *Justice Interruptus: Rethinking Key Concepts of a 'Postsocialist' Age*. New York: Routledge.

Freire, P. (1972) *Pedagogy of the Oppressed*. New York: Herder & Herder.

Fulcher, G. (1989) *Disabling Policies?* London: Falmer.

Gallagher, D. (2004) 'Educational research, philosophical orthodoxy, and unfulfilled promises: the quandary of traditional research in US special education', in G. Thomas and R. Pring (eds) *Evidence Based Practice in Education*. Maidenhead: Open University Press.

Galloway, D. (1983) 'Disruptive pupils and effective pastoral care', *School Organisation*, 13: 245–54.

Galloway, D. and Goodwin, C. (1979) *Educating Slow Learning and Maladjusted Children: Integration or Segregation?* Harlow: Longman.

Galloway, D., Martin, R. and Wilcox, B. (1985) 'Persistent absence from school and exclusion from school: the predictive power of school and community variables', *British Educational Research Journal*, 11: 51–61.

Galton, F. (1869) *Hereditary Genius, its Laws and Consequences*. London: Macmillan.

Gamble, A. (1986) 'The political economy of freedom', in R. Levitas (ed.) *The Ideology of the New Right*. Cambridge: Polity Press.

Gardner, H. (1983) *Frames of Mind: The Theory of Multiple Intelligences*. New York: Basic Books.

Gardner, H., Torff, B. and Hatch, T. (1996) 'The age of innocence reconsidered: preserving the best of the progressive traditions in psychology and education', in R. Olson and N. Torrance (eds) *The Handbook of Education and Human Development*. Cambridge, MA: Blackwell.

Garrison, J.W. (1988) 'The impossibility of atheoretical educational science', *Journal of Educational Thought*, 22(1): 21–6.

Gartner, A. and Lipsky, D. (1987) 'Beyond special education: towards a quality system for all students', *Harvard Educational Review*, 57(4): 367–95.

Geertz, C. (1975) *The Interpretation of Cultures*. London: Hutchinson.

Gelman, R. (1982) 'Accessing one-to-one correspondence: still another paper about conservation', *British Journal of Psychology*, 73: 209–21.

George, V. and Wilding, P. (1994) *Welfare and Ideology*. London: Harvester Wheatsheaf.

Gewirtz, S., Ball, S. and Bowe, R. (1995) *Markets, Choice and Equity in Education*. Buckingham: Open University Press.

Gibson, J.J. (1967) 'J.J. Gibson', in E.G. Boring and G. Lindzey (eds) *A History of Psychology in Autobiography*, Vol. 5. New York: Appleton Century Crofts.

Giddens, A. (1990) *The Consequences of Modernity*. Cambridge: Polity Press.

Giddens, A. (1994) *Beyond Left and Right: The Future of Radical Politics*. Cambridge: Polity Press.

Gipps, C. (1987) *Warnock's Eighteen Per Cent: Children with Special Needs in Primary Schools*. London: Falmer.

Gitlin, A., Siegel, M. and Boru, K. (1989) 'The politics of method: from leftist ethnography to educative research', *Qualitative Studies in Education*, 2(3): 237–53.

Goacher, B., Evans, J., Welton, J. and Wedell, K. (1988) *Policy and Provision for Special Educational Needs*. London: Cassell.

Goffman, E. ([1961] 1968) *Asylums*. London: Pelican. [First published 1961 by Anchor-Doubleday, New York.]

Goffman, E. (1963) *Stigma: Notes on the Management of Spoiled Identity*. Englewood Cliffs, NJ: Prentice-Hall.

Goffman, E. (1987) 'The moral career of the mental patient', in E. Rubington and M.S. Weinberg (eds) *Deviance: The Interactionist Perspective*, 5th edn. New York: Macmillan.

Golby, M. (1997) 'Communitarianism and education', *Curriculum Studies*, 5(2): 125–38.

Goodman, K.S. (1996) *On Reading: A Commonsense Look at the Nature of Language and the Science of Reading*. Portsmouth, NH: Heinemann.

Gordon, E.W. and Green, D. (1975) 'An affluent society's excuses for inequality: developmental, economic, and educational', in A. Montagu (ed.) *Race and IQ*. New York: Oxford University Press.

Gordon, H. (1923) 'Mental and scholastic tests among retarded children', Education Pamphlet 44. London: HMSO.

Goswami, U. and Bryant, P. (1990) *Phonological Skills and Learning to Read*. London: Lawrence Erlbaum.

Gould, S.J. (1981) *The Mismeasure of Man*. New York: W.W. Norton.

Green, D.G. (1998) *Benefit Dependency*. London: IEA Health and Welfare Unit.

Gross, J. (1996) 'The weight of evidence: parental advocacy and resource allocation to children with statements of special educational need', *Support for Learning*, 11(1): 3–8.

Haber, F.H. (1994) *Beyond Postmodern Politics: Lyotard, Rorty, Foucault*. London: Routledge.

Haldane, J.B.S. (1965) 'The duty of doubt', in A.F. Scott (ed.) *Topics and Opinions*. London: Macmillan.

Hall, S. (1977) 'Education and the crisis in the urban school', in J. Raynor and E. Harris (eds) *Schooling in the City*. London: Ward Lock.

Hall, S. and Jacques, M. (1983) 'The great moving right show', in S. Hall and M. Jacques (eds) *The Politics of Thatcherism*. London: Wishart.

Hallinger, P. and Murphy, J. (1986) 'The social context of effective schools', *American Journal of Education*, 94(3): 328–55.

Hanifan, L.J. (1916) 'The rural school community centre', *Annals of the American Academy of Political and Social Science*, 67: 130–38.

Hanifan, L.J. (1920) *The Community Center*. Boston, MA: Silver Burdett.

Harber, C. (2004) *Schooling as Violence: How Schools Harm Pupils and Societies*. London: RoutledgeFalmer.

Hargreaves, D.H. (1967) *Social Relations in a Secondary School*. London: Routledge.

Hargreaves, D.H. (1978) 'The proper study of educational psychology', *Association of Educational Psychologists' Journal*, 4(9): 3–8.

Hargreaves, D.H., Hestor, S.K. and Mellor, F.J. (1975) *Deviance in Classrooms*. London: Routledge & Kegan Paul.

Harker, R., Maher, C. and Wilkes, C. (1990) *An Introduction to the Work of Pierre Bourdieu*. London: Macmillan.

Harré, R. (1985) 'Foreword', in G. Claxton, W. Swann, P. Salmon, V. Walkerdine, B. Jacobsen and J. White, *Psychology and Schooling: What's the Matter?* London: Bedford Way Papers.

Harré, R. (1998) *The Singular Self: An Introduction to the Psychology of Personhood*. London: Sage.

Hart, S. (1996) *Beyond Special Needs*. London: Paul Chapman.

Hayek, F.A. ([1949] 1998) *The Intellectuals and Socialism*. London: IEA Health and Welfare Unit.

Hayek, F.A. (1976) *Law, Legislation and Liberty*. London: Routledge & Kegan Paul.

Hearnshaw, L.S. (1979) *Cyril Burt: Psychologist*. London: Hodder & Stoughton.

Hegarty, S. (1993) 'Reviewing the literature on integration', *European Journal of Special Needs Education*, 8(3): 194–200.

Hehir, T. (1997) 'IDEA has led to improved results for students with disabilities: a response to Lipsky and Gartner', *Harvard Educational Review*, 67(3): 596–601.

Hehir, T. and Latus, T. (1992) *Special Education at the Century's End: Evolution, Theory and Practice since 1970*. Cambridge, MA: Harvard Educational Review Reprint Series.

Heron, E. and Dwyer, P. (1999) 'Doing the right thing: Labour's attempt to forge a new welfare deal between the individual and the state', *Social Policy and Administration*, 33(1): 91–104.

Herrnstein, R.J. and Murray, C. (1994) *The Bell Curve: Intelligence and Class Structure in American Life*. New York: Free Press.

Hills, J. (1998) *Thatcherism, New Labour and the Welfare State: Case Paper 13*. London: Centre for Analysis of Social Exclusion, London School of Economics.

Hirsch, E.D. (1976) *The Aims of Interpretation*. Chicago, IL: University of Chicago Press.

Hirsch, F. (1977) *Social Limits to Growth*. London: Routledge & Kegan Paul.

Ho, E. and Willms, J.D. (1996) 'The effects of parental involvement on eighth grade achievement', *Sociology of Education*, 69: 126–41.

Hoghughi, M. (1988) *Treating Problem Children: Issues, Methods and Practice*. London: Sage.

Holt, J. (1964) *How Children Fail*. New York: Pitman.

Holt, J. (1977) *Instead of Education: Ways to Help People do Things Better*. London: Penguin.

Honneth, A. (1995) 'Foucault's theory of society: a systemic-theoretic dissolution of the dialectic of enlightenment', in M. Kelly (ed.) *Critique and Power: Recasting the Foucault/Habermas Debate*. Cambridge, MA: MIT Press.

Hornby, G. (1999) 'Inclusion or delusion: can one size fit all?', *Support for Learning*, 14(4): 152–7.

Hoskins, K. (1990) 'Foucault under examination: the crypto-educationalist unmasked', in S.J. Ball (ed.) *Foucault and Education: Disciplines and Knowledge*. London: Routledge.

Howarth, C., Kenway, P., Falmer, G. and Street, C. (1998) *Key Indicators of Poverty and Social Exclusion*. York: Rowntree/New Policy Institute.

Howe, M.J.A. (1990) *The Origins of Exceptional Abilities*. Oxford: Blackwell.

Hurt, J.S. (1988) *Outside the Mainstream: A History of Special Education*. London: Batsford.

Hutton, W. (1996) *The State We're In*. London: Vintage.

Illich, I. (1975) *Medical Nemesis*. London: Marion Boyars.

Jackson, A. and Hannon, P. (1981) *The Belfield Reading Project*. Rochdale: Belfield Community Council.

James, A. and Prout, A. (1990) 'A new paradigm for the sociology of childhood? Provenance, promise and problems', in A. James and A. Prout (eds) *Constructing and Reconstructing Childhood: Contemporary Issues in the Sociological Study of Childhood*. London: Falmer.

Jenkins, R. (1992) *Pierre Bourdieu*. London: Routledge.

Jensen, A. (1969) 'How much can we boost IQ and scholastic achievement?', *Harvard Educational Review*, 39(1): 123.

Jesson, D. and Gray, J. (1991) 'Slants on slopes: using multi-level models to investigate differential school effectiveness and its impact on schools examination results', *School Effectiveness and School Improvement*, 2(3): 230–71.

Johnson, D.D. and Pearson, P.D. (1975) 'Skills management systems: a critique', *Reading Teacher*, 28: 757–65.

Johnson, M. (1993) 'Integration, Italian style', *Education*, 18 June: 469.

Johnson, O.G. (1962) 'Special education for the mentally handicapped – a paradox', *Exceptional Children*, 29: 62–9.

Jordan, L. and Goodey, C. (1996) *Human Rights and School Change: The Newham Story*. Bristol: Centre for Studies on Inclusive Education.

Joynson, R.B. (1974) *Psychology and Common Sense*. London: Routledge & Kegan Paul.

Kamin, L.J. (1977) 'Burt's IQ data', *Science*, 195: 246–8.

Kauffman, J.M. and Hallahan, D.P. (2005) *Special Education: What it is and Why we Need it*. Boston, MA: Pearson/Allyn & Bacon.

Kavanagh, D. (1987) *Thatcherism and British Politics: The End of Consensus?* Oxford: Oxford University Press.

Kay, J. (1996) *The Business of Economics*. Oxford: Oxford University Press.

Keating, D.P. and Hertzman, C. (1999) 'Modernity's paradox', in D.P. Keating and C. Hertzman, *Developmental Health and the Wealth of Nations: Social, Biological and Educational Dynamics*. New York: Guilford Press.

Kendrick, A. (1997) 'Safeguarding children living away from home from abuse: a literature review', in R. Kent, *Children's Safeguards Review*. Edinburgh: The Stationery Office.

Kendrick, A., Simpson, M. and Mapstone, E. (1996) *Getting it Together: Changing Services for Children and Young People in Difficulty*. York: Joseph Rowntree Foundation.

Kenny, A. (ed.) (1994) *The Wittgenstein Reader*. Oxford: Blackwell.

Kevles, D.J. (1985) *In the Name of Eugenics: Genetics and the Uses of Human Heredity*. New York: Alfred A. Knopf.

Kewley, G.D. (1999) *Attention Deficit Hyperactivity Disorder: Recognition, Reality and Resolution*. Horsham: LAC Press.

Kingston, P.W. (2001) 'The unfulfilled promise of cultural capital', *Sociology of Education*, 74: extra issue: *Current of Thought: Sociology of Education at the Dawn of the 21st Century*: 88–99.

Kitayama, S. and Marcus, H.R. (2000) 'The pursuit of happiness and the realization of sympathy: cultural patterns of self, social relations, and well-being', in E. Diener and E.M. Suh, *Culture and Subjective Well-being*. Cambridge, MA: MIT Press.

Klein, P. (1997) 'Multiplying the problems of intelligence by eight: a critique of Gardner's theory', *Canadian Journal of Education*, 22(4): 377–94.

Knight, C. (1985) 'New Right and education', in A. Seldon (ed.) *New Right Enlightenment*. Sevenoaks: E. and L. Books.

Koch, S. (1964) 'Psychology and emerging conceptions of knowledge as unitary', in T.W. Wann (ed.) *Behaviorism and Phenomenology*. Chicago, IL: University of Chicago Press.

Kogan, M. (1975) *Educational Policy Making*. London: Allen & Unwin.

Kohler, W. (1947) *Gestalt Psychology*. New York: Liveright.

Kounin, J.S. (1967) 'An analysis of teachers' managerial techniques', *Psychology in the Schools*, 4: 221–7.

Kramer, J. (2005) 'Review of provision for children and young people with emotional, social and behavioural disorders in Worcestershire'.
www.whub.org.uk/consultation_docs/edu-sch-consultdoc-esbd-June2005.pdf

Kuhn, T. (1970) *The Structure of Scientific Revolutions*, 2nd edn. Chicago, IL: University of Chicago Press.

Laing, R.D. (1965) *The Divided Self*. London: Penguin.

Lamont, M. and Lareau, A. (1988) 'Cultural capital: allusions, gaps and glissandos in recent theoretical developments', *Sociological Theory*, 6(2): 153–68.

Lave, J. and Wenger, E. (1991) *Situated Learning: Legitimate Peripheral Participation*. Cambridge: Cambridge University Press.

Layard, R. (2003) 'Happiness: has social science a clue? Lecture 1: What is happiness? Are we getting happier?' Lionel Robbins Memorial Lectures, London School of Economics, 3 March.

Layard, R. (2005) *Happiness: Lessons from a New Science*. London: Allen Lane.

Lee, T. (1990) *Carving out the Cash: LMS and the New ERA of Education*. Bath: Centre for the Analysis of Social Policy.

Lee, T. (1996) *The Search for Equity: The Funding of Additional Educational Needs under LMS*. Aldershot: Avebury.

Lemert, E. (1967) *Human Deviance, Social Problems, and Social Control*. Englewood Cliffs, NJ: Prentice-Hall.

Leontiev, A.N. (1978) *Activity, Consciousness, and Personality*. Englewood Cliffs, NJ: Prentice-Hall.

Levacic, R. (1995) *Local Management of Schools: Analysis and Practice*. Milton Keynes: Open University Press.

Levine, D.U. and Lezotte, L.W. (1995) 'Effective schools research', in J.A. Banks and C.A. Banks, *Handbook of Research on Multicultural Education*. Nebraska, NE: Macmillan.

Levitas, R. (ed.) (1986) *The Ideology of the New Right*. Cambridge: Polity Press.

Leyden, G. (1978) 'The process of reconstruction: an overview', in B. Gillham, *Reconstructing Educational Psychology*. London: Croom Helm.

Linehan, C. and McCarthy, J. (2001) 'Reviewing the "community of practice" metaphor: an analysis of control relations in a primary school classroom', *Mind, Culture and Activity*, 8: 129–47.

Lippmann, W. (1922) 'The mental age of Americans', *The New Republic*, 25 October. 213–15.

Lipsky, D. and Gartner, A. (1987) 'Capable of achievement and worthy of respect', *Exceptional Children*, 54(1): 69–74.

Lipsky, D. and Gartner, A. (1996) 'Inclusion, school restructuring and the remaking of American society', *Harvard Educational Review*, 66(4): 762–96.

Lipsky, M. (1980) *Street Level Bureaucracy*. New York, London: Sage.

Locke, J. (1964) *Some Thoughts Concerning Education*. Woodbury, NY: Barren's.

Loxley, A. (1999) 'The impact of LMS on the policy and provision for special educational needs', unpublished PhD thesis, University of Bath.

Lucas, D. and Thomas, G. (2000) 'Organising classrooms to promote learning for all children: two pieces of action research', in S. Clipson-Boyles, *Putting Research into Practice in Primary Teaching and Learning*. London: David Fulton.

Lunt, I. (1993) 'The practice of assessment', in H. Daniels, *Charting the Agenda: Educational Activity after Vygotsky*. London: Routledge.

Lunt, I. and Evans, J. (1994) *Allocating Resources for SEN Provision*. Stafford: NASEN.

Lyotard, J.-F. (1984) *The Postmodern Condition: A Report on Knowledge* (trans. G. Bennington and B. Massumi). Minneapolis, MN: University of Minnesota Press.

MacIntyre, A. (1985) *After Virtue*. London: Duckworth.

Macintyre, B. (1992) *Forgotten Fatherland*. London: Picador.

Macmillan, M. (1997) *Freud Evaluated: The Completed Arc*. London: MIT Press.

Marmot, M. (2004) *Status Syndrome: How your Social Standing directly affects your Health and Life Expectancy*. London: Bloomsbury.

Marquand, D. (1996) 'Moralists and hedonists', in D. Marquand and A. Seldon (eds) *The Ideas that Shaped Post-War Britain*. London: Fontana.

Marshall, T.H. (1965) *Social Policy*. London: Hutchinson University Library.

Marx, K. (1995) *Capital*. Oxford: Oxford University Press.

Matza, D. (1964) *Delinquency and Drift*. New York: John Wiley & Sons.

McBriar, A.M. (1966) *Fabian Socialism and English Politics 1884–1918*. Cambridge: Cambridge University Press.

McClelland, D.C. (1973) 'Testing for competence rather than for "intelligence" ', *American Psychologist*, 28, 1–14.

McClelland, D.C., Baldwin, A.L., Bronfenbrenner, U. and Strodtbeck, F.L. (1958) *Talent and Society*. Princeton, NJ: Van Nostrand.

McLynn, F. (1999) 'History isn't always a cock-up', *New Statesman*, 20 September: 25–7.

McManus, M. (1987) 'Suspension and exclusion from high school – the association with catchment and school variables', *School Organisation*, 7(3): 261–71.

Meekosha, H. and Jacubowicz, A. (1996) 'Disability, participation, representation and social justice', in C. Christensen and F. Rizvi (eds) *Disability and the Dilemmas of Education and Justice*. Buckingham: Open University Press.

Meiklejohn, A. (1966) 'Knowledge and intelligence', in R.D. Archambault (ed.) *Dewey on Education*. New York: Random House.

Mercer, J.R. (1970) 'Sociological perspectives on mild mental retardation', in H.C. Haywood (ed.) *Sociocultural Aspects of Mental Retardation*. Englewood Cliffs, NJ: Prentice-Hall.

Midwinter, E. (1977) 'The professional–lay relationship: a Victorian legacy', *Journal of Child Psychology and Psychiatry*, 18: 101–13.

Miller, E. (1996) 'Changing the way we think about kids with disabilities: a conversation with Tom Hehir', in E. Miller and R. Tovey, *Inclusion and Special Education*. HEL Focus Series No. 1. Cambridge, MA: Harvard Educational Publishing.

Miller, J. (1993) *The Passion of Michel Foucault*. London: HarperCollins.

Morgan, E. (1996) *The Descent of the Child: Human Evolution from a New Perspective*. London: Penguin.

Mortimore, P. (1997) *The Road to Success: Four Case Studies of Schools which no longer require Special Measures*. London: DfEE.

Mortimore, P., Sammons, P., Stoll, L., Lewis, D. and Ecob, R. (1988) *School Matters: The Junior Years*. Exeter: Open Books.

Mousley, J.A., Rice, M. and Tregenza, K. (1993) 'Integration of students with disabilities into regular schools: policy in use', *Disability, Handicap and Society*, 8(1): 59–70.

Mouzelis, N. (1995) *Sociological Theory: What Went Wrong?* London: Routledge.

Munro, R. (1997) 'Ideas of difference: stability, social spaces and the labour of division', in K. Hetherington and R. Munro (eds) *Ideas of Difference: Social Spaces and the Labour of Division*. Oxford: Blackwell.

Nagel, E. (1959) 'Methodological issues in psychoanalytic theory', in S. Hook (ed.) *Psychoanalysis, Scientific Method and Philosophy*. New York: New York University Press.

Neisser, U. (ed.) (1986) *The School Achievement of Minority Children*. Hillsdale, NJ: Lawrence Erlbaum.

Newcomer, P.L. and Hammill, D.D. (1975) 'ITPA and academic achievement', *Reading Teacher*, 28: 731–42.

Newell, P. (1988) 'Children's rights after Cleveland', *Children and Society*, 2(3): 199–206.

Newman, J. and Clarke, J. (1994) 'Going about our business: the managerialisation of public services', in J. Clarke, A. Cochrane and E. MacLaughlin (eds) *Managing Social Policy*. London: Sage.

Newman, T. and Roberts, H. (1996) 'Meaning well and doing good: interventions in children's lives', in P. Alderson, S. Brill, I. Chalmers, R. Fuller and P. Hinkley-Smith, *What Works? Effective Social Interventions in Child Welfare*. London: Barnardos.

Nietzsche, F. ([1886] 1990) *Beyond Good and Evil*. London: Penguin.

Noddings, N. (1996) 'On community', *Educational Theory*, 46: 245–67.

Noddings, N. (2005) *Happiness and Education*. Cambridge: Cambridge University Press.

Norwich, B. (1991) *Reappraising Special Needs Education*. London: Cassell.

O'Brien, J. and Forest, M. (1989) *Action for Inclusion: How to Improve Schools by Welcoming Children with Special Needs into Regular Classrooms*. Toronto: Inclusion Press.

Oakeshott, M. (1967) *Rationalism in Politics and Other Essays*. London: Methuen.

Oakeshott, M. (1989) 'Education: the engagement and the frustration', in T. Fuller (ed.) *The Voice of Liberal Learning: Michael Oakeshott on Education*. London: Yale University Press.

OECD (1994) *The Integration of Disabled Children into Mainstream Education: Ambitions, Theories and Practices*. Paris: Organisation for Economic Co-operation and Development.

Offord, D.R., Chmura Kraemer, H., Kazdin, A.E., Jensen, P.S., Harrington, R. and Gardner, J.S. (1999) 'Lowering the burden of suffering: monitoring the benefits of clinical, targeted and universal approaches', in D.P. Keating and C. Hertzman, *Developmental Health and the Wealth of Nations: Social, Biological and Educational Dynamics*. New York: Guilford Press.

Ofsted (Office for Standards in Education) (1999) *LEA Support for School Improvement: Framework for the Inspection of Local Education Authorities*. London: Ofsted.

Oliver, M. (1995) 'Does special education have a role to play in the twenty-first century?', *REACH Journal of Special Needs Education in Ireland*, 8(2): 67–76.

Olson, D.R. and Bruner, J.S. (1996) 'Folk psychology and folk pedagogy', in D.R. Olson and N. Torrance (eds) *The Handbook of Education and Human Development*. Cambridge, MA: Blackwell.

Orbach, J. (1982) *Neuropsychology after Lashley*. Hillsdale, NJ: Lawrence Erlbaum.

Outhwaite, W. (1990) 'Hans-Georg Gadamer', in Q. Skinner (ed.) *The Return of Grand Theory in the Human Sciences*. Cambridge: Canto.

Palincsar, A. S., Brown, A.L. and Campione, J.C. (1993) 'Dialogues among communities of first grade learners', in E. Foreman, N. Minnick and A. Stone (eds) *The Institutional and Social Context of Mind: New Directions in Vygotskian Theory and Research*. Oxford: Oxford University Press.

Parker, M. (1997) 'Dividing organisations and multiplying identities', in K. Hetherington and R. Munro (eds) *Ideas of Difference: Social Spaces and the Labour of Division*. Oxford: Blackwell.

Parsons, C. (1999) *Education, Exclusion and Citizenship*. London: Routledge.

Parsons, S., Daniels, H., Porter, J. and Robertson, C. (2006) 'The use of ICT by adults with learning disabilities in day and residential services', *British Journal of Educational Technology*, 37(1): 31–44.

Pawson, R. (2006) *Evidence-based Policy: A Realist Perspective*. London: Sage.

Penna, S. and O'Brian, M. (1998) *Theorising Welfare: Enlightenment and Modern Society*. London: Sage.

Philp, M. (1990) 'Michel Foucault', in Q. Skinner (ed.) *The Return of Grand Theory in the Human Sciences*. Cambridge: Canto.

Plant, R. (1996) 'Social democracy', in D. Marquand and A. Seldon (eds) *The Ideas that Shaped Post-War Britain*. London: Fontana.

Plender, J. (1997) *A Stake in the Future: The Stakeholding Solution*. London: Nicholas Brealey.

Popper, K.R. (1977) 'On hypotheses', in P.N. Johnson-Laird and P.C. Wason (eds) *Thinking: Readings in Cognitive Science*. Cambridge: Cambridge University Press.

Popper, K.R. (1989) *Conjectures and Refutations*, 5th edn. London: Routledge.

Porter, G. (1995) 'Organisation of schooling: achieving access and quality through inclusion', *Prospects*, 25(2): 299–309.

Postman, N. (1995) *The End of Education*. New York: Alfred A. Knopf.

Power, M. (1997) *The Audit Society*. Oxford: Oxford University Press.

Premack, D. and Premack, A.J. (1996) 'Why animals lack pedagogy and some cultures have more of it than others', in D.R. Olson and N. Torrance (eds) *The Handbook of Education and Human Development*. Cambridge, MA: Blackwell.

Pullman, P. (2005) 'Common sense has much to learn from moonshine', *The Guardian*, 22 January.

Putnam, R. (1995) 'Bowling alone: America's declining social capital', *Journal of Democracy*, 6: 65–78.

Putnam, R. (2000) *Bowling Alone: The Collapse and Revival of American Community*. New York: Simon & Schuster.

Quine, W.V. (1963) *From a Logical Point of View*. New York: Harper & Row.

Rajagopalan, K. (1998) 'On the theoretical trappings of the thesis of anti-theory; or why the idea of theory may not, after all, be all that bad: a response to Gary Thomas', *Harvard Educational Review*, 68(3): 335–52.

Rawls, J. (1971) *A Theory of Justice*. Oxford: Clarendon Press.

Reay, D. (2004) 'Gendering Bourdieu's concept of capitals? Emotional capital, women and social class', in L. Adkins and B. Skeggs (eds) *Feminism after Bourdieu*. Oxford: Blackwell.

Reid, K. and Valle, J. (2005) 'The discursive practice of learning disability: implications for instruction and parent-school relations', *Journal of Learning Disabilities*, 38, 62–78.

Rennie, D. and Flanagin, A. (1998) 'Congress on biomedical peer review: history, ethics and plans for the future', *Journal of the American Medical Association*, 280(3): 213–14.

Reynolds, M.C. (1988) 'A reaction to the JLD special series on the Regular Education Initiative', *Journal of Learning Disabilities*, 21(6): 352–6.

Riddell, S. (1996) 'Theorising special educational needs in a changing political climate', in L. Barton (ed.) *The Sociology of Disability: Emerging Issues and Insights*. London: Longman.

Riddell, S., Brown, S. and Duffield, J. (1994) 'Parental power and special educational needs: the case of specific learning difficulties', *British Educational Research Journal*, 20(3): 327–43.

Rieser, R. and Mason, M. (1992) *Disability Equality in the Classroom: A Human Rights Issue*. London: Disability Equality in Education.

Rizvi, F. and Lingard, B. (1996) 'Disability, education and the discourses of justice', in C. Christensen and F. Rizvi (eds) *Disability and the Dilemmas of Education and Justice*. Buckingham: Open University Press.

Roaf, C. (1988) 'The concept of a whole school approach to special needs', in O. Robinson and G. Thomas (eds) *Tackling Learning Difficulties*. London: Hodder & Stoughton.

Roaf, C. and Bines, H. (1989) 'Needs, rights and opportunities in special education', in C. Roaf and H. Bines (eds) *Needs, Rights and Opportunities: Developing Approaches to Special Education*. London: Falmer.

Roaf, C. and Lloyd, C. (1995) 'Multi-agency work with young people in difficulty', Social Care Research Findings, 68, June. York: Joseph Rowntree Foundation.

Rorty, R. (1982) *Consequences of Pragmatism (Essays: 1972–1980)*. Minneapolis, MN: University of Minnesota Press.

Rorty, R. (1991) *Essays on Heidegger and Others: Philosophical Papers*, Vol. II. Cambridge: Cambridge University Press.

Rorty, R. (1998) *Advancing our Country: Leftist Thought in 20th-century America*. Cambridge, MA: Harvard University Press.

Ross, L.D., Amabile, T.M. and Steinmetz, J.L. (1977) 'Social roles, social control and biases in social-perception processes', *Journal of Personality and Social Psychology*, 35: 485–94.

Rothstein, R. (2000) 'Equalizing educational resources on behalf of disadvantaged children', in R.D. Kahlenberg (ed.) *A Notion at Risk: Preserving Public Education as an Engine for Social Mobility*. New York: Century Foundation.

Rousseau, J.-J. ([1762] 1993) *Émile* (trans. B. Foxley). London: J.M. Dent.

Rubington, E. and Weinberg, M.S. (eds) (1968) *Deviance: The Interactionist Perspective; Text and Readings in the Sociology of Deviance*. London: Macmillan.

Rueda, R. and Mehan, H. (1986) 'Metacognition and passing: strategic interactions in the lives of students with learning disabilities', *Anthropology and Education Quarterly*, 17: 145–65.

Rustemier, S. (2002) *Social and Educational Justice: The Human Rights Framework for Inclusion*. Bristol: Centre for Studies on Inclusive Education.

Rutter, M. (1995) 'Clinical implications of attachment concepts: retrospect and prospect', *Journal of Child Psychology and Psychiatry*, 36(4): 549–71.

Rutter, M., Maughan, B., Mortimore, P. and Ouston, J. (1979) *Fifteen Thousand Hours: Secondary Schools and their Effects on Children*. London: Open Books.

Ryle, G. (1990) *The Concept of Mind*. London: Penguin.

Sacks, O. (1995) *An Anthropologist on Mars*. London: Picador.

Sammons, P., Nuttall, D. and Cuttance, P. (1993) 'Differential school effectiveness: results from a re-analysis of the Inner London Education Authority's Junior School Project Data', *British Educational Research Journal*, 19(4): 381–405.

Sapolsky, R. (1999) 'The physiology and pathophysiology of unhappiness', in D. Kahneman, E. Diener and N. Schwarz (eds) *Well-being: The Foundations of Hedonic Psychology*. New York: Russell Sage Foundation.

Sayed, Y. (2002) 'Exclusion and inclusion in the south with reference to education: a review of the literature: learning about inclusion and exclusion in education: policy and implementation in India and South Africa'. www.ids.ac.uk/ids/pvty/Inex/Discpaper1.pdf

Sayer, K. (1993) 'Language matters: the changing vocabularies of special needs', unpublished MA dissertation, Oxford Brooks University.

Scardamalia, M. and Bereiter, C. (1999) 'Schools as knowledge-building organizations', in D.P. Keating and C. Hertzman, *Developmental Health and the Wealth of Nations: Social, Biological and Educational Dynamics*. New York: Guilford Press.

Scholes, R. (1998) 'The case against phonemic awareness', *Journal of Research in Reading*, 21(3): 177–88.

Schön, D.A. (1991) *The Reflective Practitioner: How Professionals Think in Action*. Aldershot: Avebury.

Schweinhart, L.J. and Weikart, D.P. (1997) 'Lasting differences: the high/scope preschool curriculum comparison through age 23', *Early Childhood Research Quarterly*, 12: 117–43.

Scruton, R. (1980) *The Meaning of Conservatism*. Harmondsworth: Penguin.

Sen, A. (1992) *Inequality Reexamined*. Oxford: Oxford University Press.

Sen, A. (1999) *Development as Freedom*. New York: Alfred A. Knopf.

Senf, G.M. (1987) 'Learning disabilities as sociologic sponge', in S. Vaughn and C.S. Bos, *Research in Learning Disabilities*. London: Taylor & Francis.

Sennett, R. (2003) *Respect in a World of Inequality*. New York: W.W. Norton.

Shilling, C. (2004) 'Physical capital and situated action: a new direction for corporeal sociology', *British Journal of Sociology of Education*, 23(4): 475–87.

Singer, B. and Ryff, C. (1997) 'Racial and ethnic inequalities in health: environmental, psychosocial and physiological pathways', in B. Devlin, S.E. Fienberg, D.P. Resnick and K. Roeder (eds) *Intelligence, Genes and Success: Scientists Respond to the Bell Curve*. New York: Springer-Verlag.

Singer, P. (1999) *A Darwinian Left: Politics, Evolution and Cooperation*. London: Weidenfeld and Nicolson.

Skinner, B.F. (1972) *Beyond Freedom and Dignity*. London: Jonathan Cape.

Skrtic, T.M. (1991) 'The special education paradox: equity as the way to excellence', *Harvard Educational Review*, 61(2): 148–206.

Slee, R. (1998) 'The politics of theorising special education', in C. Clark, A. Dyson and A. Millward (eds) *Theorising Special Education*. London: Routledge.

Slee, R. (2001) ' "Inclusion in practice": does practice make perfect?', *Educational Review*, 53(2): 113–23.

Smail, D. (1993) *The Origins of Unhappiness*. London: HarperCollins.

Smith, A.J. and Thomas, J.B. (1992) 'A survey of therapeutic support for children with emotional and behavioural disturbance (EBD) in special schools in the United Kingdom', *School Psychology International*, 13: 323–37.

Smith, F. (1973) *Psycholinguistics and Reading*. New York: Holt.

Smith, F. (1994) *Understanding Reading*, 5th edn. Mahwah, NJ: Lawrence Erlbaum.

Smith, F. (1995) *Between Hope and Havoc: Essays into Human Learning and Education*. Portsmouth. NH: Heinemann.

Smith, F. (1998) *The Book of Learning and Forgetting*. New York: Teachers' College Press.

Söder, M. (1989) 'Disability as a social construct: the labelling approach revisited', *European Journal of Special Needs Education*, 4(2): 117–29.

Speck, B.W. (1993) *Publication Peer Review: An Annotated Bibliography*. Westport, CT: Greenwood Press.

Spencer, B.L. (2004) 'Just one more way to fail: the "conditions of impossibility" of standardized literacy testing'. Paper presented to the Annual Meeting of the American Educational Research Association, San Diego, 16 April.

Stanovich, K.E. (1994) 'Does dyslexia exist?', *Journal of Child Psychology and Psychiatry*, 35(4): 579–95.

Stenhouse, L. (1975) *An Introduction to Curriculum Research and Development*. London: Heinemann.

Stevenson, R.L. (1999) 'A Humble Remonstrance', in G. Norquay (ed.) *R.L. Stevenson on Fiction: An Anthology of Literary and Critical Essays*. Edinburgh: Edinburgh University Press.

Strachey, L. (1971) *Eminent Victorians*. London: Penguin.

Suppes, P. (1974) 'The place of theory in educational research', *Educational Researcher*, 3(6): 3–10.

Swann, W. (1985) 'Psychological science and the practice of special education', in

G. Claxton, W, Swann, P. Salmon, V. Walkerdine, B. Jacobsen and J. White, *Psychology and Schooling: What's the Matter?* London: Bedford Way Papers.

Szasz, T.S. (1972) *The Myth of Mental Illness*. London: Paladin.

Tarr, J. and Thomas, G. (1997) 'The quality of special educational needs policies: time for review?', *Support for Learning*, 12(1): 10–14.

Tawney, R.H. (1964) *Equality*. London: George Allen & Unwin.

Taylor, C. (1992) *Multiculturalism and 'The Politics of Recognition'*. Princeton, NJ: Princeton University Press.

Taylor, D. (1998) 'Social identity and social policy: engagements with postmodern theory', *Journal of Social Policy*, 27(3): 329–50.

Terman, L.M. (1924) 'The possibilities and limitations of training', *Journal of Educational Research*, 10: 335–43.

Thayer, H.S. (1995) 'Newton', in *The Cambridge Dictionary of Philosophy*. Cambridge: Cambridge University Press.

Thomas, G. (1990) *Setting up IMS: A Study of LEAs' Submissions to the DES*. Milton Keynes: Open University Press.

Thomas, G. (1992) 'Ecological interventions', in S. Wolfendale, T. Bryans, M. Fox, A. Labram and A. Sigston (eds) *The Profession and Practice of Educational Psychology*. London: Cassell.

Thomas, G. (1997a) *Exam Performance in Special Schools*. Bristol: CSIE.

Thomas, G. (1997b) 'What's the use of theory?', *Harvard Educational Review*, 67(1): 75–105.

Thomas, G. (1998) 'The myth of rational research', *British Educational Research Journal*, 24(2): 141–63.

Thomas, G. (1999a) 'Hollow theory: a reply to Rajagopalan', *Harvard Educational Review*, 69(1): 51–66.

Thomas, G. (1999b) 'Reviewing peer-reviewing', *Research Intelligence*, 69, July: 18–21.

Thomas, G. (2007) *Education and Theory: Strangers in Paradigms*. Maidenhead: Open University Press.

Thomas, G. and Davis, P. (1997) 'Special needs: objective reality or personal construction? Judging reading difficulty after the Code', *Educational Research*, 39(3): 263–70.

Thomas, G. and Glenny, G. (2002) 'Thinking about inclusion: whose reason? what evidence?', *International Journal of Inclusive Education*, 6(4): 345–69.

Thomas, G. and Tarr, J. (1999) 'Ideology and inclusion: a reply to Croll and Moses', *British Journal of Educational Studies*, 14(1): 17–27.

Thomas, G. and Vaughan, M. (2004) *Inclusive Education: Readings and Reflections*. Maidenhead: Open University Press.

Thomas, G., Tarr, J., Webb, J. and Taysum, M. (1996) *The Monitoring and Evaluation of Schools' SEN Policies (Report of Research for DfEE)*. Bristol: University of the West of England.

Thomas, G., Walker, D. and Webb. J. (1998) *The Making of the Inclusive School*. London: Routledge.

Thompson, S. and Hoggett, P. (1996) 'Universalism, selectivism and particularism: towards a post-modern social policy', *Critical Social Policy*, 16(1): 21–43.

Thomson, P. (2002) *Schooling the Rustbelt Kids*. Nottingham: Trentham Books.

Times Educational Supplement (2000) 'False sympathy for inclusion', letter signed by Maggie Chambers and 12 others, 17 March.

Tizard, J., Schofield, W.N. and Hewison, J. (1982) 'Collaboration between teachers and parents in assisting children's reading', *British Journal of Educational Psychology*, 52: 115.

Toffler, A. (1970) *Future Shock*. London: Pan.

Tomlinson, S. (1982) *A Sociology of Special Education*. London: Routledge.

Tomlinson, S. (1985) 'The expansion of special education', *Oxford Review of Education*, 11(2): 157–65.

Tomlinson, S. (1987) 'Critical theory and special education', *CASTME Journal*, 7(2): 33–41.

Touche Ross (1990) *Extending Local Management to Special Schools*. London: Touche Ross for DES.

Toulmin, S. (1972) *Human Understanding*, Vol. I. Oxford: Clarendon Press.

Troyna, B. (1994) 'Blind faith? Empowerment and educational research'. Paper presented at the International Sociology of Education Conference, University of Sheffield.

Troyna, B. (1995) 'Beyond reasonable doubt? Researching "race" in educational settings', *Oxford Review of Education*, 21(4): 395–408.

US Department of Education (1998) Twenty-first Annual Report to Congress on the Implementation of the Individuals with Disabilities Education Act.

US Supreme Court (1954) Brown et al. v. Board of Education of Topeka et al. Appeal from the United States District Court for the District of Kansas, 347 U.S. 483.

Vickers, G. (1965) *The Art of Judgment: A Study of Policy Making*. London: Chapman & Hall.

Vincent, C. (2000) *Including Parents?: Education, Citizenship and Parental Agency*. Maidenhead: Open University Press.

Vincent, C., Evans, J., Lunt, I. and Young, P. (1995) 'Policy and practice: the changing nature of special educational provision in schools', *British Journal of Special Education*, 22(12): 4–11.

Vincent, C., Evans, J., Lunt, I. and Young, P. (1996) 'Professionals under pressure: the administration of special education in a changing context', *British Educational Research Journal*, 22(4): 475–92.

Vygotsky, L.S. ([1934] 1986) *Thought and Language*. Cambridge, MA: MIT Press.

Vygotsky, L.S. (1978) *Mind in Society: The Development of Higher Psychological Processes*. Cambridge: Harvard University Press.

Wacquant, L.D. (1989) 'Towards a reflexive sociology: a workshop with Pierre Bourdieu', *Sociological Theory*, 7: 50.

Wacquant, L. (1992) 'Towards a social praxeology: the structure and logic of Bourdieu's sociology', in P. Bourdieu and L. Wacquant (1992) *An Invitation to Reflexive Sociology*. Cambridge: Polity Press.

Wahlstein, D. (1997) 'The malleability of intelligence is not constrained by heritability', in B. Devlin, S.E. Fienberg, D.P. Resnick and K. Roeder (eds) *Intelligence, Genes and Success: Scientists Respond to the Bell Curve*. New York: Copernicus.

Walkerdine, V. (1983) 'It's only natural: rethinking child-centred pedagogy', in A.M. Wolpe and J. Donald (eds) *Is There Anyone Here from Education?* London: Pluto.

Wang, M.C., Reynolds, M. and Walberg, H. (1987) *Handbook of Special Education: Research and Practice, Vol. 1: Learner Characteristics and Adaptive Education*. Oxford: Pergamon.

Wang, M.C., Reynolds, M. and Walberg, H. (1995) 'Serving students at the margins', *Educational Leadership*, 52(4): 12–17.

Waterhouse (2000) *Committee of Enquiry into Abuse at Children's Homes*. London: HMSO.

Weatherley, R. and Lipsky, M. (1977) 'Street level bureaucrats and institutional innovation: implementing special educational reform', *Harvard Educational Review*, 47: 171–97.

Weil, S. ([1949] 2002) *The Need for Roots*. London: Routledge.

Wheeler, L.R. (1970) 'A trans-decade comparison of the IQs of Tennessee mountain children', in I. Al-Issa and W. Dennis (eds) *Cross-cultural Studies of Behaviour*. New York: Holt, Rinehart & Winston.

Williams, F. (1992) 'Somewhere over the rainbow: universality and diversity in social policy', in N. Manning and R. Page (eds) *Social Policy Review*. Canterbury: Social Policy Association.

Willis, P. (1977) 'Learning to Labour: how working-class kids get working-class jobs', Farnborough: Saxon House.

Willms, J.D. (1999a) *Inequalities in Literacy Skills among Youth in Canada and the United States. (International Adult Literacy Survey No. 6)*. Ottawa: Human Resources Development Canada and National Literacy Secretariat.

Willms, J.D. (1999b) 'Quality and inequality in children's literacy: the effects of families, schools and communities', in D. Keating and C. Hertzman (eds) *Developmental Health and the Wealth of Nations: Social, Biological, and Educational Dynamics*. New York: Guilford Press.

Wilson, D. (1990) 'Integration at John Watson School', in D. Baker and K. Bovair (eds) *Making the Special Schools Ordinary*, Vol. 2. London: Falmer.

Wilson, J. (1999) 'Some conceptual difficulties about "inclusion"', *Support for Learning*, 14(3): 110–12.

Winkelmann, C.L. (1991) 'Social acts and social systems: community as metaphor', *Linguistics and Education*, 3: 1–29.

Wolf, A. (2001) *Does Education Matter? Myths about Education and Economic Growth*. London: Penguin.

Wolfensberger, W. (1990) 'Human service policies: the rhetoric versus the reality', in L. Barton (ed.) *Disability and Dependency*. London: Falmer.

Wood, S. and Shears, B. (1986) *Teaching Children with Severe Learning Difficulties: A Radical Re-appraisal*. London: Croom Helm.

World Bank (1999) 'What is social capital? PovertyNet'. www.worldbank.org/poverty/scapital/whatsc.htm

Wright Mills, C. (1970) *The Sociological Imagination*. London: Pelican.

Young, I.M. (1990) *Justice and the Politics of Difference*. Princeton, NJ: Princeton University Press.

Zigmond, N. (2003) 'Where should students with disabilities receive special education services? Is one place better than another?', *Journal of Special Education*, 37: 193–9.

Ziman, J. (1991) *Reliable Knowledge*. Cambridge: Canto.

Index

INCLUSIVE EDUCATION
READINGS AND REFLECTIONS

Gary Thomas and Mark Vaughan (eds)

Over the past centuries research and practice has supported the use of inclusive practices as opposed to segregation. Political events relating to equality for all have spurred these changes. This book provides a valuable journey of exploration into these processes that have brought us where we are today – slow but steady progress towards inclusive practices within mainstream schools.

International Journal of Disability, Development and Education

Everyone believes in inclusion – or do they? This excellent new book takes readers on a compelling historical journey which explores the beliefs, the barriers, the evidence and the practice that surrounds the pursuit of a more inclusive education system. Historically 'the time never seems to have been right' for a fully inclusive education system in Great Britain. Perhaps the climate and context of the first decade of the 21st Century has the potential to make it the 'Age of Inclusion'. If so – this book will certainly help us to achieve this elusive goal.

Tony Dessent, Luton Borough Council

Ten years after the Salamanca Statement, this book helpfully brings together a broad range of texts to stimulate all of us to reflect on the progress made towards more inclusive education. Particularly impressive is the way that Thomas and Vaughan locate discussion of inclusion in wider debates about the nature of society.

Mel Ainscow, University of Manchester

This book examines the key influences behind the moves towards inclusive education and inclusion in mainstream society. The first of its kind anywhere in the world, this seminal work features more than 50 extracts from key documents and classic texts, alongside illuminating commentaries by two experts in the field.

Inclusive Education: Readings and Reflections demonstrates that moves to inclusion have come from many directions: research; the imperative for greater social justice; calls for civil rights; legislation that prohibits discrimination; original, distinctive projects started by imaginative educators; and the voices of those who have been through special education. These sources are marshalled and organised in this book. It is essential reading for students on a range of courses in inclusive education and special educational needs, and for anyone wishing to understand the development of inclusive education, including teachers, headteachers, educational psychologists, and parents.

Contents
Series editors' preface – Preface – Acknowledgements – Introduction – PART I: The context – rights, participation, social justice – PART II: Arguments and evidence against segregation – 1960s to today – PART III: Legislation, reports, statements – PART IV: Inclusion in action – Conclusion – References.

240pp
978–0–335–20724–4 (Paperback)   978–0–335–20725–1 (Hardback)

THE MICRO-POLITICS OF INCLUSIVE EDUCATION
AN ETHNOGRAPHY

Shareen Benjamin

This book is sustained and significant in its argument, complex in its analysis and highly original. It is extremely well written and a pleasure to read stylistically as well as sociologically.

Professor Sheila Riddell, Director, Strathclyde Centre
for Disability Research, University of Glasgow

Shereen Benjamin's work opens up new ways of thinking about learning difficulties. This beautifully written book explores the school lives and identities of young women who find school work extraordinarily difficult for a range of reasons. It is a book to read, and read again for the rich vein of thinking about schooling and special needs that it opens up. All who are involved in teaching, policy making or school management and who are concerned about these young people should read it.

Professor Debbie Epstein, Head of the Department of
Educational Studies, Goldsmiths College, University of London

How is 'inclusive education' being translated into practice at school and classroom level?

This book is a detailed account and analysis of students' experiences of 'inclusion' in a girls' comprehensive school. It uses theories associated with feminist post-structuralism to explain and critique the micro/political processes through which students identified as having ';special educational needs' make sense of the school and of themselves as school students. Central to the argument of the book is a critical engagement with current notions of school effectiveness and school improvement. *The Micropolitics of Inclusive Education* looks at how governmental policy initiatives – on school improvement and SEN/inclusion – are translated into practice by the school, and at how this practice is lived and understood by the girls. The book also explores the significance of multiple sites of difference – including social class, race, gender/sexuality and physical appearance – in the girls' schooling experiences. This book shows how 'effective' schooling can have unintended and inegalitarian effects for some of the most vulnerable students in schools, and unravels some of the complexities facing students and teachers as schools move towards inclusive education.

Contents

176pp
978–0–335–21048–0 (Paperback)   978–0–335–21049–7 (Hardback)

SPECIAL TEACHING FOR SPECIAL CHILDREN?
PEDAGOGIES FOR INCLUSION

Ann Lewis and Brahm Norwich (eds)

- What, if anything, is 'special' about teaching children with special or exceptional learning needs?

This book addresses this question, looking at pupils' special learning needs including low attainment, learning difficulties, language difficulties, emotional and behavioural problems and sensory needs.

Some special needs groups (for example dyslexia) have argued strongly for the need for particular specialist approaches. In contrast, many proponents of inclusion have argued that 'good teaching is good teaching for all' and that all children benefit from similar approaches. Both positions fail to scrutinise this issue rigorously and coherently, and it is this aspect which distinguishes this book.

Leading researchers in each special needs field defend and critique a conceptual analysis of teaching strategies used with particular learner groups with special educational needs. Summaries by the editors after each chapter link pedagogic strategies, knowledge and curriculum to key points from the chapter and pave the way for discussion.

This book is indispensable reading for students, policy makers, researchers and professionals in the field of special educational needs and inclusion.

Shortlisted for the TES / NASEN Book Awards 2005

Contents
How specialised is teaching pupils with disabilities and difficulties? – Deafness – Visual impairment – Deafblindness – Severe learning difficulties – Profound and multiple learning difficulties – Children with Down's Syndrome – English as an additional language and children with speech, language and communication needs – Autistic spectrum disorders – AD/HD – Dyslexia – Dyspraxia – Social, emotional and behavioural difficulties – Moderate learning difficulties – Low attainment – Overview and discussion: overall conclusions.

256pp
978–0–335–21405–1 (Paperback)   978–0–335–21406–8 (Hardback)